Studies
in the
Gospels

Volume 1

Studies
in the
Gospels

Volume 1

EMIL BOCK

Floris
Books

Translated by Val Jones
Edited by Tony Jacobs-Brown

First published privately in German in 1927–29
as a series of study letters entitled
Beiträge zum Verständnis des Evangeliums
First published similarly in English in the 1930s
This edition first published by Floris Books, Edinburgh in 2009
Second printing 2022

British Library CIP Data available
ISBN 978-086315-711-0

Contents

Unless otherwise stated all quotations from the New Testament are from the translation by Jon Madsen (Floris Books, 1994), which is closest to Bock's own translation into German. Quotations from the Old Testament are from the Revised Standard Version.

Preface

Emil Bock was one of the founders of The Christian Community in 1922. From the beginning he was a driving force behind the group of forty-five people who had asked Rudolf Steiner to help them bring a renewal to Christian life. When Friedrich Rittelmeyer, the well-known Lutheran preacher who led this new movement, died in 1938, Emil Bock took over the leadership.

Between 1927 and 1929 Emil Bock wrote this series of "contributions to an understanding of the gospels" as newsletters accompanying his efforts to retranslate the New Testament into language for his day which would also convey some of the depth of meaning of the original Greek text. A second series was written in 1930–33. In the ensuing years he worked on his series of books about the Old and the New Testament. Some of his earlier material was reworked into these volumes. In 1950, responding to repeated demands for these typed newsletters to be available again, Bock revised them but still saw them as unfinished, and did not want them to be properly printed. They appeared in similar form in English in the 1930s and again later.

In these studies Bock explores the images of the gospels, combining his intimate knowledge of the Greek text with his wide-ranging studies both of theology and of Rudolf Steiner's anthroposophy. With the greatest reverence he shows the relevance of the gospels for today, often bringing fresh light to apparently contradictory texts.

For this edition the text has been revised from the earlier translation.

Christian Maclean

CHAPTER ONE

Introduction

Secrets of composition

If we wish to study a painting from an artist's point of view we must first, before taking in the detail, reverently stand back and there take stock. Only then, and from that distance, should we contemplate the painting, take it in as a whole, see it as a kind of exalted design. Were we first to consider detail, no matter how admirable, we would find the body but not the soul of the painting, since every work of art does have a soul. It is woven through and through with the revelation of supersensible existence. Only when we have opened our soul to the soul of the whole work of art can we worthily appraise its detail.

Something which is nowadays generally taken for granted in relation to the study of art has yet to be won when it comes to reading the gospels. The gospels are works of art — but they are at the same time infinitely more. They are the works of art of God. As we recognize their higher design, we gaze right into a symbol which, by its intrinsic ordering and composition, reveals the sacred ordering of the divinely spiritual world, that world which essentially makes up the mighty body of God within and above the world of the senses.

In contemplating the secret of the gospels' composition, a key is vouchsafed to us, able to unlock depths in them of which we had no inkling. Nevertheless, the key will not function if it is handled mechanically by the kind of intellect that today describes itself as 'scientific.' Truly artistic contemplation of a work of art differs from the more mechanical examination of mere detail by its attitude of mind; by greater reverence. To fix the attention on the structure of the gospels is an activity which points to something far beyond merely artistic intent; science and art must be lifted to the plane of religion. In the new theology of the gospels, science, art and religion are interrelated. We are going to dare to gather together building stones to erect this new theology.

Too much attention has hitherto been given to isolated passages of the gospels, no matter whether we have been pursuing a moral and religious understanding of them or a scientific and historical one. It could not be otherwise because of the laws of evolution of human consciousness. It was moreover inevitable that the further we went along those paths, the more we became bogged down in dead ends in trying to comprehend the gospels. What sense we made of them was too restricted. There are nowadays many people to whom this is very evident. The profundity of the gospels reaches right down into every word. How can we expect to exhaust those wells? Our studies will be carried forward at every stage by awareness that we can never completely understand the gospels, that again and again new depths will be revealed to reverent, unprejudiced study.

The narrow view of Bible study has hitherto shown — and still does — that a rather more religious and moralistic interpretation invariably inclines to dogmatism. Isolated gospel verses turn into restrictive rules for human thought and behaviour. Constant quoting of biblical passages is always a symptom of this particular dead end. Clearly, only someone with superficial and narrow understanding would be likely to scatter biblical quotations far and wide in the manner common in our day, since every word of the Bible, seen against the fullness of its own context, is like a single brush stroke of colour within a painting where it acquires a depth to compel reverent silence.

The narrowness of biblical research to date shows itself on the other hand in approaches to it along rather more historical and scientific lines. Just as in the first instance detached biblical passages become dogma, so now they were often regarded as legend. The gospels were seen mainly as historical accounts of external happenings and it was thought possible to distinguish between what was historical and what was unhistorical, legendary and erroneous. The obvious result of all this was that the whole gospel for many an enquirer became open to doubt. People set themselves up as judges of God's artistic creation. They measured it by human standards and examined the 'authenticity' of passages out of context. No wonder that they were left with nothing in hand but fragments.

There have undoubtedly been efforts of quite another kind to understand the gospels, efforts which are different from those mentioned above. There is, however, a reason why whatever hardened into dogma, or led to mere evanescent legend, had somehow to come to a full stop. The gospels do not really describe events which took place only on earth, or which belong in the main to an earthly setting. They are messages from the supersensible, divinely spiritual world, which dominates the world of our senses, entering it in a unique way through the person of Jesus Christ. We can — indeed we must — translate the word *'evangel'* as more or less, 'message from the realm of angels.' That is why an age which does not recognize the existence of a supersensible world, which has no desire to know it and which denies it, cannot help being pulled up short.

Rudolf Steiner's anthroposophy has breached the wall of materialism; it has opened up a mighty prospect of the reality of the supersensible world; it provides a base for continual advance into understanding the gospel. These studies of ours admittedly rest on Rudolf Steiner's foundations, firstly, as to their general approach, and, secondly, as to much of the detail. They link up with the riches poured out by him in his lectures on the gospels and on other books of the Bible. We could not, without Rudolf Steiner's spiritual achievement, turn our gaze — strong and far reaching — upon the wholeness of the gospel revealed in its divine composition.

The concept of composition occurs in modern Protestant theology in a form totally different from the concept we have in mind here. It has been observed that from chapter nine on, the Gospel of St Luke places everything into the framework of a journey by Jesus to Jerusalem in a manner that seems to contradict the other gospels. We are led to conclude: the writer of the Gospel of St Luke lacked accurate particulars of the latter part of the life of Jesus of Nazareth; so he fell back on a model, a framework, by way of literary device, in order to compose into a coherent whole such disjointed stories as were handed down to him and were at his command. The journey to Jerusalem is supposed to have served the author as such a framework. According to that view, the sequence of events in the various sections from chapter nine on is assumed not to be historical; not to be the order in which the various episodes actually took place, nor that in which the alleged words of Christ were in fact uttered. The

sequence is more probably a piece of literary composition invented by
the author of the gospel.

In the following studies what we understand as 'composition' is
something quite different. We mean divine, not human, composition.
We do not mean a subjective kind of composition, perhaps even one
that flippantly manipulates historical truth — something a man could
have put together from notions of his own, thereby violating that very
truth. Composition, as we understand it, need not even have existed
within the evangelist's full consciousness. It is the inmost order of spiritual realities reflected in the evangelists' souls.

Whether Raphael deliberately composed his painting of the Sistine
Madonna so that the masculine figure of Pope Sixtus is on the same
side as the Jesus child, while the feminine figure of St Barbara is on the
mother's side, is a question we do not take seriously any more.
Raphael's composition is no longer due to human arbitrariness; it is
divine truth.

Here we approach the old question of how the gospels came into
being, the question of inspiration. We must not discuss that question
as if it were dogma. Only where knowledge of a higher, divine world
and familiarity with its laws of life has been lost, can the inspired character of the gospel become rigid, incomprehensible dogma. Through
anthroposophy we attain to tidings of beings of that higher world and
of its laws; thereby, light is cast once again on the manner in which
human souls can become bearers of divine revelation. Inspiration is no
longer a miracle beyond understanding, rather a stage in higher consciousness into which human beings can lift themselves. In these preliminary considerations we shall have more to say, and with greater
precision, about inspiration. The following will suffice for the present:
Inspiration is actually the source from which the gospels flowed.
However, this concept is wrong if we mean that the human consciousness of the evangelists was in some wonderful way blotted out, and
their hand and pen guided from outside to write down the gospels.
Rather, we should think of it in the following manner.

There were human beings in early Christendom in whose souls
was present not merely the common consciousness based on the
senses reflecting a sense-world, but, as well, through destiny and
training, a heightened consciousness which reflected a supersensible
world. Such a consciousness enabled these people not only to look

back into the past, but also to penetrate into the future, to rise to the hierarchical levels of divine beings. Awareness of earthly things remained constant in their thoughts and memory, while at the same time this exalted form of consciousness was receptive to the revelation vouchsafed it.

The difference between the consciousness of the several evangelists depended upon the destiny and training of each one. At what heights, how harmoniously and clearly the spiritual world could reflect its own image within human consciousness, depended upon those differences. That is why we have four evangelists since the full *evangelium aeternum* — the eternal gospel inscribed in the spiritual world — desired to express itself in human words; it had to reveal itself simultaneously to four different souls, to four radically different aspects of exalted humankind. All four gospels, taken together, are needed before we can gain a dim perception of the eternal evangel. Nor should we count up or add together the content of the four gospels; we should allow their higher pattern, the secrets of their composition, gradually to coalesce into one grand design. That design consists of imprints on earth of the rhythms, levels and circles of existence of the divinely spiritual world.

If we try to understand the inspiration of the evangelists and their consciousness, then it will not be dogmatism that emerges from the inspired character of the Bible. No longer can we demand 'belief in the Bible.' We can only appeal for the greatest reverence in face of the gospel. On the other hand, untrammelled searching and thinking about the Bible are not only permissible but essential. Understanding of the gospels comes not at the beginning of the search for Christ but as the end-achievement. After all, revelation bestowed upon heightened awareness can become fully accessible only in response to conscious struggling towards a sublime state. The beginning of a likeness to the Christ, indeed of gospel reading, lies not in dogmatic acceptance of the gospel, but in reverence before what it reveals. As for continuity, this depends upon striving, upon active longing to grow deeper and deeper, more and more clearly into the divine revelation. This is the justification for the studies we are about to begin.

The three stages of spiritual revelation in the Apocalypse

Before entering on a detailed discussion of St Matthew's Gospel, we shall be looking at the New Testament as a whole in order to demonstrate, by examples, the nature of its structural secrets.

It is no coincidence that the Revelation to St John, the Apocalypse, stands at the end of the New Testament; it is the very summit of the heightened consciousness of inspiration. The spiritual world's circles of existence are mirrored here with great clarity and power. If we can understand the composition of the Revelation to St John, then we have gained many a key to the composition of the gospels. The structure of the Apocalypse lies before us marvellously illumined. John, the Seer carries us like an eagle soaring higher and higher in great and holy spirals through four vast circles to the heights of the heavenly Jerusalem. Each of these four circles is made up of seven stages:

The seven letters

The seven seals

The seven trumpets

The seven vials of wrath

The seven churches to whom the seven letters are directed are to be found on earth. The first mighty circle of the eagle's flight soars over something already in earthly existence.

Beginning with the second circle, which leads through the seven seals, we are carried beyond earthly consciousness. The first level of existence opens for us; it is that of the divinely spiritual, transcendent world. The scenes that well up as the seals of the Book of Life are loosed, are no longer earthly perceptions but visions of the spirit, images in which things divinely spiritual make themselves known.

The trumpets of the seven angels sound in the third great circle. A new level, transcending earthly existence, must be climbed. Heightened hearing is now added to heightened sight. The trumpets do not sound inarticulately; they utter divine words of revelation, perceptible to the ear of the soul. The sounds of the trumpet, like their words, are not of this world. The earthly ear is deaf to them. Those who possess only earthly hearing hear nothing, no matter how mightily the angels cause those voices to ring out. They do not penetrate the human soul before the third circle of apocalyptic experience is reached.

The last and highest circle of St John's apocalyptic eagle's flight leads up into regions where the seven vials of wrath are poured out. Here a third supersensible element is added to those of heightened sight and hearing; it is the power of directly touching beings and forces of the spirit world. The immediate contact is always a cosmic judgment, a separation of spirits. At this touch, whatever is good in man feel the divine love, even as it bursts into flame. By that same touch, whatever is evil in man feels the divine wrath which burns it up. This revelation can then culminate in the heavenly Jerusalem shining forth from the adversaries' fall, brought to pass by the wrath poured out by God.

Something of the utmost importance to a general understanding of the gospels follows from this review of the composition and structure of the Revelation to St John. Firstly, every book of the Bible leads the human soul along a way that rises in stages. The gospels are not merely books to be read. They are not historical accounts that remain at all times on the same level. They are books that aim always to guide the souls of humanity, step by step, along a journey upward. Every portion of the gospels, and indeed of every other book of the New Testament, requires that those who approach them shall have climbed the steps which precede them. You cannot read two passages of any one of the gospels in the same frame of mind. The later passage demands greater reverence, greater purification of the soul, than did the earlier one. We have sinned enormously against the gospels in this respect. Properly understood it may be said that the gospels are books of initiation, meaning that by them the soul is led to ascend the steps of initiation.

The second point to emerge from the structure of the Apocalypse is this: There is a recognizable cosmic order in the sequence of letters, seals, trumpets and vials of wrath, just as there is in that of earthly consciousness — spiritual vision proceeding to spiritual hearing and spiritual hearing proceeding to spiritual touch and contact. That world order does not change wherever entrance to it is sought and found in the right way. The world of spirit is like a three-storeyed edifice towering above earthly existence. There, pictures take up the first level, words the next, and beings the third.

A precipitate of the threefold character of these three stages in spiritual experience, derived from a genuine wish to ascend, is traceable right down into works of art that are creations of the spirit. An example is Goethe's *The Secrets*. Brother Marcus reaches the portal of the monastery to which he has been sent, after a long journey fraught with trials. Above the entrance he sees the Rose Cross. He is received into the company of the twelve wise elders of the community who now surround him and tell him wonderful things about their own lives with *Humanus*. *Humanus* is the thirteenth, the mysterious leader who has already bidden farewell to his own life in order to pass through the gates of death.

Instruction in the company of the twelve brethren is Marcus' preparation for the three stages of spiritual experience towards which he is moving. That instruction is to him the same as what the seven letters are for a neophyte of the Revelation to St John.

After a meal, the aged brethren lead young Marcus to a sacred precinct. Thirteen chairs are ranged in a circle around the walls; above each chair he sees a heraldic design which, like a seal, imprints itself deeply upon his soul. The design above the thirteenth, central chair is that of the Rose Cross. As he looks upon the thirteen designs, Marcus passes through a reflection of that pictorial stage which the Revelation to St John represents through the seven seals. The next stage takes possession of Marcus when he wakes from a short sleep in a quiet cell. The sound of bells reaches his ears.

> And as he listens he hears something strike thrice on hollow
> steel; this is no clock chiming, nor is it the pealing of bells;
> mingling with those sounds are notes of a flute. The sound,
> strange, solemnly inviting and difficult to interpret, moves and
> delights the heart, and happy couples sing as they dance,
> winding their way in and around each other.

The sounds Marcus hears are not physical. They are 'Harmonies of the Spheres,' the round-dance of spirit worlds. Even as he becomes aware of the word, of the tonality, so he advances into the region of the seven trumpets. The visual impression becomes to him the word; the three rays of light that emanated from the image of the Rose Cross are transformed into three ghostly sounds. The third spiritual stage is to Marcus like a delicate intimation.

He hurries to the window to catch a glimpse of whatever it may be that bewilders and so strangely moves him. He would like to recognize those beings who have revealed themselves to him in sound. He peers into the twilight between night and day and there in that border region between worlds he does recognize them. The three lights turn into as many sounds and now they manifest themselves as beings:

> He watches as day greys the far east, as the horizon becomes
> streaked with a faint veil of mist. And — can he believe his
> eyes? — a wondrous light touches the garden; and then he sees
> three youths with torches in their hands, in haste following the
> winding avenues. Distinctly he sees their garments, gleaming
> white, clinging to their bodies in comely wise; he sees their
> locks wreathed with flowers, the roses that are their girdles. It
> would seem they have come from dancing by night, refreshed
> and beautified by their exertions. And now, quickly they
> quench their torches like stars and vanish into distance.

Goethe's poem — unfinished yet complete — breaks off with this hint concerning the experiencing of three angelic beings and of the emotions of Easter. Brother Marcus has reached the threshold of that spiritual region where divine love and divine anger confront humanity in substantial form. He has been led through the stages of spiritual vision, of word, and of being.

Rudolf Steiner has described these three stages of spiritual perception as a kind of exalted theory of awareness. This he has done from many points of view, including that of the internal organization and composition of the Apocalypse. He distinguishes three faculties of the heightened consciousness as Imagination, Inspiration and Intuition.

> Imagination — the faculty of perceiving what is visual.
> Inspiration — the faculty of perceiving words.
> Intuition — the faculty of touching spiritual beings.

The above distinction is going to be very important to us in our studies of the gospels. It will also help us to find the answer in ever fuller and more concrete terms to the long standing question concerning inspiration. We recognize that there were stages in the consciousness of the evangelists, that inspiration was for them no rigid, supernatural condition, but a living, fluid phase in the process of transformation of consciousness — and of its exaltation. The struggling human soul rises as it grows into the region of self-bestowing revelation. The gospels are not recorded tradition but the fruits of human initiation and at the same time of the revelatory gifts of God. And the earthly awareness of human beings persists within human thought and memory in just the same way as the letters to the churches in the Revelation to St John persist and are still audible in the seals, the trumpets and the vials of wrath. The evangelist wrote down the sacred texts from a consciousness in which personal recollection, spiritual vision, hearing and contact functioned in living harmony.

We shall have a good deal to say about the questions we have opened up but we shall not necessarily be doing so in theoretical discussions — although such discussion is essential to the present introductory considerations. The gospel will offer many examples and opportunities to clarify our questions more and more.

An accurate grasp of the difference between the gospels in relation to the three stages of consciousness (Imagination, Inspiration and Intuition) is extraordinarily illuminating to the question of inspiration. This is where we approach the basic difference between the first three gospels on the one hand and the Gospel of St John on the other. That difference is not one of historical material, nor is it one of historical reliability. The difference is one of the nature of consciousness and of stages of cognition.

The first three gospels derive mainly from imaginative perceiving, whereas St John's Gospel flowed from a cognizance that embraced all three stages: Imagination, Inspiration and Intuition.

Should we wish to define accurately the inspirational character of the different gospels, we would have to say: only the Gospel according to St John is in the true sense 'inspired.' It is in fact more than inspired; it is woven through and through with Intuition. The first three books, Matthew, Mark and Luke, are *seen*, 'imaged.' Inspiration in the fullest sense of the word resounds in them, as it were, only from a distance and into their 'pictorial' form.

The difference between these stages is best recognized by comparing the Gospel of St John with that of St Matthew. Here we are approaching a concrete topic which is to be basic to our studies. In order to reach that end, we shall try to take a brief look at the general structure of St John's Gospel, then that of St Matthew in relation to the composition of the Revelation to St John.

The three stages in the Gospel of St John

The first half of the Gospel according to St John, comprising eleven chapters, is built around the seven great Johannine miracles of Christ.

> Turning water into wine.
> Healing of the nobleman's son.
> Healing of the man at the pool of Bethesda.
> Feeding of the five thousand.
> Walking on the waters.
> Healing of the man born blind.
> The raising of Lazarus.

That number, seven, is not due to chance, any more than it is in the 4×7 of the stages of the Apocalypse. The ordering and rhythm of the number seven is a fact of the spiritual world, just as the seven tones of the octave, the seven colours of the rainbow, and the seven days of the week are facts.

The seven miracles of Christ in St John's Gospel confront us as powerful images that sweep our souls along with them. They set out to impress themselves upon our souls like the seven seals of Revelation, having been unsealed in spiritual regions by perceptive imaginative consciousness. If we really follow the miracles, we will find that they were not unique, historically complete events, but that they bear within themselves the original phenomenon of a soul transformed in consequence of spiritual perception. Our own existence as human beings is changed into the pitchers at the marriage in Cana — inside them the water turns to wine. We ourselves are the youth healed through his father's prayers. The sick man by the pool of Bethesda is within us. Even as we are seen, so we see the images taken from the life and work of Christ become a mirror in which we see ourselves; we see the miracles of Christ through which we have passed.

The world of Imagination opens out even as images of earthly events turn to mirrors of spiritual happenings. The first stratum of supersensible experience spreads out. The seven deeds of Christ, accomplished by him on earth, turn to seven seals; as these are unlocked, so seven stages of experience gush forth. Human souls may

pass through them anywhere and at any time. Those sacred and historical occurrences in the Holy Land express themselves as parables,
not in words, but in deeds. They become visions of spiritual seeing,
while never ceasing to be definite, uniquely historical events in the
earthly life of Christ.

The sequence of seven pictorial events reaches its climax with the
raising of Lazarus; from then on, a wholly new element takes over in
the second half of St John's Gospel. From chapters twelve and thirteen
onward, the Christ performs no more miracles. To some extent he
withdraws with his disciples to a holy place, there to plant words of
divine teaching and knowledge — seed in the disciples' hearts.

The tremendous transition from picture to word emerges quite
clearly in chapter thirteen, following the washing of feet. Now begin
what are known as the farewell discourses of Jesus. The cathedral of
Christ's words rises ever more holy and more powerfully on the foundation of the washing of feet and of the Last Supper. At last, in the high
priestly prayer of chapter seventeen, the sacred and innermost completion of the cathedral is achieved, 'so that they may all be one; as
you, Father, are in me and I in you, so they shall be one in us ...' (John
17:21). The church of the spirit is the cathedral of Christ's words.

While taking the broad view of St John's Gospel as a whole, we
must become inwardly attentive to the great transition from picture to
word which comes after the raising of Lazarus, that is, from chapter
twelve to chapter seventeen. Here, as in Revelation, we now feel ourselves borne aloft by an eagle who strives towards the heights through
three immense circles. The great farewell discourses of Jesus are the
second circle. They traverse the actual region of Inspiration, of spiritual hearing. Here the seven trumpets have assumed the voice of
Christ.

To be sure, the first portion of the gospel, the part of the seven miracles, is also interwoven with inspirational word elements. The deeds
of Christ grow more and more powerfully into the revelatory speech
of Christ. In the intervals between the miracles which he performs, the
Christ speaks now to the common people, now to the Jews or the disciples. But the significance of the Word, of the Logos by itself, emerges
only after the seventh, the supreme miracle.

The eagle soars to the heights, touches the world of the Logos from
which all creation emanates. It is the world from which flows the evan-

gel even as its first disciples emanate from it: 'In the beginning was the Word.'

With chapter 18, the Gospel of John rises to the third circle of the eagle's flight. Now the suffering, death and resurrection of Christ begin; no longer does he speak externally in words of revelation. This is when he performs his supreme spiritual deed; even while humanity acts against him, scourges and crucifies him and lays him in the grave, he pours out the draught of the love of God — his own being, his own soul. He sacrifices his own self, uniting his soul with that of his flock and with the earth. From now on, true Intuition penetrates all existence; *it is permeated by an essential contact with the divine world* — the Christ has sacrificed himself. He can from now on be close to the whole of creation; all creation can feel his nearness, actually feel his very essence and touch it.

No other gospel recreates as does the Gospel of St John the intuitive character of the suffering, dying and rising again of the Christ. Much within those four last chapters is quite incomprehensible unless we recognize in them an expression of intuitive experience. Here is just one example taken from the resurrection stories.

Thomas thrusts his hand into the wound inflicted by the spear upon the side of Christ, his finger into marks made by the nails; Christ himself invites him to do so. This is all the more remarkable because shortly before the story is told how the Risen Christ appears to Mary Magdalene. When she recognizes the Christ she stretches out her hands to take hold of him. Out of the depths of her nature, the soul of Mary Magdalene confesses — not in words but with her hands — that the Christ even now, after death and resurrection, still has a body. The hands of Mary Magdalene confess belief in the bodily resurrection of Christ. But Christ says, 'Do not touch me, for I have not yet ascended to the Father.' (John 20:17).

To Thomas, Christ says the very opposite, but Thomas does not doubt that the Christ, having passed through death, is present among the disciples in the spirit. He does doubt whether he has a body: he wants to make sure by touching that body of the Resurrection. And Christ says to him, 'Touch me.'

These scenes have a peculiar, delicately weaving atmosphere of Intuition. They have been taken in a material sense and in consequence either interpreted as purely dogmatic 'miracles,' or else sceptically dismissed as legend. When this happened it was because people had no notion of the secret of their composition. Had those scenes been placed at the beginning of the gospel, then an earthly material understanding of them might have been acceptable. But they are in that last 'holy of holies.' They should not be pulled from their context, nor should they be dragged from the level they have attained after all that has gone before. One assumes that those who seek to understand them have in fact lived through what the gospel has given earlier: the seven miracles, the farewell discourses, the stories of Christ's passion and death. Anyone who has inwardly passed along the way indicated by the preceding nineteen chapters, who has, above all, drawn into himself the true breath of the passion and of the death on Golgotha, cannot conceive of the Thomas scene in grossly material terms. A grossly materialistic mind moves at ground level; but the object of its interest has gone ahead and climbed three high flights of stairs, to the level of a world where different life conditions prevail, into a region where vials of divine love and divine wrath are poured out and where the soul is washed by the tides of divine strength.

In his encounter with the Risen Christ, Thomas attains the stage of Intuition. Only at that stage can humanity become aware of, become a partaker in, the new body created by the resurrection of Christ. That body is not a material one, nor is it earthly. It is an imperishable spiritual body, the building material of the heavenly Jerusalem. It was no earthly hand of Thomas that reached out towards Christ's body. It was the organ of intuition that groped for the wounds of Christ; it was the soul's power of touch, Thomas' spiritual hand. Whatever movements he made with his physical hands were no more than accompanying phenomena. There are those who know that in the human hand, especially in the fingertips and the palm, there dwells a delicate, etheric sense of touch associated with the soul. That sense of touch far excels the merely physical, nor is it tied as closely to the physical hand. Such people may attain to a faint understanding of what Thomas experienced.

The word 'Intuition' in its exact meaning as we understand it here is assuredly the key to the Mary Magdalene and Thomas scenes, insofar as they are experiences of touching the body of Christ. The same scenes can also be examples of what is encompassed in St John's Gospel by the third circle of the eagle's flight. The Gospel of John proffers the most profound, the grandest expression of an intuitional experience where it speaks of John the disciple himself. It tells how at the Last Supper he 'leaned on Jesus' bosom.' Here we have the description of a physical posture which the disciple assumes at the supper table. But it is first and foremost a pictorial expression of an inward state of intuition wherein the soul-nature of John directly contacts the spirit-soul nature of Christ. John has means not open to the other disciples of obtaining answers from Christ, because he is able to listen to the heart of Christ with nothing coming between. That is why Peter bids John ask Jesus 'who should betray him.' If the answer could have been given in audible words, Peter would have been able to put the question himself. John hears the Christ speaking in a different region from the one where the lips move. This he could do through Intuition.

The supper scene is not in the last four chapters — the Intuition chapters — but in the middle portion, that of Inspiration. Just as the word element is discernable in the first pictorial part, so, in the second part the essential intuitional element shows through the inspirational word element. John is the 'disciple whom Jesus loved,' the disciple into whom is poured the cup of divine love. He is related to the Christ through Intuition. That is why his gospel is able to ascend so clearly into the third circle of the eagle's flight. We shall see later that St Matthew's Gospel differs from it.

The second stage of the gospel, that of the Word, once again reaches heights from which, through the prologue, the whole gospel descends: 'In the very beginning was the Word.' In the third stage we approach yet again the archetypal worlds proclaimed in the prologue. Wherever we hear that sound rising loud and clear of how John leaned on the bosom of Jesus, there was fulfilled on earth something of the heavenly Intuition existing between God the Father and God the Son. There is a hint of this in the prologue where it says, 'No human being has ever seen the divine Ground of the World with eyes. The only Son, who was in the bosom of the Father, he has become the guide in such seeing.' (John 1:18)

We can recognize accordingly from the general composition of the Gospel of St John as a whole that it is derived from a consciousness embracing Imagination, Inspiration and Intuition. The clearest embodiment of each is to be found in:

— The Johannine Imagination (John 1–11), the seven miracles.
— The Johannine Inspiration (John 12–17), the farewell discourses.
— The Johannine Intuition (John 18–21), Passion and Resurrection.

It would be possible to illustrate this right down into the details of St John's Gospel. Our concern however is to acquire a foundation from which to survey the book in general, just a few broad guidelines. We could summarize what we have seen so far in this way:

— The seven miracles according to John are seven deeds of Christ —
   namely the seven seals.
— The seven trumpets resound with the voice of Christ in the
   farewell discourses.
— In the life and death deed on Golgotha the seven vials of wrath
   are turned by Christ into the great vessel of sacrifice and love,
   poured out for the salvation of the world.

The three stages in Matthew's Gospel

Armed with the key we have gained in our study of the composition of the Book of Revelation and of St John's Gospel, let us now approach the Gospel according to St Matthew. It is much more difficult to recognize its composition than in the case of the other two — it seems to have been part-buried; and yet it emerges more and more distinctly before our eyes in response to wide-ranging and penetrating study.

What we are about to indicate should be accepted freely as a summary of statements, the proofs for which can only become evident from a number of separate studies that are to follow. We shall have to accept a simple statement so that a genuinely comprehensive view of the whole of the Gospel of St Matthew may emerge.

What is the essential difference between the first and the fourth gospel? Both are initiation books; both describe the way by which human souls can rise towards the spiritual world. But those two worlds differ. Two different kinds of human beings, two different types, are shown differing paths to Christ. We can say that St John's Gospel describes the path of Johannine man; St Matthew describes that of Petrine man. To Johannine man it is vouchsafed to pass through all three stages of Imagination, Inspiration, and Intuition, that is, of picture, word and being; to pass on, completely clear to the very end. This is he whom God loves, the disciple whom the Lord loves and who on that account seems to have been predestined to communion with the divine, to true and total Intuition. He walks through those stages of the soul that are the seven miracles of Christ undoubting to the end. That is to say, he is strong enough to pass through death and resurrection, for such is the content of the seventh and last stage of the first circle. Lazarus, who dies and rises again, is the true man of John. Anthroposophy tells us that Lazarus himself is the disciple whom Jesus loved; Lazarus is John; the Gospel of St John is fruit of the death and resurrection of Lazarus. We need go no further here. One thing in any case is clear: the Johannine human being, whose way is described in the Gospel of John, could not have attained to an unimpeded experience of inspirational words, nor to inward hearing of the farewell of the Christ, had he not previously passed through the seventh miracle; through death and resurrection. He struggled across the most difficult threshold because he summoned the strength to return at the word of Christ from beyond the grave to earthly existence; he has truly fought his way through to Inspiration, to hearing the spiritual word of Christ, to feeling the touch of the Christ's spirit.

The first eleven chapters of St John correspond to the first sixteen of St Matthew. Here we see Petrine man instead of Johannine man on his way through the seven stages of the deeds of Christ. He does not pass that way with any consistent assurance. The human element is stronger in him than it is in Johannine man, in whom the angelic predominates. His human temperament sends Petrine man storming and blustering to the heights only to drop him into depths all the deeper.

At first glance, we can recognize two of the seven circles of John in the Gospel of Matthew. They are the fourth and fifth stages with the feeding of the five thousand and the walking on the waters (John 6; Matt.14).

If we compare in particular the account of the walking on the waters in John and in Matthew, we shall find the difference between them clear before us. John tells us that when the disciples saw Jesus walking on the waters they felt fear. They see him. They do not as yet recognize the vision, the Imagination, for what it is. They see Jesus but do not recognize him; that is what makes them afraid. But then hearing is added to seeing, the word to the vision. Jesus speaks: 'I am' (The Greek *eg eimi* is a mighty runic word; it should not be translated by the trivial, 'It is I.') And as that word brings about recognition, so fear leaves them. The story relates: 'Then they willingly received him into the ship; and immediately the ship was at the land whither they went.' By that experience of vision and of word the disciples are prepared for essential union. We shall see more fully later on that the whole event is a spiritual experience of the disciples; but the experience comes to an end, the ship reaches land, the sea of the spiritual world now lies behind the disciples. They are back on the *terra firma* of earthly existence. That is how John passes through this stage, the stage of walking on the waters.

Peter's experience is altogether different and this is what Matthew describes. Having recognized the Christ after all the fear and dismay, Peter is carried away by his own effervescent nature, 'Lord, if it is you, bid me come to you over the water.' And he said, 'Come.' But then, as he sets out to walk upon the sea just like the Christ, Peter is again overcome by fear of storm and waves; he begins to sink, cries out to the Lord to help him and clings to the hand of Christ. He has to be told that he was not able to walk upon the sea because his faith was wanting.

The scene with Peter occurs only in St Matthew's Gospel and we shall realize more and more clearly that throughout that gospel, and not only in this passage, St Matthew shows us the way of Peter. If he is to enter upon spiritual regions he must be able to walk upon the sea. Whether the sea be stormy or calm depends upon each individual human soul. If a soul be cleansed and harmonious, the surface of the water will be as still as a mirror. But for the passionate stormy soul the waves of that sea will be high and storm-tossed. Peter is the man of the stormy sea. He desires to walk on the waves but is not strong enough. John and Peter pass through the fifth and seventh stages of their journey differently. John goes forward in unquestioning confidence of soul; his way lies unencumbered no matter what lies ahead. One can foresee that he will be able to pass through the crucial seventh stage which brings death and resurrection. As he passes through the fifth stage, Peter is overcome by uncertainty and fear that spring from a weakness in his own soul. He seems to be stumbling along his path. While the Gospel of John, after the walking on the waters, goes forward unclouded and exalted, Matthew's Gospel confronts us with the question: How will Peter, how will Petrine man (whom after all, we meet everywhere) — how will he stand up to the ordeal of the sixth

and seventh stages, seeing that when Peter walks upon the water only
the grace of the hand of Christ makes up for Peter's flagging faith.

We can recognize the seven seal stages, that is, the miracles of
Christ, in their correspondences to St Matthew's Gospel — the feeding
of the five thousand and the walking on the water are obviously anal-
ogous. As for other stages, we will discuss them later in more detailed
studies. Once again, in order to gain a general view, parallel gospel
passages have been set out below:

First stage	Wedding in Cana (John 2)	Sermon on the Mount (Matt.5–7).
Second stage	Healing of the noble-man's son (John 4)	Healing of the centu-rion's servant (Matt.8).
Third stage	Healing the man at pool of Bethesda (John 5)	Healing the man sick of palsy (Matt.9).
Fourth stage	Feeding the five thou-sand (John 6)	Feeding the five thou-sand (Matt.14).
Fifth stage	Walking on the sea (John 6)	Walking on the water (Matt.14).
Sixth stage	Healing of the man born blind (John 9)	Peter's acknowledgment at Caesarea Philippi (Matt.16).
Seventh stage	Raising of Lazarus (John 11)	

The way of John leads into the mystery of the seventh stage. Peter
breaks down before the seventh stage, having already stumbled at the
fifth. The raising of Lazarus according to John has no analogy in
Matthew. It is most important for the further study of the composition
of the Gospel of St Matthew to look more closely at this. We shall be
discussing this passage in greater detail later on. For the present we are
only going to indicate what is necessary for the appreciation of its general structure.

Let us look into the sixteenth chapter of the gospel. Somewhere near
the town of Caesarea Philippi Jesus asks the disciples about the secret
of his own identity. Peter bursts out with the answer: 'You are the
Christ, the Son of the Living God.' Peter is not subscribing to an article
of faith. His confession springs from vital and sudden recognition.

Hitherto his physical eyes have seen only the Master, the man Jesus of Nazareth. But now Jesus' question at one stroke rends apart the veil of the sense world; for a moment the portals of the spirit world swing open. Radiant light gushes from them. Peter's soul-eyes open at the same time as the doors. He gazes into the light. He sees the human form of Jesus surrounded and filled by the light-figure of the Christ being. His soul's eyes, blind hitherto, now see and he realizes that Jesus is indeed the Christ, the exalted being, the Son of God.

It is there, near Caesarea Philippi, that Peter actually relives in his own soul the healing of the man born blind; he himself in his own soul is the man born blind. Peter is consecrated by this experience and he receives through it the divinely appointed task of Christian priesthood. Jesus says to Peter, 'You are Peter, the Rock. On this rock I will build my congregation, and the gates of the abyss shall not swallow it up. To you I will give the keys to the kingdom of the heavens.' We might say, however, that the Christ gives Peter only what Peter already had in that moment when he confessed the Christ, that is, he gives to Peter the key that opens the gates of realization, the gates of vision. Much has been said, throughout the centuries, which leads in the opposite direction concerning Peter's power of the key. The image of the key presupposes an image of gates, of a door. For Peter has with the open eyes of his soul seen the Christ being through a chink in that door. Thereafter the church of Christ to be founded upon Peter, the rock; it enters upon life through the open gates of the kingdom of heaven. The image of the gates, of the door, is further stressed by that word, 'gates.' The gates of hell shall not prevail against it. That which constitutes the church of Christ dwells between two gates — the gates of the kingdom of heaven and the gates of hell. The first gate is to be victorious over the other because the key to it has been given to Peter.

And now the sixth stage has been carried out for Peter by the healing of blindness and by priestly consecration. The Christ makes ready for the fulfilment of the seventh mystery whose content is death and resurrection. This he does by beginning to speak to the disciples of what lies ahead. He utters the first intimations of suffering. By looking ahead to the death of Christ and to his resurrection, the souls of the disciples, but especially that of Peter, are to be prepared to pass through the Lazarus stage, towards the stage of death and resurrection. 'From then on Jesus Christ began to tell his disciples that he must go to Jerusalem, that much suffering from the elders and high priests and scribes lay before him, that he must be killed and that he would be raised on the third day' (Matt.16:21).

How does all this affect Peter? How does he find admittance to the seventh hall of the sanctuary? We see Peter rise up in protest against the mystery of death and resurrection. He has admittedly beheld the Christ and recognized him as a living being, but he is far from realizing that the Christ is on earth for the sole purpose of passing through death and resurrection. He is able to acknowledge Christ alive, but not Christ's death. 'Then Peter took him aside and began to remonstrate with him, "I mean well, Lord; do not allow this to happen to you".' (Matt.16:22).

This time the Christ answers differently from the way in which he answered earlier. We should get this radical change of attitude quite clear in our minds. He had said earlier, '... you have not received this revelation from the world of the senses but from the world of my Father in the heavens.' (Matt.16:17). But now: 'You are no longer thinking heavenly thoughts; now you are only thinking as earthly Man.' (Matt.16:23). Earlier it was: 'On this rock I will build my congregation and the gates of the abyss shall not swallow it up.' But now: 'Leave me, power of Satan.'

This contrast enables us more clearly than anything else to sympathize with Peter's sudden faltering along the way. The sixth station he had passed while richly gifted, but he broke down at the seventh stage. He lacked the strength to die and rise again.

Lazarus having emerged from the grave, Johannine man is able to mount, his spirit purified, to the second circle of the eagle's flight — he passes into the sphere of the Christ-word that sounds clear and resonant through Inspiration. The passage of the seven miracles is followed by the divine farewell discourses of Jesus and continues to the high priestly prayer.

How does Petrine man enter upon the middle circle, the circle of the Word? St Matthew's Gospel also has that middle circle. If we pay attention to the seven parables of Jesus which form the stations of this middle circle, we will discover something significant about the architecture of Matthew's Gospel and, as well, of the sequence of stages in the way of Peter. These form the stages of this middle circle. St Matthew's Gospel contains twice seven parables; seven of them are in chapter thirteen, which is between the third and the fourth stage of miracles, that is, between the healing of the man sick of the palsy and the feeding of the five thousand. The second series of seven parables is spread between chapter eighteen and the chapters of the Passion. We are here concerned with the following parables:

1. The unmerciful servant (Ch. 18)
2. Equal pay for unequal work (Ch. 20)
3. The two sons in the vineyard (Ch. 21)
4. The messengers to the husbandmen and the son (Ch. 21)
5. The royal wedding (Ch. 22)
6. The five wise and five foolish virgins (Ch. 25)
7. The talents (Ch. 25)

We will reserve discussion of these parables for a later study. For the present it is the following that interests us:

The parables are words of the Christ. However, unlike the farewell discourses in St John, the transition from picture to word is not fully accomplished in them. The word still has visual characteristics. The parables are pictures in speech. As such they are a sequel to words enacted, that is, to the miracles of the first great circle.

The pictorial character in Matthew's Gospel continues into the second, middle portion (Matt.17–25). We could say that St Matthew's Gospel does not transcend the stage of imaginative experience, whereas the Gospel according to John rises to inspiration. The whole of it is the spiritual consequence of Peter's personality. Matthew, as it were, edits his gospel in terms of the soul and the path of Petrine man. But Peter fails at the seventh stage of the first circle, that circle being at the same time the threshold to the second one. Events in the life of Christ continue to influence Peter's soul; at the end of the first great circle, they are, however, seen to fall back to the pictorial stage of that self-same circle.

At the point where the third circle begins, with events that can be fully grasped only through intuition, we see Peter sink into a kind of sleep or dream. In that condition he perceives the great intuitional events of the suffering, death and resurrection of Christ only as pictures; he lets them pass before him like so many waking dreams. Peter and John experience the Passion of Christ in ways as different as it is possible for them to be. John is the only disciple who stands beneath the cross. Peter falls asleep in Gethsemane. It is he who fights the approach of death as he does near Caesarea Philippi. He it is who cuts off Malchus' ear with a sword. At the last he denies the Christ while under the influence of that dreaming sleep into which he has fallen and which has turned all things for him into unfamiliar and remote pictures.

A deeply moving human drama is that of Petrine man. It reveals itself more and more distinctly in that the Gospel of St Matthew stops short at the pictorial stage, at Imagination. It remains there even when events are struggling to rise from picture to word, that is, Inspiration, and from word to inmost essence, to Intuition. It is Pentecost that rouses Peter awake and free of his pictorial dream into the region of the spirit-word. The end of St Matthew's Gospel can be to us a prelude to the word-miracle of Pentecost. On the Mount, the Risen Christ speaks, 'Go forth and be the teachers of all peoples and baptize them in the name and with the power of the Father, and of the Son and of the Holy Spirit.' (Matt.28:19).

It is there, at the end, that the soul of Petrine man — and with it St Matthew's Gospel — finds its way out of Imagination up into the world of Inspiration.

The Gospel of St John	*The Gospel of St Matthew*
Chapters 1–11 The Seven Miracles of Christ IMAGINATION	*Chapters I–26* The Seven (Six) Miracles IMAGINATION
Chapters 12–17 The Farewell Discourses INSPIRATION	*Chapters 17–28* The Seven Parables INSPIRATION in form of IMAGINATION
Chapters 18–21 Passion, Death, Resurrection INTUITION	*Chapters 26–28* Passion, Death, Resurrection INTUITION in form of IMAGINATION

CHAPTER TWO

Secrets of the Genealogy

The Relationship of the New Testament to the Old

The New Testament emerges from the Old, spiritually as well as externally, as soon as we open the Gospel of St Matthew. The Gospel of St
Matthew, by its very structure, provides a transition from the writings
of the Old Testament to the new covenant. This is manifest in that St
Matthew's Gospel was originally written down in Hebrew, as we
know from early Christian tradition. That first gospel then, in Hebrew,
is the bridge from the Hebrew of the Old Testament to the Greek of the
later books of the New. Had the original Hebrew version been preserved along with its Greek translation, then the rich veins of intimate
knowledge, through which that gospel is bound to the sacred books of
Judaism, would doubtless lie open to our gaze even more clearly. We
could more easily have found an answer to the question: what does the
Old Testament mean to us today?

There is no element of chance in the sequence or the arrangement
of the New Testament. For this there are profound reasons. We may
not change the order of the gospels. St Matthew's is the foot of the
New Testament tree by means of which the New Testament is
grounded and rooted in the Old.

Let us look at the first chapter of St Matthew. At first glance it
seems to be no more than an endless list of names. After that, it sets out
the story of the birth of Jesus in a concise style, in words so much more
austere and terse than those of St Luke which are spiritually so rich.
Since the genealogy is assumed to be more or less extraneous material,
we have got into the habit of skimming through that first chapter,
especially through the larger, first part. We expect nothing from it in
the religious sense.

The gospel, however, holds nothing that could be taken as merely

externally historical. All of it is important. Everywhere the secret language of its composition touches on the weightiest secrets; very important paths are shown to us.

The gospel explains its own structure in words. Having listed the
forty-two generations from Abraham to Jesus it says: 'So all the generations from Abraham to David are fourteen generations; and from
David until the carrying away into Babylon are fourteen generations; and from the carrying away into Babylon unto Christ are fourteen.' Those are the rungs of the ladder which lead down from
Abraham to Jesus of Nazareth: six times seven, or three times fourteen rungs.

It is made clear to us that in addition to other implications in those
numbers, three great epochs of Jewish history, or we could say of Old
Testament history, are embraced by those thrice fourteen generations.
The names in the forty-two generations are a condensed recapitulation
and summary of the whole of the Old Testament. Every name strikes
the bell of Old Testament mysteries. The genealogical tree is neither
boring nor merely statistical for those to whom characters in the Old
Testament are familiar and vivid. People, pictures, scenes rise before
them. They pass through the narthex of the temple where many a character greets them. It resembles the vast and marvellous portals of
medieval cathedrals about whose arches are grouped figures of the old
and new covenant. All who pass through such a portal in the right
spirit can apprehend that the sacred precinct they are about to enter
rests on the shoulders of thousands of years of human history, in the
course of which God already spoke to human souls through the mouth
of his servants.

And the genealogy is indeed the portal to a cathedral, the ante-
chamber to a temple. If we are to understand the feeling of awe with
which early Christian centuries passed through those portals towards
the message of the gospel, then this is what we must think about.
Names in ancient times were always significant. They were bestowed
from out of an instinctive knowledge, or even out of actual vision of
the recipient's nature. Nowadays naming has become abstract. Family
names are without significance, whereas during the Middle Ages they
did have a meaning — a man's occupation, for instance. Many a man
is today called 'Smith' without being one by profession. It was different in ancient times. Now first names are given idly, maybe because of

some family tradition; in most cases, on this account, the true intention of the name fails — that is, to strengthen and help the recipient in his inmost nature.

The old names, such as those of the Jewish world, reflected pictorially a person's spiritual nature. Names in the genealogical table are Hebrew names; to us today they are foreign words. In the Greek text of St Matthew's Gospel they are still foreign. But if we imagine them as Hebrew words in their original Hebrew context, then we understand that they did at one time carry powerful pictorial force.

In Hebrew every name is a picture. Could we but see each name as an image, then the genealogical table would lose its dry, statistical character. We would have before us a series of forty-two pictures, down which we could descend as if down a flight of well ordered stairs. In this study we shall give a few examples of translations of names which illustrate what we mean.

While the genealogical table is a concentrated recapitulation of the Old Testament, in St Matthew's Gospel it occupies the same place as do the seven letters in the Revelation to St John of which we said in our first study that they were the historical entrance hall to the seven seals, the seven trumpets and the seven vials of wrath. To go back once more to Goethe's poem *The Secrets*, before being led to the hall of the thirteen armorial bearings and thence to his other adventures, Brother Marcus is seated at the round table of the twelve sages, each of whom recalls and narrates something from another epoch of humanity. We have to be led in the same way into the company of those thrice fourteen personages, before we can embark on our spiritual pilgrimage through St Matthew's Gospel. Each of them will tell us another portion of sacred prehistory.

The women in the genealogy of Jesus

The genealogical table gives to us, in four places, more than we would have expected. It mentions in those places the name of the woman as well as that of the man.

> Tamar, wife of Judah
> Rahab, mother of Boaz
> Ruth, wife of Boaz
> The wife of Uriah, Bathsheba, wife of David.

We might at first think that there is nothing special about an unusual mention of the mothers. There are however two points to be noticed which show that here too there is nothing coincidental in the gospel; on the contrary, in naming those four women chastely, inconspicuously, secretly, the intention is to point to very definite secrets which could not be expressed in words.

In the first place we recognize, thanks to those four names, that certain characters and pictures inwardly belong together. Tamar plays the harlot towards Judah. Rahab is the harlot of Jericho, whose house Joshua's two spies enter and where they take refuge. Ruth is the young Moabite woman who, in order to raise up heirs to her late husband, lies down in bridal array at the feet of the sleeping Boaz. Bathsheba is the woman with whom David commits adultery and who in time becomes the mother of Solomon.

As we consider the stories grouped about those four names it is essential totally to ignore any moralistic feeling for values and judgments which all too easily turn out to be prejudices. We must hold ourselves in unalloyed contemplation of the scenes that rise up before our eyes at mention of those four names. It may surprise us to note that just these four women should have been named in the lineage of Jesus. Too hasty a moral appraisal could come up with the question: why was Jesus descended from so doubtful a line?

Those who read the genealogical table as if they were gazing into a wisdom filled picture book may come upon a further observation: the naming of the four women is not haphazard but meaningful. They will ask themselves, is not Mary's name the fifth of the series? And is not the naming of the four Old Testament women, (however strange the idea may seem) a marvellously quiet yet eloquent pointer on the gospel's part to the secret of Mary, to the secret of the birth of Jesus; a gesture offered to those able to decipher a key to the mystery of the virgin birth?

The whole of the first chapter begins to reveal its inmost spiritual affiliation, its visage. A delicate golden bridge leads from the first half-chapter, so like a dry list of names, into the second half-chapter which recounts the birth of Jesus. The theme of the eternal feminine is established as the images of the five women rise; they are more then individuals, they are women who belong to humanity, they represent womanhood. The expectation comes to life in the hope that we may be able to understand the immemorial problem of the virgin birth.

To be sure, there is much more to be said before we can understand a chapter such as the first chapter of St Matthew. In this study, however, we will confine ourselves mainly to the line drawn through those five women, and we shall allow ourselves to be led quietly by the first of them back into the Old Testament; with that example before us we may recognize something of the relationship of St Matthew's Gospel to the Old Testament and at the same time the relationship of the whole New Testament. We shall only say here that the secret pattern of the first chapter of the New Testament, which finds expression in those five characters, is virtually never taken seriously in theology, nor even taken notice of.

Tamar

Grouped about the name of Judah, ancestor of the tribe of Judah, are additional names, normally so rare in the genealogical tables; here wives of the fathers are mentioned by name, as are brothers of the sons. By this means the narrow line of descent is extended. Abraham and Isaac having been named as originators of the line, the table goes on: 'Jacob begat Judah and his brethren; Judah begat Perez and Zerah of Tamar.' The line of descent comes down through Jacob, Judah, Perez. In mentioning Jacob's twelve sons, Tamar, and Zerah the twin brother of Perez, the pictures set before our souls images which we must take into account if we are to understand what follows: namely, the story of their birth.

These scenes are to be found in Genesis (37–39). The chapters vividly contrast Joseph and Judah of all the twelve sons of Jacob.

Chapter 37 tells how Joseph is sold by his brothers at Judah's instigation to Ishmaelite merchants. In the Old Testament Judah stands in a similar relationship to Joseph as Judas does to the Christ. In the New Testament, the dark one confronts the bright one, but it is not Joseph who becomes the ancestor of the tribe of Judah, the messianic race. Even though Judah's position among his eleven brothers resembles that of an Iscariot, it is he who becomes that ancestor — in uncleanness. Chapter 38 describes this, putting great stress on the difference in the content of chapters 38 and 39 which tells how Joseph in Egypt resisted the temptation of Potiphar's wife. Chapters 38 and 39 — the Judah and Joseph chapters — oppose the sexual aberrations of Judah and his sons to the sexual purity and chastity of Joseph in Egypt. The question arises again: why does the dark one, the unclean one, become the founding father of the messianic line, rather than the bright and pure one?

Let us look more closely at the Judah chapter. Judah is presented with three sons by his Canaanite wife — Er, Onan and Shelah. Judah marries his eldest son to Tamar. Er is killed by Yahweh because he is evil. Tamar becomes a widow. The second son, Onan, takes Tamar to wife but he forsakes the ancient holiness and destiny of the race. He is united to Tamar but he does not want a son to come of the union since, according to the old law, such a son would continue the race of Er, not his own. So Onan wastes his semen. For this he is slain by Yahweh. Judah is afraid that death threatens his third son, Shelah, through marriage with Tamar. He consoles her temporarily against the time when Shelah will have grown up, but he does not intend to marry Shelah to Tamar. He intends to break the racial law according to which, following the death of a childless man, his nearest male relative must take the widow to wife in order to raise up heirs to the dead.

Judah's wife dies. Tamar disguises herself as a harlot and sits down by the way along which Judah must travel. Judah takes her as a harlot without recognizing her as Tamar. By way of a pledge instead of a ram (a harlot's fee) he leaves her his sacred symbols: his signet ring, staff and bracelet. The messenger who is to redeem the pledges cannot find the harlot. Three months later Tamar is accused before Judah, having become pregnant through harlotry. Judah has her brought before him in order to have her burnt on a pyre. She shows him his own pledges, whereupon he realizes that she is pregnant to him.

Tamar has achieved continuation of the race by subterfuge, a sacred duty which Judah as well as his sons has betrayed. She has achieved her aim even though she had to turn whore. What deep reason prompted her to do it? From the very beginning the destiny has hung over the Jewish people through all the generations of their history: to help build the physical body in which in due course the divine messianic being would be able to incarnate. The sacred racial destiny must have passed down through the souls of the women in a particular way. No such word could as yet have been coined in those days but the mothers of Israel felt themselves, thanks to the consecrated authority of their femininity and to the prophecy that rested on the race, as being 'Mothers of God.'

This peculiar instinct for the future, for the secret of the Mother of God, came to life with unusual strength in the soul of Tamar. Judah and his sons had disregarded the divine command. Tamar tricks him into obedience, but not in order to ensure observance of a formal decree; it is so that a mystery rite should be fulfilled. Tamar feels that the future of the world will be at risk if she does not become a mother. She has a strong presentiment of the messianic line as a whole and she feels the presence of the Messiah himself within her womb wanting to be called awake. Tamar becomes a harlot in order to become the mother of God. She saves the exalted destiny of Israel. The line of Judah comes into being although not at the wish of Judah. The messianic line arises through the will of a woman. Here we see the first dawning in the Old Testament of the secret of Mary. The genealogical tree of the chosen one grows out of the unconsciousness, the error of his ways, of a man.

The genealogical table in St Matthew does more than name Tamar the mother and Perez the son: Zerah, the twin brother, is also brought to our notice, and we are made to envisage the scene where Tamar gives birth to the twins, to Perez and Zerah.

The hand of Zerah is the first to stretch forth from the maternal body of Tamar and the midwife marks it with a thread of scarlet in order to distinguish the firstborn. But Perez, the other boy, forces Zerah back and it is he who is born first and so continues the line of descent. The scene is a pictorial solution of profound cosmic riddles. The names reveal as in a picture what is taking place there at the human level. 'Tamar' signifies a lofty 'palm,' one that resembles a pillar and carries an ample crown of leaves. 'Perez' means a 'breach,' one who rends. He receives that name because in pushing his brother out of the way as he comes to birth, he tears his mother's body. 'Zerah' means the 'sunrise.'

In Tamar humanity is still both virginal and maternal, pure with the purity of a plant; like a palm tree soaring heavenward, heavenly innocence is still hers; what is coming to birth is like a glowing sunrise.

A future as beautiful as paradise is already heralding itself. Then the sinister brother of the bright boy pushes himself forward. Something pertaining to the ego asserts itself. An image of egotism presses forward. Man's plant-like innocence, man's sunny brightness, passes away at the sullen rise of egotism. Pre-ego humanity is rent asunder. Harmony comes to an end with egotism. A rending replaces harmony not only in the community but also in the individual.

The scene of the birth of Perez and Zerah has something in common with the story of Cain and Abel. Earthly man, the competent one, kills Abel, the man of heaven. It is Cain, not Abel, who becomes the forefather of a branch race, from which later on the messianic line is derived.

If humanity is to find earth, the whole earth, then humanity must forego heaven. The future belongs to Cain, the ego-man, not to Abel, the man of soul. The Fall marches on stage by stage. Earthly competence, an earthly future, ego-evolution — all these must be paid for by guilt, by hardening, by fratricide.

A further stage in the Fall is the cheating of Esau by Jacob. Esau still bears an ancient, natural link with cosmic spirituality. Jacob, on the other hand, is the bearer of human intelligence. Lies and deceit are the price of Man's future as the bearer of intellectuality.

We see yet another stage of the Fall in the sale of Joseph by Judah. Joseph is still endowed with visionary powers, his dreams are those of a seer. Judah it is who has forgotten all about the world of spirit. That is why he has not kept himself sexually clean. Individual personality must be bought for the future by impurity.

The birth of Perez and Zerah belongs in the sequence of scenes of the Fall's advance.

> Cain and Abel,
> Jacob and Esau,
> Judah and Joseph,
> Perez and Zerah.

Why does Judah rather than Joseph, why Perez and not Zerah, become the founder of the messianic line? That question answers itself pictorially if we can envisage these four pairs of brothers at the same time. Man descends step by step from heaven to earth through all the stages of the advancing Fall in order thereby to achieve ego-strength. The divine passes into the depths at the same time as humanity, from

Abraham to Jesus, through all the forty-two generations enumerated by St Matthew's Gospel: men do not grow to be more heavenly, they grow more earthly; not more angelic but more ego-centric. The Christ being can, when the time comes, be incarnated only in a human body wholly ego-centred, utterly earthly. In no other way was the Christ able to transform and redeem earthly man.

We can gain some understanding of why the genealogical table in Matthew travels from above downwards. It is an earth-bound ladder, not a heavenly ladder. A comparison with the genealogical table in Luke (which is of course not identical with Matthew's) reveals at a glance that it is set up in reverse order, that is, from the bottom up. It begins with Jesus, rises to Abraham, Adam and at last to God. How is it that St Luke's Gospel presents the genealogy as a ladder to heaven and not, like St Matthew's, a ladder to earth? The answer, which only needs to be indicated at this stage, can be found in the position which the genealogies occupy in the two gospels. In St Matthew it stands at the very beginning, linked to the birth of the Jesus child. In St Luke, on the other hand, it follows the Baptism in Jordan by John. The story of Christmas is the story of the birth of the Jesus child; the Baptism in Jordan is the birth of the Christ. It was then that the Christ, the messianic being, was actually born, incorporated in Jesus of Nazareth, the human being. That is why for over three and a half centuries, early Christians, who still preserved vital knowledge of these things, celebrated the birth of Christ not on December 25, but on January 6 — the day of the Baptism in the Jordan. It was after the incarnation of the Christ on earth, that is, after the Baptism in the Jordan, that the downward movement of humanity — its descent — was turned back again to ascent. The step by step advance of the Fall is changed; it becomes world transformation, world redemption. The birth of Jesus is the last rung of the earthbound ladder; the birth of Christ is the first rung of the heavenly one.

We have seen Tamar, the first of the four women in the genealogical table, stationed at an important juncture of the descent of man to earth; she was the custodian of the sanctuary although in the guise of a harlot. Even when for Judah and his sons the inevitability of the ancient custom and with it of innocence itself is lost, as one heavenly heirloom after another had to be lost to them — so it is Tamar who keeps alive the stream of innocence, and she finds out in her own body the way in which the ego-impulse works its way to the outside, how it displaces and tears apart both custom and innocence. Her body is rent as she gives birth to Perez the render.

Rahab

Rahab is the second woman mentioned by name in the genealogical register. Her name brings to life the story in the second chapter of the Book of Joshua. Joshua, the successor of Moses, is leading the children of Israel into the Promised Land. They must conquer the land step by step. Above all Jericho, the city of the moon, must be overcome. Joshua sends two spies into Jericho. The spies enter the house of Rahab. Rahab hides them on the roof of the house and sets the pursuers on the wrong trail. That night Rahab comes to the men and by her words reveals an intimate link with the spirit and destiny of Israel: 'I know that the LORD has given you the land, and that the fear of you has fallen upon us, and that all inhabitants of the land melt away before you. For we have heard how the LORD dried up the water of the Red Sea before you when you came out of Egypt. ... for the LORD your God is he who is God in heaven above and on earth beneath.' (Josh.2:9–11). The spies swear to Rahab that at the destruction of the city her house will be spared. Then follows the pictorially memorable scene of the rescue: Rahab lets the two men out of the house by a rope. Since the house is situated upon the city wall, they are immediately out of the danger zone of the hostile city.

In all the Old Testament Rahab appears only in this story of Joshua's spies and in the account of the destruction of Jericho, in which we are told that the house of Rahab was indeed spared. The New Testament in the genealogical table names Rahab as the mother of Boaz. The name is mentioned almost casually, without the smallest addition. But it is just this pithy mention that shows the name was familiar to all. In the New Testament her deed on behalf of the spies is used as an example of 'faith' (Heb.11:31, James 2:25). Here is one of those places where we can but admire the artistry and wisdom of the way in which the Old Testament is integrated with the New. What would the name of Rahab be without the story of the spies in the Book of Joshua? Indeed — and this is even more significant — what would the Old Testament scene be, were the name of Rahab, so easily overlooked, not mentioned in the Gospel of St Matthew? The house of Rahab the harlot has to be spared during the sack of the city because Rahab is to be a 'Mother of God,' ancestress of the Messiah.

Let us try to penetrate into the meaning of the story of Rahab and, as in the case of the Tamar-Perez-Zerah story, let us enquire into the meaning of the name. Rahab is a word that indicates at one and the same time both something inward and something external. It cannot for that reason be translated by a single word. In more modern languages the concepts of 'external' and 'internal' have fallen apart. The words are either abstract or else concrete. In Greek the single word *pneuma* still means 'air,' 'wind' — that is, something concrete, but also 'spirit,' that is, a so-called abstraction. Rahab in its inward meaning signifies something like 'freedom,' but externally implies 'space.' Rahab is a mantric pictorial word. Its inferences can be illustrated by the deep breath that a man draws who has been released from a constricting prison and steps forth to freedom a free man.

With that, the word takes us back to the scene of Rahab and the spies. The two spies experience 'Rahab' when they are set free of the city by means of the rope out of the house. The picture expressed twice over in the name of Rahab and in the Rahab story is more than just another isolated insignificant tale. It is the pictorial expression of the fact that humanity is reaching an important parting of the ways in human evolution. Humanity is passing from heaven to earth, from paradise to desert. Man loses God-supported fellowship in order to find freedom in the loneliness of the ego. When Moses led the children of Israel into wandering in the desert, he was a leader to freedom. In Egypt, Israel was embedded in a world of voluptuous cults. Those temple rituals however were by that time becoming decadent — as were the related cults of Babylon — because they were no longer appropriate to the time. Their era was over: the evolution of human consciousness had advanced beyond them. What had earlier been holy had become a desecration, degenerate. That was especially so in the case of all manner of sexual mysteries, which played a part in a variety of Egyptian and Babylonian temple ritual. The spirituality of Egypt and Babylon was transformed into temptation for human beings, into a force that sought to hold men back in the past. That is how there came into being that which in time John, the writer of the Apocalypse, designated as the 'whore of Babylon.' The Exodus from Egypt was the forsaking of the cloying sleep-inducing religious culture; it meant forsaking the magic circle of the whore of Babylon. Humanity could not escape that exodus. Without it, in spite of the fact that the way led into the wilderness, or perhaps because it did, there could have been no awakening from the all-enfolding dream, and no escape into freedom.

And now the children of Israel, having ended their wandering in the wilderness, were reaching the approaches of the Promised Land. Were they inwardly quite free from Egypt, having left behind them the dream culture? Were they able to build up a culture of the individual? In the Holy Land the Israelites again came up against peoples who practised rituals similar to those they had left behind in Egypt; theirs were Baal and Astarte cults, dream cults of the moon. The people of Israel were to be tested as they entered into the land of Canaan as to the extent to which they had freed themselves from Egypt and its twilight moon-world. That was the reason why Joshua had first of all to overcome Jericho. Jericho means 'city of the moon.' We must think of it as a city completely governed by the practices of Egypto-Babylonian moon rituals.

It is well known to students of the history of religions that there were low-grade priestesses in the Astarte temples of Asia and decadent Greece who, in performing their duties, also served as prostitutes. Since this is known from history, we often think of the temple cults today with disapproval. We forget that all sexual aberrations carried on within those temple precincts were symptomatic of the degeneration of mysteries that had at one time been truly venerated.

We may assume that Rahab was called a harlot because she belonged to some such moon cult of Astarte. If we are right in this assumption, then the sojourn of the spies in Rahab's house is a piece of religious history. Israel, having left Egypt and having passed through the wilderness, returned nevertheless in a spiritual sense to Egypt. In the person of these two men, Israel passed through something like a relapse into the world of Egypt. It was, however, a relapse that enabled Israel to struggle quite free of the dream world and to enter into the world of freedom. When the spies were released from the city through the window of Rahab's house, they left behind them not only the enchanted circle of the moon city, but also the enchanted circle of the world of the Egypto-Babylonia cults. The experience was 'Rahab' — freedom of space. They stepped forth from enveloping night into day.

And it all happened so strangely. The spies unexpectedly found in the person of Rahab not a representative of the whore of Babylon, but a witness to Israel's spiritual mission. The servant of the goddess Astarte testified for Yahweh, the god of Israel, 'For the Lord your God, he is God in heaven above and in earth beneath.' The two Israelites enter an unfamiliar house and find — themselves. In the house of the moon they find the sun!

Her meeting with the spies sinks deep into Rahab's destiny. It may be that one of the spies was that Salmon whose wife she became and to whom she bore Boaz. It may even be that the union which led to the birth of Boaz was a part of the worship brought in that house in Jericho to the moon and Astarte. But instead of the spies meeting the whore of Babylon in the person of Rahab, it was Rahab who met Yahweh in the person of the two men. She imbued herself with the perception of Yahweh and of the spiritual mission of Israel. By apprehending the spirit of Israel, she gains a share in the dimly perceived and distant secret of the Mother of God, the secret kept alive by the women.

Destiny caught the spies unawares in their disloyalty. It let them come up against Yahweh in the soul of the very woman with whom they were about to betray Yahweh. Instead of Israel paying tribute to Astarte, Israel received through Rahab a fresh contribution to its genealogy. Astarte brings tribute towards the building of the temple of the body which the Messiah would in time inhabit.

Ruth

Ruth is the third name of a woman in the genealogical table. The story of Ruth leads us into intimate proximity to the secret of Mary. We are taken to Bethlehem, the house of bread, the scene of the Christian story.

There is famine in Bethlehem. Elimelech and Naomi flee with their sons before the famine to the land of Moab. The sons take Moabite women to wife — Orpah and Ruth. Then Elimelech and his sons die, all three of them, and the three women are left widowed. In time the famine in the house of bread comes to an end and Naomi sets out for home. She suggests to Ruth and Orpah that they integrate back among their own people, return to their old gods. Orpah accepts the advice but Ruth has felt too much of the spirit and the mission of Israel; she does not allow herself to be sent back into the past. She follows Naomi to the land of Bethlehem in Judah — 'for where you go I will go, and where you lodge I will lodge; your people shall be my people, and your God will be my God' (Ruth 1:16). We must not regard Ruth's decision as an act of personal loyalty or of affection for Naomi, in the way in which it is often presented in sentimental literature. Ruth would have turned back to the gods of her homeland, as did Orpah, had not Yahweh, the spirit of Israel, taken strong possession of her. There is an inward link between the words of Ruth to Naomi and of Rehab to the spies. 'For the LORD your God, he is God in heaven above and on earth beneath,' and 'Your people shall be my people, your God will be my God.'

Alien folk souls reach a point of contact with the Yahweh-Israelite stream. Rahab and Ruth are bearers of experiences of the godhead, of contact with Yahweh. 'Your God will be my God.' Here is the inmost soul of the Book of Ruth.

In what way did Ruth experience Yahweh? Within the inmost, hidden recesses of her soul she felt that divine being who would one day incarnate on earth; she felt the approach of the Messiah, the god who was in heaven above and who would one day be on earth beneath. She apprehended that facing that god were the people of Israel, the line of Judah, the town of Bethlehem, and the Mother of God who one day would bear the Son. In holiest devotion to this divine being, Ruth saw herself called upon to assist maternally in the building of the temple of the body. We can say it was a Marian experience through which Ruth was destined to follow Naomi in order to belong to the next of kin in his own homeland, Bethlehem; and this is true even though it may all have taken place with Ruth herself deeply unconscious of it. The vision of a virgin who bears the son was alive in Ruth's soul. A very delicate element of Advent and of Christmas wove itself about Ruth. She was ready to become the handmaid of the Lord.

The image of Mary with the Child is not that of an historical character who lived two thousand years ago. It is the image of every human soul that gives birth within itself to the spiritual, to the ego. It is a prototype. Those who see a spiritual picture in an 'imagination' (see earlier considerations of this term) of their own soul and spirit nature, behold the virgin mother and child. From this standpoint Ruth's name acquires marvellous light. Ruth can be translated 'the beloved who loves,' or more explicitly 'she who sees visions is seen in a vision,' 'she who sees herself in a vision.'

Mary comes to life in the soul of Ruth. In the person of Ruth the Old Testament foreshadows Mary in terms realistic and exalted.

How did Ruth become an ancestress of the Messiah? We see Ruth gleaning in the barley field of Boaz in Bethlehem. Boaz sees her among the maidens and hears her story. To see her and to know her story moved him so much that he showed her special favours. Now Naomi realized that fate has led Ruth to the 'heir,' the blood relation of her dead husband and Ruth follows the mother's advice; garbed in bridal array, she lays herself that night at Boaz' feet as he sleeps on the threshing floor. 'Spread your skirt over your maid-servant, for you are next of kin' (Ruth 3:9).

An indescribable breath of Christmas passes across the scene of the gleaners on the barley field, and of Ruth, all decked out, on the threshing floor. It is as if she were saying, 'See, I am the handmaid of the Lord. May your word be fulfilled upon me.' (Luke 1:38). Mary's robe billowed about Ruth in Bethlehem. The people commented on the marriage of Boaz and Ruth 'May the LORD make the woman, who is coming into your house, like Rachel and Leah, who together built up the house of Israel. May you prosper in Ephrathah and be renowned in Bethlehem; and may your house be like the house of Perez whom Tamar bore to Judah, because of the children that the LORD will give you by this young woman.' (Ruth 4:11f). And Ruth bore to Boaz a son, Obed, father of Jesse and grandfather of David.

The name of Boaz must have had a sacred connotation for every Israelite, for it was the name of one of the twin pillars in the temple of Solomon. These pillars were called Jachin and Boaz and were the work of Hiram the master builder. Jachin was the bright pillar of day, of birth. Boaz was the solemn, dark pillar of night and death. The sounds of Boaz' name enable one to feel the process when in sleep or death the soul forsakes the bodily vessel (the letter B) as it were through a gateway (letter O), to ray out into the cosmos (letter A), there to be swallowed up by and wedded to the cosmos (letter Z).

If we assume that those names — Ruth and Boaz — are more than coincidental, that they are in fact spiritual pictures, then we are tuned in by them to the fervent spirit that emanates from the veil of night and sleep. This is the soul's veil that covers the marriage of Boaz and Ruth.

A solemn unawareness and virginity hover above the birth of Obed in Bethlehem.

'Obed' restates with greater emphasis what is contained in the word 'Ebed' — 'Ebed Yahweh' — servant of the Lord. This is the designation by which the Book of Isaiah (especially from chapter 53 onwards) points to the Messiah. The word 'servant' implies more or less what we could express by the following picture: 'A certain lord had a servant who was devoted to him in boundless loyalty, so much so that when the master died he was able to live on in his servant.' 'Servant' here has the force of 'vessel.' The servant of Yahweh is the human being who is utterly the vessel, the incarnation of Yahweh; Jesus of Nazareth became the vessel, the covering of the Christ. He became Obed, Obed of the Christ. A prophecy is thus contained in the name Obed of the messianic incarnation of the Christ in a human body. The 'servant,' the 'vessel' proceeds from the marriage of Boaz and Ruth, and Obed became the father of Jesse. 'Jesse' is only the name of Jesus in its Old Testament preliminary form.

The further we look ahead in the genealogical table the clearer whatever the whole is striving towards stands out, in words and pictures. It becomes a step higher up a rising stairway. If we wish to draw nearer to the secret of God made Man, then we must enter into each name, we must ourselves become Judah, Tamar, Perez and Zerah; we ourselves must be Rahab and Salmon, Boaz, Ruth and Obed. The genealogical table is a path to guide us through many forms and metamorphoses. And in every one of those metamorphoses that we have discussed, the theme music of Mary is clearly audible.

Bathsheba

The fourth woman to be named in the genealogical table is Bathsheba, wife of David. Admittedly, she is referred to not by her own name but by that of her husband, Uriah. The story of David and Bathsheba is especially puzzling. What stage of human development has here been transformed into story, into picture?

Those two names, Uriah and Bathsheba, point a way. Bathsheba means 'daughter of seven-ness.' The name directs us into the world of stars, or rather of the planets. According to the ancient view, the planets are 'the seven': 'seven-ness.' We are therefore to think of Bathsheba as being in some way linked to the planets. Uriah means 'Yahweh is my light,' otherwise 'Yahweh, Light of the Ego.' The woman's name has brought us to some kind of general concept of the planetary world; the name of the man indicates more explicitly a place within that world. The source of light in the realm of planets is the sun. As the other seven planets — and more especially the moon — reflect that light, so they become imbued with ego forces; they are individualized. The moon gives forth light of the ego, Uriah, the Yahweh light.

Man has accepted everything he now has and is. Nevertheless, he must learn to say 'I.' But every utterance of 'I' is an act of ingratitude, a denial of the primordial light. That denial, however, is an inevitable step if man is to attain to freedom. The light of the cosmic sun cannot without an intermediary become the force of ego development. It must first change into moonlight; moonlight which thinks it is itself light, although it is only light reflected from the sun. Human ego-consciousness resembles moonlight when it thinks of itself as light in its own right and forgets the true source of its light. Human self awareness could not come into existence without yet another significant step forward by the Fall, namely the moon's ingratitude to the sun.

The moon's entry into the human soul means the separation of man from the true sources of human nature. The human being brings this about through self-awareness born of cosmic ingratitude and, linked to that, brings something else to pass — we can call it personal sexuality. It happens when human beings, awakened from that moon-derived awareness of self, imagine that their body is themselves. Human beings identify themselves with their own physical body. They experiences themselves physically. In the same way they experience other people physically. They see the other's body as that person's true self instead of as a vessel wherein the soul and spirit sojourn. Just as the moon enters into the self-awareness of the individual, so too does it enter into the relationship of the sexes to one another. Hitherto sex life pertained to the race; it was cosmic, ritualistic, because people still experienced themselves and also others as being one with the cosmos and not as ego beings.

The moon entered into the human soul at the same time as self awareness and personal sexuality came into existence; that event in the evolution of the Jewish race was transformed into the history of David' adultery with Bathsheba.

David says Bathsheba is his wife but actually she is the wife of Uriah. That is the same as if the moon were to say 'I shine,' while in fact the moon only reflects the sun's light. It is also the same as man saying 'I' when in fact he owes everything he has or is to the cosmos.

The story goes like this (2Sam.11–12). David rises during the night from his bed and climbs to the roof of his house. There he sees a woman of surpassing beauty bathing. Next day he sets enquiries afoot to find out who the woman might be. He is told she is Bathsheba, wife of Uriah. David has her brought to him and he sleeps with her. When she becomes pregnant she goes to the king to tell him.

David sends for Uriah. Uriah evidences utmost loyalty and swears that he is more closely bound to his king than to his wife. In so doing Uriah gives utterance to a wish to belong to his king with everything that he has — including his wife. On David's orders Uriah is placed in the most dangerous position in battle, and he is killed.

Thereupon David takes Bathsheba to wife and she bears him a son. Nathan the priest reproves David and proclaims the punishment: 'Behold, I will raise up evil against you out of your own house; and I will take your wives before your eyes, and give them to your neighbour and he shall lie with your wives in the sight of the sun. For you did it secretly; but I will do this thing before all Israel and before the sun.' (2Sam.12:11). The son of David and Bathsheba must die. The boy's death marks the end of David's time of remorse. The second son of David and Bathsheba lives. He is Solomon.

The night scene in which David first sees Bathsheba may have been either an external event or a visionary experience of the spirit. In either case the details are relevant to the inward event bound up with it. The representation of David on the roof stresses that his spiritual nature has ascended to his brain. (If the human body is a dwelling, then the head, the brain, is its roof). The brain is totally dominated by lunar powers. On the roof there is moonlight, and it is sultry. There it is that personal sexuality is born, the sister of ego-orientated intellectuality, influenced by the moon. Sexuality is derived from the sensuality of individual physical bodies who feel themselves to be the ego. It is also the very thing from which this kind of experience of self draws especially strong nourishment.

Wherever the soul out of its ingratitude to the cosmos imbues itself with moon-feeling, there the spiritual ego dies, the firstborn is strangled. The son's death is punishment for adultery if a man possesses himself of another man's wife. The second son, born following the remorse, after gratitude to the cosmos has been restored — he can survive. That is when the moon again becomes cognizant of the sun. The very first breath of a higher nature passes through the soul as 'peace.' Man becomes Solomon — the bearer of peace.

These soul processes into which inmost human development as it was taking place flowed like a tributary into the mainstream — these processes become historical events in the external life of David. David's life was at one and the same time an external phenomenon and a pictorial version of inmost soul processes. The stage in the advance of the Fall of Man, when the moon entered into the soul, became visible in David's adultery.

If we look back at the four Old Testament dramas, pictures of which rise up before us with the names of the four women in the genealogical table — then we can clearly recognize a difference between the first three and the fourth. Actually it is only the fourth that leads us into the region of personal sin. The names of Tamar, Rahab and Ruth are still woven round about the soul world which carries them along, which precedes the individuality.

It is significant that the genealogical table is divided into three groups, each with fourteen generations. The gospel itself has arranged them in this way. The names of Tamar, Rahab and Ruth occur in the first third of fourteen, while Bathsheba's, wife of Uriah, is placed where the genealogical table descends into its next third. We find no more names of women in the second or in the third and last group. The second and the third groups, each of fourteen ancestors, set before us no more pictures pertaining to the story of the eternal feminine. The transition into personal sin, that is, the descent from heaven to earth, having been attained, the gospel is silent on the fate of Eve. It is content to follow the eternal feminine along its descent to the point where it becomes earthly womanhood. The gospel shrouds the destinies of earthly womanhood with a mantle of silence until the time when it will be able to speak of Mary, the fifth woman. Eternal womanhood, having sunk utterly into the depths, comes to life again in Mary.

We find women entering the ancestral table only in the first grouping of the forty-two generations; what is the significance of this?

We can describe the history of humankind before David (*c.* 1000 BC, the time of Homer) as the childhood of the human race. The significant fact in childhood up to the age of nine or ten is that the soul is occupied in incarnation. The soul is seeking earth while it labours to give form to the body. The process goes on in a certain way right up to puberty. That is why a child urgently needs nature, the world of the senses, as an island for its own religious life. This is especially the case up to the age of ten. The direction of the child's religious life begins to turn back on itself only after the body is completely shaped; that is, after puberty. The direction from above downwards is reversed, moving from below up. A child's religion is the opposite of an adult's.

Much confusion in modern religious teaching stems from failure to recognize this vital fact. We mention this in passing; in bringing the religion of adults to children we tear them prematurely out of their bodies — in the natural course of events they would sink deeper into them. We impede their complete incarnation. Rudolf Steiner has uttered an extraordinarily illuminating statement in his foundations for a new education: 'A child's religion is physical.'

Up to the time of David and Homer, humanity was engaged in a process of incarnation rather like what a child goes through up to the tenth or fourteenth year. Humanity was looking for earth. That is why man's religion was physical. It was right and in keeping with what pertains to the spirit that it should have been so. It is wrong to dismiss pre-Christian eras as simply pagan. We could say that up to David's time the human earthly body, including its sexuality, was indeed the proper vessel for religious life.

Sin comes into existence when a human being matures. If, after puberty, human beings strongly experience their body — that is when sin begins. Prior to puberty they not only *may* but *should* experience the body, he should have it. Sin begins when something hitherto embedded in the womb of justifiably sustaining customs is retained beyond the onset of what pertains to the ego. We think of Tamar, Rahab and Ruth in relation to accepted custom and of Bathsheba in relation to the loss of innocence.

In the adultery of David with Bathsheba, humanity passed through a kind of puberty; humankind lost the innocence of its sex life. Man's fall into sin from that time on moves towards atonement. After David's death the Old Testament tells us of Solomon's aberrations in the form of polygamy. The curse of Bathsheba works itself out further. David marks a turning point for humanity. Similar stories to those of the four women, if they appeared in the second and third groups of the genealogical table, would reveal only sin and impurity. There are no more women's names. Where next will the world evolution of Eve's destiny become visible?

Mary

Up to this point it may seem that we have been discussing the Old Testament instead of the Gospel of St Matthew, but we come now to the subject for which the whole of the genealogical table with its many golden secrets is the foundation, namely the birth of Jesus. Mary's is the fifth name of a woman and it is placed outside the forty-two stages of the genealogy.

'And the birth of Jesus Christ took place in this way: Mary, his mother, was betrothed to Joseph; but before they were aware of having come together, she was found to have conceived a child through the power of the Holy Spirit.' (Matt.1:18). We are confronted with the problem of the virgin birth. The gospel itself rejects the crude idea that Jesus was born without a father. The genealogical list would serve no purpose if Joseph were not the father of Jesus. The mere fact of the genealogy, which of course sets out the ancestry of Joseph, is sufficiently convincing to defeat the crude, materially miraculous concept of the virgin birth, as it has emerged from the ossified dogmatism of Christianity.

But to say that is not to dismiss the mystery which is indeed woven around the birth of Jesus; it is therefore important to see the relationship between Joseph and Mary in the light of those dramas of the four women, especially of the first three. What happened between the parents of Jesus is the continuation of those stories, the fifth episode in that puzzling series; only in their light are we able slowly to arrive at an understanding of them. We must recognize that in naming the women in the genealogy there was an undoubted intention in relation to the story of Jesus' birth, if not on the part of the evangelist, then on that of the gospel.

Just as during man's primordial time in paradise sexuality took its course wholly in the region of unconsciousness, of sleep, so did the union of Joseph and Mary; they happen to have been two people in whom a childlike paradisal consciousness was destined to be a possibility. The apocryphal gospels of the childhood of Jesus tell how Mary was a temple virgin while still almost a child. It tells how by the wish of the priests and on divine indication, she was wedded within the Temple to Joseph, an old man. Because their union did not come about through any human will or consciousness, the stream of personal sin, associated with the curse of Eve and of Bathsheba, did not flow into them. The childlike purity and unconsciousness of Joseph and Mary made it possible for the union to be brought about by angelic hands, even by the Christ himself, who was even then preparing to incarnate. Joseph does not 'know' Mary. This is not a sexual act to intrude into consciousness. Human bodies became the stage for divine events. Joseph and Mary were quite unaware that they had been united by the angel. The veil of virginity was spread out over them.*

There were two nights in the lives of Joseph and Mary that belong closely together. The first night was when the angel brought about the event; the other was the night when the angel solved the riddle for Joseph in a dream. And then came the holy night when the babe was born.

The descent to earth leads through Old Testament pictures; the new ascent of the eternal feminine towards heaven begins in the New Testament scenes of Mary. Tamar, Rahab and Ruth are 'Mothers of God' within the course of the fall of man as it advances. Mary is the mother of God who, together with Jesus, brings the redeemer to earth.

The first chapter contains one more important pointer to the Old Testament: 'All this took place, so that the word of the Lord, spoken by the mouth of the prophet, might be fulfilled: See, the maiden will conceive; she will bear a son, he shall be called Emmanuel. Translated, that means: God is in our midst.' (Matt.2:22f).

This prophecy from the seventh chapter of the Book of Isaiah is not an abstract, miraculous prediction of an historical event. The mysteries already knew about the birth of the virgin's son, the birth of Emmanuel. It is the birth of the ego, of the divine child in the human

---

* About the virgin birth and the different accounts of the birth in Matthew and Luke, see *The Childhood of Jesus*.

soul. A number of people had experienced this birth prematurely in the early years of the true mysteries. In future — people like the prophets knew this well — the ego, the 'God in us,' would be born in many a human soul. Those who experienced it saw their own soul nature in the imagination of the Virgin Mary with the divine child. The ancient mystery utterance, but also the vision of the virginal mother of Emmanuel, was fulfilled by the birth of Jesus. Something that had previously taken place only inwardly now took place as an historical event. An inward event within the soul became history, while in Mary and the child history again becomes an inward event within the soul. The Madonna scenes of Christian art present themselves as mirrors before souls as they pass through that experience. Emmanuel is coming to birth in human souls.

The words of Isaiah then are a kind of epitome and crowning of all that was suggested earlier in the five stories. Among other things not touched upon here, we can now recognize the first chapter of Matthew as a story of the secrets of human sex, a story of eternal womanhood, a story of woman herself insofar as woman is a likeness of the human soul.

Six scenes take their places in turn, one after the other:

      1. The birth of Perez and Zerah to Judah and Tamar.
      2. The birth of Boaz to the harlot Rahab.
      3. The birth of Obed to Boaz and Ruth.
      4. The birth of Solomon to David and Bathsheba.
      5. The birth of Jesus to Joseph and Mary.
      6. The birth of Emmanuel to the virgin human soul.

CHAPTER THREE

The Character of Matthew,
Evangelist and Apostle

The birth of Jesus is the focal point on which many rays of vision converge. The amazing and divine bounty of these rays was to some extent obscured on the one hand by the grossly miraculous concept of the virgin birth and, on the other, by the intellectually critical view which held that the birth of Jesus had already been obscured beneath a rank growth of legend in the gospel itself.

So pure was the humanity of the parents, that they found helpers and guides who emanated from the supersensible, spiritual world; as well as from those who knew that a Messiah, the Christ, would become man. Their knowledge was derived from ancient mysteries and priestly wisdom. The help and guidance bestowed upon the parents of Jesus from out of the supersensible world, and which the gospel designates as the Holy Spirit, we could call the governance of the eternal feminine, the stream of cosmic mother-forces. The trinity of Father, Son and Holy Spirit was often more portrayed pictorially than was the trinity of World Father, World Son and World Mother. The Holy Spirit was perceived as being mother-like, the life bearing eternal feminine. The unselfconscious, pure spirituality of the parents, especially of Mary, made it possible for the Holy Spirit to bring about conception from above. Even as Mary conceived on earth, so the world mother, the soul of humanity, the earth's soul, conceived in the world of spirit. Our previous study was concerned with the part played by the spiritual world, by the eternal feminine, a part that could only be hinted at haltingly in images rather than in concepts.

This, our third study, will be linked to the second chapter of the Gospel of St Matthew and will deal with that other stream, which we could call the stream of the eternal masculine, of the forces of fatherhood. We shall be speaking of the way in which mystery centres participated in the birth of Jesus of Nazareth through priests and wise men.

Let us begin by setting before ourselves Matthew the disciple and evangelist. At first glance we do not seem to know much about him from the gospel; only one scene is described for us, when Jesus calls him to follow him; in his joy, Matthew prepares a feast for his fellow tax-collectors to which he invites Jesus and the disciples. And yet a wealth of spiritual currents of that time can come to life for us in the person of Matthew if the question is put concerning the riddle of his identity.

The Gospel of St Matthew is the only one which at the time of the calling of the disciples refers to Matthew by that name: 'As Jesus walked on, he saw a man called Matthew sitting at the tax office; and he said to him, "Follow me!" And he got up and followed him. And as he sat at table in the house, see, many tax-collectors and outcasts came and shared in the meal with Jesus and his disciples.' (Matt.9:9f).

St Mark's gospel calls him by another name: 'And as he went on he saw Levi the son of Alphaeus sitting at the tax desk and said to him: "Follow me!" And he stood up and followed him.' (Mark 2:14).

St Luke's gospel uses the same name as St Mark but omits the 'Alphaeus'; instead, the name Levi is used, and repeated with all the more emphasis: 'As he went on after this he saw a tax-collector called Levi sitting at his tax office. And he said to him, "Follow me!" And he left everything, got up and followed him. And at his house Levi prepared a great banquet in his honour ...' (Luke 5:27–29).

And so, the tax-collector is called now Matthew, and now Levi; but we should note that elsewhere, in both St Mark and St Luke, who refer to him as Levi, we also find him called Matthew. This doubling up of the name is not without significance. Whenever one and the same character or event is differently named or described by the different evangelists, this appears contradictory to the materialistic viewpoint. The viewpoint which looks towards the spiritual content carried by the gospel right into its smallest details will be made aware of peculiar, unspoken secrets by those very so-called 'contradictions.' The contradictions between the gospels are actually the means whereby the Bible expresses the inexpressible.

Let us gather up what we know from the meagre indications in the gospel about Matthew-Levi. That name, Levi, tells us that the evangelist belonged to the tribe of Levi, which had been dedicated to the priesthood, the priestly race, ever since the days of Moses. Matthew is a Levite, and thereby a fellow-bearer of Jewish priesthood (as for the designation, son of Alphaeus, which Matthew carries, as does the brother of the younger James, who is also called 'brother of the Lord,' this we shall consider at a later stage).

If we admit that by descent Matthew was a member of the Jewish priesthood, then the riddle of his personality becomes a very pressing one. How has it come about that Matthew the Levite, instead of exercising the priestly functions open to him, associated himself with the despised tax-collectors? A story of the soul begins to reveal itself in response to our hypotheses.

The tax-collectors were looked down upon and hated by the Jews, not for any moral or social inferiority. They were despised on religious and ritualistic grounds. In considering New Testament history we greatly underestimate the enormous power and consequence of the Caesar cult. Rome's world empire was enmeshed in ritual observances because the emperors had forced initiation for themselves at already decadent mystery centres. By so doing each emperor became the vehicle of supersensible forces and thereby had himself worshipped as a god. These 'gods,' however, were not beneficent divinities but rather demons, whose tools the emperors became. All political, military, judicial institutions received a religious colouration. Every aspect of life was to become, according to the Roman view, a service of the gods insofar as it was carried out in the service of divine Caesar. The object was to set up on earth, in the name of Rome's god, Caesar, a divine, a sacred state. This was to be achieved by declaring whatever was profane and worldly to be religious and cultic.

Wherever the Romans entered as conquerors, there they compelled the local gods to Emperor worship; they destroyed temples, carried off idols and sacred vessels, and bore traditional ritual back to Rome; by declaring himself *Pontifex Maximus*, Caesar made himself high priest of the religious observances which had hitherto been vital in the land. But the Romans did not enter the Jewish region as conquerors. They came when Judas Maccabeus called them in as allies and helpers against the Seleucid oppression. That is why the Jewish people retained the right to continue observance of their own religion and ritual. The Temple in Jerusalem remained with the people, although their leaders lived in constant dread lest the Romans find an excuse to seize it for themselves and so deprive the people of the free exercise of their religion.

But in the administrative field, especially in that of taxation, Judah had fallen wholly under Roman domination. In order to keep the Temple, the Jews had to agree to more and more compromises and concessions in matters 'worldly,' and this led to endless internal conflict because in the Roman sense there were no 'worldly' issues. Custom dues, taxes which they demanded from their 'allies,' the Jews, were in Roman eyes temple offerings, sacrificial gifts, made to the god, Caesar. By carrying out the collection of taxes on behalf of the Emperor, the Jews became partakers in Emperor worship. In their anxiety, they actually went along with Roman ritualistic demands in setting up money changers' and tax collectors' tables inside the precincts of the Temple in Jerusalem, even though to Roman thinking it made them altars of Caesar. They served two gods — Yahweh and Caesar. What we have indicated here is the key to a number of significant scenes in the gospel, and we will have to come back to them in greater detail.

The tax-collectors who served Rome, some of them Romans and some Jews who had entered Roman service, were in fact to Roman perceptions a kind of low-ranking clergy, a humbler priesthood, since what they had to collect were temple taxes, sacrificial offerings.

The more the Jews compromised with Emperor worship, the worse their hatred and disdain grew for those who carried out the will of Caesar in the land of Judah, and first and foremost among those were the tax-collectors. They were despised because they served the cult of the foreign, demonic god. If those who, obedient to the law, served Yahweh in the right way were the righteous ones, then the man who served the Emperor was a sinner.

We can understand why Jewish popular feeling vented its hatred especially against those who, being members of the Jewish race, entered Roman service and became tax-collectors. The Jews were all of them guilty of serving Caesar in consequence of their own attitude. As for the Jews among the tax-collectors, they could be seen as deserters from the Jewish faith! By scorning the tax-collectors, Pharisees and Jews covered up their own bad conscience.

How they must have looked down upon the man who, though a member of the Jewish priestly caste, had joined the servants of the

Emperor, and had become a temple servitor of money and of Mammon!

Here we meet the riddle of Matthew. What could have induced him, a priestly representative of the Jewish stream, to place himself within the Caesarian stream of Rome as a tax-collector, and thereby bring down upon himself the hatred of his own countrymen? Perhaps the answer to that question can only be found if we take into account a third stream. We can recognize Levi the tax-collector through his name of Matthew as belonging to that third stream.

Matthew and the Essenes

The name Matthew reveals Levi to be an adherent of the Essene stream. 'Matthew' approximates in meaning to 'a pupil of Matthai.' Matthai was one of five personalities who played an important part in esoteric Judaism about a century before our era: Matthai, Nakai, Nezer, Boni, Thodah. These five names are transmitted to us in the historical documents of Jewish history. Rudolf Steiner speaks of them in his lecture course on the Gospel of Matthew. He describes them as disciples of a great prophetic reformer of late Judaism — of one Jeshu ben Pandira, said to have been crucified and stoned about 100 BC by fanatical opponents. This Jeshu ben Pandira is said to have been a great Essene teacher who prepared for the work of Christ in a decisive fashion in that he orientated the order of Essenes towards the imminent coming of the Messiah.*

We have very scanty historical traditions concerning the order of Essenes. We only know that its origins stretched back into the evolution of Egyptian and Babylonian civilization, where it was part of the ancient stream of esoteric wisdom. Its members described themselves as Therapeutae, that is, as 'healers.' We also know that the order of Essenes suddenly disappeared at the beginning of our own era, at around the time of the mystery of Golgotha. That is why it is often utterly overlooked in historical records; it is even asserted that the order never existed and is no more than a legend.

We must, however, realize that the order of Essenes played a

---

* More about the Essenes and Jeshu ben Pandira is in *Caesars and Apostles*. The Appendix of that book also contains accounts from the Dead Sea Scrolls which had not been discovered at the time Bock wrote these *Studies in the Gospels*.

significant part in Palestine at the very time of the birth of Jesus. Members of this order looked forward to the birth of the Messiah in assured expectation and awed reverence; that group who were often referred to as 'the quiet ones in the land' should be seen as having been closely linked to the Essenes.

Essenes and Therapeutae: Matthai and Nezer

Philo, the Hellenistic-Jewish philosopher and scholar who at the time of Christ was living in Alexandria, wrote a book about them. In his biography of Moses, he states that the young Moses was a priest among the healers in the same circle where Miriam, his sister, was a priestess. Up to the time of Moses, Egypt was indeed the vehicle for a highly developed mystery science, which on the one hand embraced the cosmos through astrology and, on the other, humanity in a kind of anatomy, through the science of mummification. We can take it that while in Egypt, Israel absorbed a good deal of the temple wisdom of that land, permitting within its own racial interconnections, the rise of a form of Essene movement; these groups cultivated a wisdom that combined Egyptian and Israelite elements. The name, 'healer,' indicates that their wisdom was concerned with a medical stream of sorts, one that knew a good deal from Egyptian astronomy about the ways of fate, and about the secret of birth; from Egyptian anatomy of the mummy, it knew certain things about the laws of heredity. This stream of wisdom within the order of Essenes next passed through many vicissitudes, especially in the time of the Babylonian exile, when the wise men of Jewry met wise men of Greece, Babylon and Chaldea (Jewish legends are full of them). In the last stage of the Essenes, this more scientific branch of the order found a representative among the five disciples of Jeshu ben Pandira in the person of Matthai, to whose school Matthew later belonged.

Alongside these, there was a more practically ascetic branch of the Essene order which we can follow with greater clarity in Jewish history: the Nazarites. Chapter 6 of Numbers tells us how Moses instituted a form of monasticism for the order of Nazarites, a set of prescribed exercises and rules for purification, all tied to the Nazarites' oath, by which men strove towards a definite relationship to the spiritual and towards initiation. We see many a great figure of Jewish history, for example, Samson* and, later, John the Baptist, who were adherents of this ascetic branch of the Essene order. At the time of the five great Essene teachers it was Nezer (as his name tells us) who gave to this stream new content and new life. Rudolf Steiner describes how Nezer founded an Essene colony, a kind of monastic settlement, in the hills of Galilee, which received the name of 'the town of Nezer' — Nazareth. The circumstance is enormously significant to our ideas of the youth of Jesus. And it leads factually, for the first time, into chapter two of St Matthew's Gospel. The last verse reads: 'Following a revelation which he received in a dream he [Joseph] went to Galilee and settled in the town called Nazareth. The word of the prophet was to be fulfilled: He is predestined to be a Nazarene.' (Matt.2:22f). The prophecy quoted here is not to be found anywhere in the Old Testament. We have often glimpsed a word of Essene sacred tradition. The Gospel of St Matthew openly displays its Essene characteristics. Matthew reveals himself as a disciple of Matthai, an Essene.

Before turning back to the personality of Matthew, let us take a quick look at one more puzzling passage in chapter two. It is again a quotation, this time admittedly from the Old Testament prophecy, from the Book of Hosea: 'Out of Egypt have I called my son' (Hos. 2:15). The way in which the evangelist repeats the words may once again be an indication of his own Essene affiliation. The words 'He is predestined to be a Nazarene' are rather an utterance of Nezer, while 'Out of Egypt have I called my son' could belong to Matthai.

Whenever the people of Israel looked back into the past, they saw their own Exodus from Egypt. That Exodus was for the people at large no more than liberation from slavery. But when the Essenes looked back into the past, they inevitably felt that Egypt was for them the source whence flowed much of their treasured wisdom. Spiritually,

---

* Samson, whose name in English means 'son of the sun,' 'like the sun,' was regarded, by the Jews, and especially the Essenes, as a predecessor of the Messiah. They believed that they could deduce something of the destiny of the Messiah from that of Samson. The Essene utterance 'He shall be called a Nazarene,' was to some extent applied to all those whose birth was foretold by an angel, from Samson right down to John the Baptist and Jesus of Nazareth; it indicates the Essenes' expectation of the Messiah (compare Judges 13:3–5) 'And the angel of the Lord appeared to the woman and said to her, "Behold, you are barren and have no children; but you shall conceive and bear a son. Therefore, beware, and drink no wine or strong drink, and eat nothing unclean, for lo, you shall conceive and bear a son. No razor shall come upon his head, for the boy shall be a Nazirite to God from birth; and he shall begin to deliver Israel from the hands of the Philistines".'

they felt towards Egypt as would a son towards his father. At the same time, that did not preclude them from experiencing the Exodus as a liberation. The group of Essenes and healers of Moses' time must have been vividly aware that the days of the Egyptian father had run out and that the days of Israel's sons had begun. That is when the principle of sonship, the ego-impulse, enters history; and Israel was in a quite special way the vehicle of the ego-impulse. Through the Exodus of the children of Israel from Egypt 'the son' was indeed called out of Egypt.

Profound wisdom concerning human birth and the human body was alive in Egypt. That wisdom flowed into the peoples of Israel through the healers. As it flowed from the temples of Egypt into the Jewish schools of healers and Essenes, it passed to some extent from the fatherhood stage to that of sonship. It was transformed. What had been generalized wisdom in Egypt, concerned with star lore in its application to the human body, and with the transformation of that corporeality through heredity, was to find a unique application in Israel. For Israel was destined to bring forth the body in which the Messiah was to come, and this through a genealogy guided in a certain way.

Egypt bestowed the wisdom of the Incarnation.

Israel itself was to bring about the Incarnation.

Egypt possessed knowledge that it was to be the appointed task of Israel to realize. That is why Israel had to fetch from Egypt the awareness and the knowledge concerning its own task. It may well be that clear realization of what was to be Israel's destiny became actual only with the rise in Egypt of the order of healers. The decision to leave Egypt had to mature on the basis of this realization. The commission which Moses received before the burning bush coincided with what the healers must have accepted as inevitable.

Israel had to be led from the land of wisdom concerning the body of the Messiah, the son, into the land of birth of the son's body, of the Messiah's body. Egypt was the land of wisdom concerning the Father. The Holy Land was the land of the Son's birth. In the time that followed that of Moses and Joshua, the children of Israel were led by the influence of the order of healers and Essenes towards their destiny as sons.

Rudolf Steiner's accounts provide us with evidence that the order — its scientific as well as its practical ascetic side — was very well aware of the laws according to which Jewish destiny was fulfilling itself.

We shall touch only briefly on some of that evidence. Rudolf Steiner tells us that Nazarene exercises consisted in following certain rules, ascetic and ritualistic, whereby, step by step, the disciple rendered the sum total of physical heredity transparent; he thus strove towards the spiritual world by penetrating his own physical world. That is, the disciple had to move up the ladder by which his forefathers had come down to him — first to his father, then to his grandfather, and so from ancestor to ancestor. His own physicality became more and more transparent in relation to the spiritual which is after all our ultimate ancestor. Steiner suggests that having passed through seven receding generations, a certain subdivision was reached, in a sense a new level, separated from those lower down by a stairway of seven grades. Having attained a place immediately before the spiritual region, the disciple felt that he was on the seventh level, having climbed 6 × 7 steps. We can look upon the genealogical tree as a table of the Essene soul discipline as it applies to the Nezer stream of the order. Let us take a hypothetical view from there over to the Matthai stream. This being in a sense the stream of realization and of science, its eyes were turned in the opposite direction. The Nezer discipline rises from the present into the spiritual heights of the past, by way of the genealogical ladder. It goes back from son to father.

The disciple of Matthai descends from Father Abraham down to the sons; thanks to an Egyptian heritage of wisdom, he watches the gradual transformation of the physical body and arrives in the end always at 'the son.' That is the direction in which Matthew, the Matthai disciple, looks. He enumerates the ancestors from father to son, from Abraham to Jesus.

We are deeply moved if we entertain the incredible thought that there may have been people who consciously followed the march of generations from Abraham down, knowing that on reaching the seven times seventh generation, the Messiah would be born into a quite definite family. The nearer the time, the greater must have been the tension and the expectation among such people, of whom there were probably very few. Here we reach the point where we begin to perceive an incredible possibility: there may have been people who kept themselves in the background, for they were 'the quiet ones in the land,' yet in the light of the wisdom we have been discussing the task of bringing about the marriage of such as Joachim and Hannah and of

Joseph and Mary had been given to them. Apocryphal tradition gives us an inkling of all this in its word pictures.

For the disciples of Matthai the great question and the expectation was this: When will the Son be born beneath the sign of that number, the six times seven?

For the disciple of Nezer the question went like this: When will we have reached the stage where the ladder with the six times seven rungs can lead even me to the Father?

The school of Nezer strove to ascend to the purity of the godhead by climbing the forty-two grades of discipleship. Each grade corresponded to one generation in the genesis of the messianic race. All those who climbed one single rung of the ladder regained what humanity had lost in descending one such rung of that ladder which led down to earth. Men knew — success in ascending all forty-two rungs would mean that they had found their way back to the essential character of God the Father, from whom step by step humanity had fallen away. If they were to get part of the way back to Abraham, up the forty-two spiritual generations, they would not meet God the Father in the person of Abraham; nor would they even had they struggled on as far as Abraham himself. There would still be a painfully nostalgic way left to go. 'The Father' could not really be found before 'the Son' appeared.

Men felt poised between the Father and the Son. And yet, they had neither Father nor Son. The Father would have to reveal himself in the Son. Here was the dual conviction which in a manner inspired the Essene order. The Father sends forth the Son; the Son leads to the Father.

We shall not present probabilities as certainties, evidence for which may not be equally convincing to all. Nevertheless, probabilities may help us to realize the atmosphere and the environment surrounding the birth and early years of Jesus, and which the Essenes created for him, for that is the environment in which we must envisage Matthew the apostle and the whole of the Gospel of Matthew. Matthew, the tax-collector and Levite, was a member of that very circle of Essenes who looked forward and strove with such high hopes towards the coming of the Messiah.

Matthew the tax-collector

We now come to the question of why Matthew the Levite became a tax-collector.

It has often been observed that the order of Essenes disappeared completely in the first century of our era. This can be explained from what has been said above. The task of the order was accomplished with the birth of Jesus of Nazareth. Those Essenes who failed to recognize this, and who tried to keep the order going, ceased to be true Essenes. We may be permitted the proposition that Matthew gave up his activities within the orbit of the Jewish priests and of the order of Essenes because he knew that the Messiah had come, and because he awaited nothing with so much longing as to be called by him who was expected and acknowledged.

But why did he join the tax-collectors of all people? Here again we may be permitted to seek an answer through empathy into the character of Matthew and into the historical situation.

Whenever the Essenes looked into the past, they looked towards Egypt. Where did they look when they gazed into the future? They looked towards Rome. They felt themselves involved in a mighty process of incarnation, in the incarnation of the Christ. That process led from Egypt to Jerusalem. They felt that process striding forward from Jerusalem to Rome. Living as they did in Palestine, it seemed to them that they were midway between Egypt and Rome.

The source whence flowed the wisdom concerning the body of the Messiah was in Egypt. That body, in its earthly shape, would be born in Jerusalem. In Rome, humanity itself was to become the body of Christ.

As the people of Israel journeyed from Egypt to the Holy Land, they passed from a Christ wisdom that preceded his birth, into a world of the Christ to be born into the body of a man. (It is characteristic of the Essene Gospel, and is of great importance, that it tells the story of the flight into Egypt. The boy Jesus recapitulates his people's destiny. He himself is called out of Egypt as the Son, thereby taking the step from Egypt to the Holy Land). From the land of wisdom concerning the body, he reaches the land of the body itself. The step into the land of the body of all humanity lay ahead. And that land was the world of Rome. Matthew and other Essenes must have had a vital foreknowledge that Rome and its world would play a prominent part in the early days of Christianity. The secret of incarnation was the very heart of the healers' teaching. Egypt, Judea, Rome were three great stages in the incarnation of the Christ; but the unique historical event itself was to be found at the midpoint of this path, while the special mission of the Essenes was to serve during that middle period.

The Pharisees, and also the Jewish public, stood in great fear of Rome. They feared for their sacred objects which stood under the feeble protection of privileges which the Jews enjoyed by virtue of their formal alliance. 'Are we to administer the taxes on behalf of Caesar?' (In Greek 'taxes,' *telos,* also means 'consecration.') Because of Emperor worship and because of the ritual significance which Rome attached to all monetary and taxation matters, this was a constant source of anxiety for the Pharisees. That was the question confronting all Jews. Administration of the taxes was one of the compromises by means of which the Jews sought to keep in favour with Rome.

Matthew's attitude towards Rome differed from that of the Pharisees and of the Jewish people in general. They were afraid of Rome because they wanted to save the old ways. Matthew realized that antiquity had fulfilled its task; no matter how distorted the image of Rome, he saw Rome as the vehicle of the future. Others saw the Romans as mere servants of alien gods; Matthew saw in them the Christians of the future.

An answer to the question, why did Matthew become a tax-collector, may be found in that direction. He went among the Romans, inspired by the Essene within him. The second, that is, the middle step of the incarnation of Christ having been taken, he wished to help prepare the third.

Without doubt the Essenes recognized the demon in Rome as clearly as did the Pharisees. They knew, however, that by fear of the devil they would have laid themselves open to his power. From a point of view like that of the Essenes and healers, the Pharisees would have looked like our contemporaries, men who recognize the Ahrimanic nature of electricity and who strive on that account toward monastic retreats, free from technology. True Essenes were undoubtedly centred on healing. They knew that human injuries and demon possession could only be cured by compelling them to become weapons of light.

The Essenes took sickness upon themselves in order to heal it in all humanity by the strength of what was within themselves.

Matthew was a modern in the best sense. He involved himself in modernity even when modernity revealed itself at first in demonic form. We may from this distance compare Matthew's soul-attitude with the state of mind that has in our own time caused some people to ally themselves with the proletariat, even though their own origins were in other social classes. People felt that in those circumstances the proletariat was the vehicle of future cultural evolution, although at the time it had to live out its life as a movement of revolution and protest.

The words of Jesus, 'Healthy people do not need a physician, but the sick do' (Luke 5:31), aptly depict the frame of mind of Matthew, such as we have tried to describe it. For *therapeutai* means 'healer' or 'physician.' So we arrive at a basic trend of the healer's movement if we imagine that saying proceeding from the mouth of Matthew, and put it in this way: 'Those who are whole do not need the healer, but those who are sick.' We can now well understand how Matthew, the Levite, because of his membership of the order of Therapeutae, became a tax-collector.

That utterance concerning the whole and the sick takes us right into the centre of the scene of the calling of Matthew. We can picture Matthew as a kind of leader among tax-collectors, one who had collected about him quite a circle of these despised men in order to influence them. Then, when the great hope of Matthew's life had been fulfilled, when the Christ summoned him to become one of the twelve, Matthew was able to bring the Christ to that despised group where he himself had lived and laboured. He prepared a joyous meal, a sacred feast, to which he invited all who belonged to the body of tax-collectors. The Christ responded to Matthew's call, even as Matthew had responded to the call of Christ; he attended their feast. To see that scene as merely an occasion for trivial eating and drinking, or even as a banquet, would be to underestimate it. It was a hallowed meal, where the Christ blessed and distributed bread and wine. It was a sacrament. There emerges a grand symbol of human history; when the Christ distributed the sacrament of bread and wine for the first time after the call of the disciples (Matthew was the last to be summoned into that group of twelve). He gave it to Romans and to adherents of

Rome among his own people. Here was an occult yet powerful prophecy of the stature that Christianity was to assume in the first epoch of its destiny.

The Pharisees said: 'How can your teacher eat with the tax-collectors and outcasts?' Their anger was not moral but ritual. For they could not understand that the Christ was bringing into the demonic worship of Caesar the healing medicine of a ritual of transformation. They were afraid of the cultural influence of Caesar. The Christ, as the great therapist of the world, released the demon through the sacrament of his own love-nature. Accordingly, not only was he able to confound the Pharisees with that utterance, he had to do it: 'Healthy people do not need a physician, but the sick do.' For Matthew, the words were like an accolade.

What Peter did after the mystery of Golgotha, fulfilling the commission of Christ, that Matthew did by way of preparation before the mystery of Golgotha; he did it within a small group. Peter went to Rome, right into the demon's den, in order there to found for an epoch the centre of Christianity, impelled by his Essene-Manichean convictions. Matthew was the first to prepare for the descent into hell of Petrine Christianity. This was through his professional and general life style, in gathering together from among Roman tax-collectors the first community of the Supper. That makes Matthew the first evangelist of Roman or Petrine Christianity. He was able to tread the way of Peter's gospel as we shall see further in this study.

Keeping in mind the three streams which Matthew combined in his own person, in that he was a Levite, an Essene and a tax-collector all at the same time, a rich and gripping drama of life is unrolled before us, even though the gospel is almost entirely silent concerning him. All we could present here as suggestion or hypothesis ought some day to be told in literary form, free and convincingly. The object of our present study would certainly not be misunderstood were someone to perceive in it a sketch for a novel about Matthew. A novel of that kind would doubtless bring us closer to an enquiry into the truth of external, historical events than would a whole string of scholarly research into extant historical documents. Virtually no historical document exists and yet in few words the gospel affords us a view into whole dramas of soul destinies.

Matthew came of Jewish stock. In his soul he advanced to a humanity that embraced all. He bore within himself, besides Judaism, what emanated from Egypt and what belonged to Rome, each in its own way. That is what makes him the 'Man' among the evangelists. John is the Eagle, Luke the Bull, Mark the Lion. Matthew is the Man. Judaism gave him Levitical thinking, Egypt's culture gave him Essene feeling, Rome gave him will as a tax-collector — Judaism, Egypt, Rome: these three add up in him to world humanity.

Finally, in order to round out the portrait of Matthew, we are going to throw out a question concerning the point in the gospel story at which the calling of Matthew and the feast of the tax-collectors is told, and just what finds expression in the episodic structure. Naturally, the answer can only be given as it were diagrammatically, since the structure of the gospel is to be discussed more fully in the course of future gospel studies.

Matthew was the last of the disciples to be called. The group of the twelve was completed by that call. Those summoned before him had already had a variety of experiences in the course of the journeys with the Christ; they had passed through many grades. Could it be that Matthew had passed through grades the other disciples lived through before him, in order to become a disciple of the Christ? Was it his destiny, such as we have tried to recount it, to pass through them in other ways?

Just before the calling of Matthew, the gospel tells of the healing of the man sick of the palsy. This is the scene to which the third miracle in John's Gospel corresponds, that is, the healing of the sick man at the pool of Bethesda. So Matthew joins the circle of disciples as the third stage is reached and the transition is being prepared to the fourth — the feeding of the five thousand where the transition is made from man the individual, to man the member of the human community, to man the member of all humanity. As we have seen, Matthew realized some part of this stage of his transition through his destiny. We are able to apprehend how significant and how moving a part of the gospel's composition is in the way in which the scene of Matthew's summons leads into the scene of the feast, that supper which the Christ and the twelve disciples celebrated together with the tax-collectors. And now the way is to be prepared for the fourth stage, the miracle of the feeding, and also for the sacrament of bread and wine. The feast which Matthew made ready in joy at his calling may at the same time be presented as a first step towards that mystery:

First step:

    Marriage in Cana   The Sermon on the Mount

Second step:

    Healing of the nobleman's son   The centurion in Capernaum

Third step:

    Healing at the pool of Bethesda   The healing of man sick of palsy

Fourth step:

    Feeding of the Five Thousand   The tax-collectors' feast.

                                        Feeding of the Five Thousand

The Essenes

Thanks to the concept to which our study of the personality of Matthew has brought us, we have built up a basis upon which to consider the second chapter. We have already touched on two Essene utterances: 'Out of Egypt have I called my son,' and 'He shall be called a Nazarene.' We are going to consider the second chapter further, paying attention to direct or even merely indicated links with the Old Testament.

We have seen that the first chapter of Matthew's Gospel presents wanderings which eternal womanhood had to pass through in the history of humanity. The second chapter reveals how the greatest masculine streams of pre-Christian humanity combined to flow into the earliest earthly destinies of the Jesus child: that is, the streams of Zarathustra and of the Essenes.

Two Old Testament prophecies are uttered in the second chapter of Matthew's Gospel which we shall touch on briefly since in them an inward bridge is thrown, as it were, from the first to the second chapter:

'Bethlehem in the land of Judah, you are not the least among the leading places in Judah; for from you shall come the ruler, the shepherd of my people Israel.' (Matt.2:5f). 'A voice is heard in Ramah, wailing and great lamentation; Rachel weeps for her children, and she refuses all consolation, because they are no more.' (Matt.2:18).

The first of these prophecies is spoken to the three priest kings who came to honour the child and to enquire after the place of his birth. The second occurs following the story of Herod's murder of the innocents. Herod stands there, a fourth king beside the three wise men from the Orient. He is the sinister one. The three wise men come to worship the child. Herod is related to the three priest-kings in the way the fourth, the mixed king in Goethe's fairy tale of the *Green Snake and the Beautiful Lily*, is related to the three other kings of the Rock Temple — the golden king, the silver and the bronze king.

To what do the prophecies point? There could be a great deal to say on that. What follows will suffice here. Bethlehem is a city woven about in a very special way by the secrets of motherhood. Not only because Ruth and Mary both bore their sons here; but Bethlehem is also the place where Rachel died when Benjamin was born, and where she was buried. It is the site of the son's birth and of the death of the mother. The two wives of Jacob make up a significant duality: Rachel is the vehicle of eternal womanhood, Leah of earthly womanhood. 'Rachel' means 'sacrificial lamb' — 'Leah' means 'a letting go,' a loss of vital forces. Rachel bears only Joseph and Benjamin, the youngest of the sons. The inheritance passes to the sons of Leah as does the continuation of the line. Joseph and Benjamin do not continue the messianic line. Joseph and Benjamin carry within themselves, like their mother Rachel, forces of eternal womanhood. But eternal womanhood must be sacrificed, it must become the sacrificial lamb 'Rachel' — it has to die. The national destiny is taken from the Rachel sons and given to the sons of Leah, vehicles of eternal masculinity. That is the theme of Rachel's lament on the heights of Bethlehem. The death of the youthful force of humanity, the death of eternal womanhood, strides onward. When the Jesus child is born of Mary in Bethlehem, Rachel the sacrificial lamb is thereby redeemed, the lament falls silent, Bethlehem is pure again, the place of birth. The bearers of the kingly masculine strain come with their offerings to the woman and child. A new enemy of soul forces, of the childhood forces of humanity, arises in the person of Herod. The demonic-masculine arises as the enemy of eternal womanhood and makes Bethlehem the site of the murder of the innocents. The lament of Rachel rises again on the site of Rachel's grave. From now on there is only slow death, only slow resurrection of eternal youth, of eternal womanhood. But there is also the struggle between the new childhood forces of the Christ and Herod's murder of the children, the struggle between eternal womanhood and the demonic masculine; between those who bear and worship the child forces, and those who destroy them; between the three kings and the fourth, King Herod.

And so we come to some words which — apart from the Bethlehem-Rachel quotations — are cited directly as prophecies. These are the two Essene utterances that frame the story of the flight into Egypt; of these, only the first is an Old Testament quotation, the other being taken from purely Essene tradition:

'Out of Egypt have I called my son.'

'He shall be called a Nazarene.'

The first quotation occurs when, on the angel's command, Joseph takes the child to Egypt; the second comes when, after returning home, he brings the child to Nazareth. Egypt is the land where the Essenes originated; Nazareth was probably the principal settlement of Essenes in Palestine at the time of the birth of Christ. The history of the Essene order passed from Egypt to Nazareth.

Just as the strongly masculine, paternal stream found expression in the forty-two generations of the first chapter, so too it did in the two prophetic sayings: that is to say, within the order of Essenes.

However, as we have tried to show, the Essene order was no more than a kind of exponent of Israel's national history from the time of the Exodus out of Egypt up to the birth of Jesus.

The birth of the Son is the fruit of the Exodus from Egypt. At the time of Moses the children of Israel were the Son. The Son still slumbered within the loins of his fathers. That is why the story of Israel is the same as the life of Jesus. The one pertains to the destiny of a people, whereas the other is the destiny of an ego. And the life of Jesus is the recapitulation by a single individual destiny of a national destiny. The flight to Egypt under threat of famine by Jacob and his sons is repeated in the flight of the Holy Family into Egypt because of Herod's massacre of the children. The Exodus from Egypt under the leadership of Moses is repeated in Nazareth. Passing beyond the limitation of chapter two, we could find a repetition of the crossing of the Red Sea in the Baptism in the Jordan; the forty years of wandering in the desert are paralleled by the forty days of the temptation of Jesus in the desert.

From the time of the Exodus from Egypt to that of the birth of Jesus the people of Israel had lived through destinies of their own. The healers and Essenes cultivated awareness of the significance and of the prophetic value of every individual destiny of their people. In their awareness of national destiny they looked prophetically to the future, towards the messianic fate. And when the messianic fate began, it was the Essenes, and Matthew among them, who understood why all things had to happen in the way they did; it was they who were able to contribute much to the education and guidance of the Jesus child, especially later on in Nazareth. They understood the meaning of those moves of the boy from Egypt to Nazareth. They knew of the transition from the era of the Father to that of the Son. They felt that they themselves were the bridge from Egypt to Nazareth, from Moses to Jesus, from Father to Son. They knew themselves to be one of the great streams of humanity that leads from Father to Son.

Moses

That brings us to a wealth of Old Testament echoes in the second chapter of Matthew's Gospel. These echoes are, however, not the exact words of the prophets; they are pictures which bring to life the writings of the Old Testament in some degree of secrecy, but none the less forcefully for that.

Two scenes in particular link the destiny of Jesus with that of Moses.

Pharaoh causes children to be murdered. A baby boy, Moses, is saved by being placed in an ark of bulrushes and confided to the waters of the Nile. At Herod's behest children are slaughtered in Bethlehem. The baby Jesus is saved by flight into Egypt. In both instances, child murder is an image of black magical cults which rely on abuse of the childhood forces of murdered children. So we recognize that the rescue of each boy was the rescue of childhood forces of quite special significance to humanity.

The other contact between the story of Moses and that of the Jesus child lies in the following. Moses having undergone his experience in Midian in the house of Jethro the wise priest, Yahweh spoke to him thus: 'Go back to Egypt, for all the men who were seeking your life are dead.' (Exod.4:19). And we are given the picture of Moses, with the ass upon which Zipporah and her son are mounted, returning home to Egypt. Herod having died, an angel appears to Joseph in Egypt and speaks to him saying: 'Get up, take the child and his mother and journey to the land of Israel; for now those who hunted for the child's life and soul are dead.' (Matt.2:20). And the picture rises before us of Joseph leading the ass upon which Mary is riding with the child.

We perceive in these scenes a second masculine stream enter the destiny of Jesus. At first it may appear to us a Mosaic stream. It may well be an Essene stream insofar as Moses himself belonged to the Therapeutae and founded the Nazarene order. It may also be akin to a third stream of which there will be more to say. We may be permitted to introduce at this stage something of the results of Rudolf Steiner's spiritual science which is able to throw more light onto the spiritual background of the flight of the Jesus child into Egypt and also onto the pictorial contacts between the destinies of the Moses babe and the Jesus child.

Rudolf Steiner speaks of the first Zarathustra, founder of Persia's earliest civilization, and he shows how the most significant cultural impulse emanated throughout pre-Christian history from this great leader of humanity. Hermes, founder of Egypt's earliest wisdom, and Moses the leader of the children of Israel, he calls Zarathustra's two greatest disciples. Rudolf Steiner tells how they had indeed been disciples of Zarathustra. When in later epochs each was to fulfil his own high mission, the one as Hermes and, somewhat later, the other as Moses, they were guided and inspired by the nearness of their teacher (See the lectures, including those on Zarathustra, Hermes and Moses, published as *Turning Points in Spiritual History*).

We recognize as the strongest influence upon the career of Moses the circumstances between the baby's exposure in the little ark at the time of the child murders under Pharaoh and his return home from Jethro, the wise priest. By these means an intimate communion between Moses and Zarathustra was renewed and established as an overriding spiritual power.

Rudolf Steiner's spiritual science also reveals that the Jesus child of whom St Matthew's Gospel speaks was a reincarnation of Zarathustra. If we can accept such a finding of spiritual science, then we shall also be able to accept what follows. There was alive in the Jesus child a certain element that had once taken part in those works of Hermes which brought into existence Egypt's temple culture but, as well, an element that had taken part in those works of Moses which, towards the end of

Egyptian temple culture, rescued the children of Israel and brought them back into the land of their fathers. The Jesus child's flight into Egypt and his return home, is thus the spiritual link with what the individuality now alive in the child had long ago achieved through Zarathustra's two disciples. Through the coming of the Jesus child to Egypt, where the essence of Hermes' work was dominant, Zarathustra, as it were, received back what he had given to Hermes. In that the boy Jesus came home from Egypt, re-enacting thereby the Exodus of the people of Israel, the Zarathustra individuality received back what had been given to Moses.*

What we had observed as the Mosaic stream flowing into the destiny of Jesus, we can now describe more accurately, in the light of the above, as the stream of Zarathustra's great disciples, of Hermes and Moses.

Zarathustra

A third stream was carried to the child Jesus by the three kings before he was plunged into Egypt in order to gain an inmost link with the stream of the great disciple of Zarathustra. It was the stream of the first Zarathustra himself.

Once again we find ourselves before a long series of Old Testament allusions. The Balaam story surfaces with the same star as the one the three kings saw. The children of Israel, led by Moses, were on their way out of Egypt. Balak, King of Moab, wanted to bar their way by spiritual means. He summoned Balaam, the prophet from Mesopotamia, out of the lands of eastern ancient civilizations, and demanded that Balaam curse the Israelites. But Balaam who wanted to curse, was constrained instead to bless, and his blessing culminated in a foretelling of the star: 'I shall see him, but not now, I shall behold him, but not nigh. There shall come a star out of Jacob and a sceptre shall rise out of Israel.'

The name 'Zarathustra,' 'Zoroaster,' has been repeatedly translated as 'The Star of God.' We can therefore accept Balaam's prophecy as one foretelling the return of Zarathustra who would indicate his presence by the appearance in the heavens of the Zarathustra star. That is quite

* See also 'The Flight to Egypt' in *The Childhood of Jesus*.

probable if we represent to ourselves the traditions that went right back to the first Zarathustra, and were still alive in Babylonia and Chaldea, Balaam's homelands. In Balaam we can see a vessel of that primordial Zarathustra tradition.

By their sojourn in Egypt and by their Exodus from it, the people of Israel had become bearers of whatever it was that emanated from Zarathustra's mighty disciples, Hermes and Moses. When Balak set out with Balaam's help to intercept the Israelites, he undertook to play off the Zarathustra stream against that of Zarathustra's disciples. But Balaam blessed Israel against his own will, as well as Balak's. We could say that Zarathustra put up no struggle against his sons. Balaam, a disciple of the golden star, wanted to oppose Israel and yet he was forced to promise those very Israelites the return of the star of God. He perceived that Zarathustra desired to go from Persia to Israel. As the Essenes felt that they were between the Father and the Son, between Abraham and Jesus, even so must Balaam have felt that he was between the Father Star and the Son Star, between Zarathustra and Jesus. The Essenes could see the earthly Father-to-Son line. Balaam saw the spiritual Father-to-Son line in which the Father became his own Son.

Beginning with Balaam, there existed in the East, in the region of the ancient Zarathustra culture, a prophetic tradition of the return of the great teacher, the Star of God, within the race. In the time of Jesus, it was from this tradition that the three wise magi-kings drew their knowledge of the star, of the star of Zarathustra. Its reappearance indicated the return of Zarathustra. Medieval legends concerning the three holy kings in every case traced their wisdom back to the prophecies of 'Bileam,' or Balaam. The apocryphal Arabian Gospel refers clearly to Zarathustra by name, linking him with the star of the three kings. 'And when the Lord of the Universe, Jesus, had been born ... behold, there came magi from the Orient to Jerusalem, even as Zarathustra had prophesied.'* The three kings were priestly magi from temples where the wisdom of Zarathustra was cultivated; they were disciples of Zarathustra.

Spiritual scientific research shows that Zarathustra returned once in the interval of time between Balaam and the three kings. He came as the great teacher, Nazaratos. Nazaratos lived at the time of the

---

* See *The Childhood of Jesus*, p. 282.

Babylonian exile and later became the teacher of great Hebrew prophets, as well as of such mighty wise men as Pythagoras, who travelled the world. Something of these encounters is echoed in the rich legends of Judaism.

Jewish history as a whole acquires from awareness of such things a marked unity. We can therefore describe it as a mutual search between the people of Israel and the personality of Zarathustra. In being sent into exile to Egypt, the Israelites were actually being drawn by Zarathustra, who desired to take them up into the stream of his two disciples, Hermes and Moses.

When Israel was led forth into exile to Babylon, Zoroaster was drawing the people to him for the second time, this time not towards his disciples but towards himself. The significance of that meeting lay in the meeting between Israel and himself. The significance of that encounter was that Zoroaster himself took the place of his disciples with Israel. He himself became the teacher of the prophets in place of Moses. He renewed Balaam's prediction for the people. From that time on, the prophets enunciate ever more clearly the messianic prophecy.

The third great meeting between Zarathustra and the people of Israel did not take place through Zarathustra calling them to him. He went to the people himself and was born a son of the people in the person of Jesus of Nazareth. And now, seeing that he was no longer drawing Israel to Egypt and Babylon in order to learn there, he drew Egypt and Babylon towards himself, so that they might learn of Israel. That is the story of the three kings. In them Egypt and Babylon came to Bethlehem. The three kings were disciples of the line which continued from the first Zarathustra through Balaam and Nazaratos. They brought to the Zarathustra Jesus child offerings of gold, frankincense and myrrh. Basically, what was it that they brought him? They brought back to Zarathustra what they had received from him. They brought him the spiritual fruits of his own earlier works. The very greatest streams of humanity flowed into the earthly destiny of Jesus the Christ. The fruits of the Zarathustra stream were being offered to him. He who had once previously sowed them, now received the harvest.

Two Old Testament prophecies were fulfilled as the three magi-kings offered their gold, frankincense and myrrh. The first prophecy is to be found in Psalm 72; the other in Isaiah 60. Both are repeated in St Matthew's Gospel, though not in so many words:

May the kings of Tarshish and of the isles render him tribute,
may the kings of Sheba and Seba bring gifts! May all kings fall
down before him, all nations serve him! (Ps.72:10f).
All those from Sheba shall come. They shall bring gold and
frankincense.' (Isa.60:6).

'Sheba' is more than a geographical term. Its plural implies the
starry hosts of heaven and the angelic hierarchies of the heavenly
hosts, who dwell in the stars. The Shebans were the custodians of the
ancient stellar cults. They were important in Mesopotamia and
Chaldea right up into the Christian era. The Queen of Sheba was a figure who incorporated within herself the wisdom of the stars. When we
are told that the wisdom of the kings who brought offerings of gold, of
frankincense and myrrh came from Sheba, then that is a pointer that
we should seek the sacrificial gold, incense and myrrh that they bear
in the stars. They were able to bring these gifts because they came from
lands where men were still able in their rituals to hold communion
with spirits of the stars. And Zarathustra is the greatest of all star spirits. He is the Star, the Star of God, who was even then revealing himself.

We see three mighty Father-streams flowing into the destiny of
Jesus:
— the Essene stream,
— the Moses stream (that is, the stream of Zarathustra's disciples),
— and the Zarathustra stream.

The Essene stream found expression in Matthew 2, mainly in
words; that of Zarathustra mainly in pictures. The Moses stream
stands between them.

There are bridges between the Essene stream and the stream of
Moses. And, in conclusion, we may mention yet another bridge. It lies
in that name for Zarathustra, Nazaratos, and it brings us close to the
Nezer-Nazareth name. The Essene stream, which was established in
Egypt, may well have experienced a renewal through Nazaratos in
Babylon; in consequence the great teacher's name came to be propa-
gated as one sacred to the Essenes. It could therefore be that the
Essenes in Nazareth made offering to the Jesus child of the fruits of his
own earlier activities as a human being. They conferred on him his
own name when in accordance with the prophecy they called him a
'Nazarene.'

The birth and youth of Jesus is indeed a focal point in which the riches of the spiritual history of humanity are concentrated. May something like an awareness emerge from these studies of how all peoples and civilizations actually found fulfilment in Jesus Christ.

The virgin birth

We can quite understand that nowadays there are many who cling to the miraculous dogma of the fatherless birth of Jesus. People may feel that a mystery was being destroyed if processes leading to the nativity of Jesus were to be brought down to the level of what is sensual and human, in the way that happened often enough within the new theology. For the most part, only two possibilities can be envisaged: either fatherless birth, or else — a profanely sensual and human birth.

We tried at the end of chapter two to show that such an alternative is not inevitable; rather, that the gospel itself indicates a third possibility, natural and supernatural at the same time. That third alternative will only be seen where there is the realization that human sexuality bore a sacred and divine character.

Certain questions addressed to me have caused me to state what follows by way of recapitulation and expansion.

The gospel indicates clearly enough through the genealogical tree of Joseph, which precedes the story of the nativity, that externally Jesus was indeed the son of Joseph. The whole of that genealogy would be senseless and irrelevant if the dogma of a fatherless birth were correct. On the other hand, the gospel enunciates that what is maturing within Mary's body is begotten of the Holy Spirit. Joseph is the physical father. But the will to beget was the will of the Holy Spirit, not the instinctual desire of a man. The divine will of the Holy Spirit overshadowed the parents with the mysterious veil of the eternal feminine. Beneath the cloak of sacred sleep, human consciousness was silent. Divine providence had brought together Joseph and Mary, a human couple, who had been able to preserve in their essentially childlike nature and chastity those forces which humankind had lost with the advancing Fall.

In bringing about the destined meeting of Joseph and Mary, providence made use (if we can put it so) of certain persons who knew how to guide and lead. It was the priests of the Temple of Solomon who wed the elderly Joseph to the childlike Mary. Mary had been brought up as a temple virgin, wholly devoted to her vow of chastity and to her prayers. The priests were bidden by spiritual messages to wed Mary to a man who would be recognized through a miracle. Lots were cast among the twelve tribes. The tribe of Judah was chosen by lot, and all unmarried men of that tribe were summoned to the temple. Each man brought with him a staff. Joseph, an old man, was the last to take back his staff from the hands of the priest, for Joseph could not have conceived that the lot would fall on him. His was the staff that broke suddenly into leaf. Only then Joseph accepted the will of God and declared himself ready to take Mary into his house, provided that Mary might in his house have about her the protective circle of the other temple virgins. He bowed unwillingly to the higher will.

Pictorial legendary accounts such as these probably contain more historical truth than a trivial external presentation of events could give. We can in any case recognize this much: the parents were brought together through higher recognition and revelation. Their own human wills, if anything, opposed the union. Providence prevailed and fulfilled its work.

It seems to me a very likely and vivid picture that not only the wedding of Joseph and Mary should have taken place within the Temple precincts in Jerusalem, but that the night of conception did too; and that Joseph took his wife to his house only after that other night, when the angel appeared and solved the enigma.

Here, as everywhere in the gospel, it is far more difficult to resolve the question concerning what happened in exoteric history, than to solve the question concerning spiritual events in the sacred story. It would be a major illusion to think that exoteric facts in the life of Jesus can easily be established through historical and critical research. The recent materialistic view of the world leads to the opinion that scientific research into the external biographical course of events in the life of Jesus can provide a basis for unlocking the gospel.

It is the exoteric, historical events which will probably confront us most consistently as the final, the most difficult and mysterious part in our studies on the gospels.

CHAPTER FOUR

John the Baptist and Jesus of Nazareth

Essene wisdom in the working of John

The four gospels are like a great tree which sends its roots deep into the realms of earth, its branches stretching high into the heavens. In St John's Gospel, the tree has grown upwards into the eagle's heavenly heights. St Matthew's is the root gospel. It sends its roots far into the matrix of human history. From the mighty past, above all from the sacred regions of the Old Testament of Jewish history, rays converge in St Matthew's Gospel into the earthly life of Christ, as the root system of a tree converges into its trunk. We can understand that the first two chapters of Matthew bear within themselves that root character especially clearly, so that our considerations of the two chapters turned inevitably into a journey through the religious history of pre-Christian times.

The gospels do not set out to dismiss the religious existence and spiritual striving of pre-Christian times as so much unenlightened paganism. The story of the adoration of the three kings, and also the account of the flight into Egypt, contradict the narrowly confessional way of looking at Christianity, which assumes an unbridgeable contradiction between Christianity and what went before it. The Christ was the fulfilment of all men's longing, the consummation of the wisdom of all mysteries. Paganism became decadent only when it failed to realize that its time was up and that it must make way for one greater than itself.

In the early chapters of St Matthew's Gospel we can watch flowing into the tree of Christ the life of the mother-soil of all human history by way of the roots of old prophecies and of ancient pictorial echoes of sacred tales.

We are going to approach chapters three and four with this question: how do the roots grow into the trunk?

We have to transport ourselves to the scene where John the Baptist is baptizing Jesus of Nazareth in the Jordan. The two great streams of humanity, of which we spoke in the last chapter, stand before us in the person of these two figures. All that emanated from the Essene stream is gathered up in John. Everything coming from the Zarathustrian stream is concentrated in Jesus of Nazareth. These two streams unite and between them shape the vessel able to receive the heavenly content, the being of Christ.

Let us first look at John the Baptist. We recognize him by his hair shirt as a Nazarene, as an Essene. What he says to the people is Essene wisdom. But it is the kind of wisdom of Essene teaching which recognizes that its mission has run its course and that it must prepare the way, make the paths straight for one who is greater. The true Essene teaching speaks through him: 'He must increase, but I must decrease.' The task of the Essene movement was to lead humanity down the forty-two steps from Abraham, from the spiritual world into earthly life. That task has now been fulfilled. Now the need is to ascend again: 'Change your hearts.'

John is portrayed very differently in each of the first three gospels. Mark gives the shortest account, then Matthew, then Luke; and each of the gospels repeats what the preceding one has given, but adds something more. We should not, however, assume that the shortest account is the scantiest.

St Mark represents John as the angel fulfilling the priestly office of baptism. He introduces what he has to say about the Baptist with the words of Isaiah: 'See, I send my angel before you; he is to prepare your way' (Mark 1:2). Matthew passes beyond what Mark describes; he tells how John the preacher of repentance is still leading the human soul down the last stages of the descent to earth, through images that proceed from a sense of world judgment, images of the axe laid to the tree, of the winnowing fan on the threshing floor. Matthew's Gospel begins by leading from heaven to earth, even as the forty-two names in the genealogical table make up the rungs of an earthbound ladder that lead from heaven to earth. In the same way John the Baptist is the human being who completes the descent to earth by his preaching. Matthew does not at this point introduce Isaiah's words concerning the angel. Those words in relation to John cannot be uttered until the eleventh chapter. There is a path that must first be trodden from man to angel.

In St Luke's Gospel, John is the fulfiller of the baptism; he is also the preacher of repentance. But he is more. St Luke's Gospel enters fully into the upward movement of transformation which may follow man's descent to earth. It moves from below up, just as St Matthew's moves from above down. Accordingly, St Luke's heavenly ladder, leading as it does from Jesus to Abraham, and beyond Abraham to God, moves in reverse order to Matthew's genealogical table. Similarly, we are to understand what Luke gives us of John's sermons over and above what Mark and Matthew say. John answers questions from the crowds, from the tax-collectors and the soldiers, 'What must we do then?' with advice which sounds like proverbs. John stands forth as the hierophant who is not content merely to bring to a close the descent of man through his own powerful preaching of repentance. He is now directly influencing and guiding the resumed ascent. The utterances with which he replies to the multitudes are the sayings of a hierophant which prompt humanity towards personal striving for higher things.

Let us look at John the man, the preacher in the wilderness, as Matthew portrays him. 'Preacher in the wilderness' really means 'he who calls in solitude of soul.' Humanity has reached earth, a place of desolation, the place of ego-solitude. While humankind was still on the downward path, that is to say, had not yet reached earth, man was still embedded in an enveloping spiritual element. The development of the ego can really begin only on earth. That development can be bought only at the price of the ancient link with spirit. The first stage is the 'wilderness,' the experience of solitude. John is the herald of that ego-development, the painful sense of loneliness. Ruthlessly, he puts into words this stage of the soul in order, in so doing, to fulfil it.

Humanity has traversed the forty-two generations. Accordingly, man could indeed find the Father in Abraham by climbing the purifying ladder with its forty-two rungs. But of what use would that be? The line of Abraham had become as hard as stone. Unless a new life principle were to enter, Father Abraham would have only dead stones in place of sons. And how was the living to arise out of the dead?: 'Do not look for excuses by saying to yourselves: We have Abraham as our father. I say to you: The Father in heaven can just as well raise up sons of Abraham from these dead stones' (Luke 3:8). John sets out in these words to bring to the awareness of the Pharisees a sense of the poverty of soul, of the soul's hardening. They were not to withdraw through illusion from the full descent to earth. The word for 'stone' in Hebrew is *eben* or *aben*. The word for father is contained in it: 'Ab' = father, and 'Ben' = Son. 'From stones, sons' in Hebrew must have been a highly significant play on words, *abanim banim*. There was also something else sounding through it: 'Of the Father's sons' sons.' The Pharisees were those who had no desire to make the transition from the time of the Father to the time of the Son. But to halt at the Father principle meant petrification.

The Baptist's utterance on stones and sons reminds us of the divine utterance which according to Greek mythology was vouchsafed to Deucalion and Pyrrha, the only human couple to have survived the great flood: 'Cast the bones of thy great Mother behind thee.' They understand at last that the stones were meant for the bones of Mother Earth. They cast the stones behind them and from the stones there arose a new human race. Paternal forces have led to stone. A new race can be brought forth out of petrification only by the Son. Therefore, change your hearts. Such was the Essene wisdom of the Baptist, a wisdom which superseded its own self.

And now the preaching of him who calls in solitude soars to two mighty word pictures of the mystery: 'Already the axe is laid to the root of the trees, and every tree that does not bear good fruit is felled and thrown into the fire' (Matt.3:10). 'The winnowing fork is in his hand, and he will cleanse his grain of the chaff. He will gather the wheat into the barn, but the chaff he will burn in an unquenchable fire' (Matt.3:12).

But there is more alive in those words than pictorial language. The primitive strength of those words is due to the fact that the deepest world secrets can be seen in them by the inward eye. Supersensible truth in the pictures bestows magical power upon the words. What trees are those to whose roots the axe is laid? We can picture for ourselves the world-tree that is to be felled in three ways. If we look upon the macrocosm, we can say: it is the star tree. In primordial times there lived in human souls a cosmic consciousness which saw the world in mythical terms. In that ancient cosmic consciousness, man still experienced himself as a limb of the earth's body, as a branch of the tree. The soul was not locked within the narrow compass of life; it was, as it were, still poured out throughout the heavens. The stars of heaven hung in the branches of this tree. The tree must be felled, only the stump is to remain. It is all described for us in chapter 4 of the Book of Daniel:

> The visions of my head as I lay in bed were these: I saw, and behold, a tree in the midst of the earth; and its height was great. The tree grew and became strong, and its top reached to heaven, and it was visible to the end of the whole earth. Its leaves were fair and its fruit abundant, and it was food for all. The beasts of the field found shade under it, and the birds of the air dwelt in its branches, and all flesh was fed from it. I saw in the visions of my head as I lay in bed, and behold, a watcher, a holy one, came down from heaven. He cried aloud and said thus, 'Hew down the tree and cut off its branches, strip off its leaves and scatter its fruit; let the beasts flee from under it and the birds from its branches. But leave the stump of its roots in the earth, bound with a band of iron and bronze, amid the tender grass of the field. Let him be wet with the dew of heaven; let his lot be with the beasts in the grass of the earth; let his mind be changed from a man's, and let a beast's mind be given to him; and let seven times pass over him.' (Dan.4:10–16).

The root-stock remaining after the felling of the tree of ancient cosmic consciousness is human thought. From it a new cosmic consciousness, the new star tree, can one day come forth.

The hewing down of the star tree is a cosmic inevitability. It is identical with the descent of man to earth, without which there could be no freedom. By their words the prophets, of whom John the Baptist himself is the last, swing the axe against the world tree. The ancient cosmic consciousness has to give way before an earthbound thought-consciousness. The sixth chapter of Isaiah tells how Isaiah is virtually commanded to cut down the world-tree by his preaching:

> Go, and say to this people: 'Hear and hear, but do not understand; see and see but do not perceive.' Make the heart of this people fat, and their ears heavy, and shut their eyes; lest they see with their eyes, and hear with their ears, and understand with their hearts, and turn and be healed. Then I said, 'How long, O Lord?' And he said: 'Until cities lie waste without

inhabitant, and houses without men, and the land is utterly desolate, and the Lord removes men far away, and the forsaken places are many in the midst of the land. And though a tenth remain in it, it will be burned again, like a terebinth or an oak, whose stump remains standing when it is felled.' (Isa.6:9–13).

If we turn our attention to the individual human being, that microcosm, we can say: the tree to which the axe is laid is the tree of the vein of blood. Star harmonies sounded in the blood just as long as cosmic consciousness was alive. Then the tree was felled. Its root-stock became the heart which from then on grew as hard as stone, obdurate and bestial rather than human. 'Make the heart of this people fat,' and again, 'Let his mind be changed from a man's, and let a beast's mind be given to him.' Nevertheless, a new, sonorous blood tree is to sprout from that heart, and then the heart will become flesh again instead of stone, human instead of bestial, when the etheric heart within the physical heart will have re-awakened to become the physical organ for the perception of the spiritual world.

A third aspect lies between the macrocosmic and the microcosmic aspects of the world-tree; an historically human one. Here we may say: the tree being felled is the genealogical tree. In this we draw quite close to the intention of St Matthew's Gospel. The passage about the trees to whose roots the axe is to be laid follows immediately on the utterance concerning Abraham, the sons and the stones. What is said of the trees concerns the continuation of the race. It is thereby discernible as Essene wisdom. The tree to whose roots the axe is to be laid is the forty-two-limbed family tree set out in chapter one. The tree is felled, having grown from summit regions of heaven all the way down to earth. The mission of the race has been fulfilled. The time is past when blood relationships, generation sequences and physical inheritance were the vessel and the instrument of the spirit. The root-stock from which the new shoot will arise is to remain in the stony ground: 'There shall come forth a shoot from the stump of Jesse, and a branch shall grow out of his roots.' (Isa.11:1).

It has always been customary to draw a tree with branching root and bough system when depicting the genealogy of an old family. The genealogy in the gospel has been represented pictorially as a tree. There one saw 'the root of Jesse' made visible to us. The root of Jesse in this tree is what the heart is to the blood-vein tree, and what thought is to the star tree.

The root of Jesse re-opens the unfruitful, petrified womb to humankind. A new humanity comes to birth. The Christ is its ancestor.

The two genealogical tables, Matthew's and Luke's, taken together, differ from one another not only in the reversed order in which the names are listed. They also differ in the position within each gospel story at which they occur — and this is vitally important.

The family tree in Matthew stands right at the beginning. In St Luke's Gospel, the family tree is not at the beginning, nor is it in any way linked to the story of Jesus' birth; it follows immediately on the Baptism of Jesus, right in the middle of chapter three.

In this study we shall have particularly to discuss further on how the Baptism in Jordan was for the Christ being very much the same as the birth in Bethlehem was for the Jesus individuality. The physical birth of Jesus took place in Bethlehem. In Jordan it was the spiritual birth of Christ that occurred. The Jesus ego incarnated in the tiny babe born to Mary. The Christ being incarnated in the physical-spiritual entity of Jesus of Nazareth when, thirty years after birth, he received baptism at the hands of John. More detailed consideration will follow. However, we have to briefly mention this much now, in order to clarify the family tree of St Matthew and that of St Luke in their differing forms.

The genealogical table of the first gospel, leading from heaven to earth, precedes the physical nativity of Jesus in which Jesus fulfils himself: he completely attains earth. Luke's family tree follows the spiritual birth of the Christ. It leads away from earth, back towards heaven. The rise became possible again because the Christ entered the rootstock of Jesse, enabling the shoot of the new world tree to sprout.

Matthew's family tree is felled. It is the tree of Fatherhood. Luke's family tree is the tree of Life, the tree of the Son. That is why, in St Matthew's Gospel, John proclaims the end of the tree of the old world. In St Luke's Gospel, John stands forth among men as the hierophant; his words are no longer merely blows of the axe against the trunk of the tree. He gives to humankind the earliest indications of how to plant and cultivate the new world tree, in that he gives the common people mottos for spiritual striving. Matthew's tree falls, the Christ having appeared, but Luke's tree rises.

The Baptism in the Jordan

We have looked at John the Baptist, one of the figures in the holy baptismal scene in the Jordan. We turn now to the other figure, to Jesus of Nazareth.

We have lost sight of the distinction which must be made between Jesus and the Christ, in proportion to the degree to which knowledge of the spiritual world has been lost among men and, with it, of the nature of the Christ. And as this difference again becomes the vital possession of souls, so a lively understanding of the Christ will again become possible. To see the man, and only the man, in Jesus Christ, is correct for Jesus of Nazareth before the Baptism in Jordan. After the Baptism in Jordan, a being stands before us who can no longer be explained in terms of what is only human.

There was in early Christianity a clear concept of the relationship between Jesus and the Christ. It was only after Christianity had passed out of the early stages and had been declared the established religion under the Emperor Constantine, that the councils were inaugurated, that the debates and the dogmatizing began concerning the divine and the human in the Christ. Here was the symptom that the living perception of the nature of the Christ had been lost.

However, an echo of that early understanding of the relationship of Jesus to the Christ survived for a long time beyond the first council (AD 325) in the religious cultures of the first centuries of Christianity. There is a fact we have to keep pointing out. The festival of Christmas used to be celebrated in early Christianity not on December 25, but on January 6. And January 6 was the day of the Baptism in the Jordan. Not until the year 354 was the feast of Christmas moved to December 25 in Rome and its territories. In the Eastern Church the original holy day persisted until the sixth century, when the Emperor Justinian forcibly introduced December 25 in place of January 6.

The Baptism in the Jordan was experienced quite inevitably as the nativity of the Christ. It was only after the feast of Christmas was moved to December 25 that the birth of Jesus became the content of that celebration. The original content of January 6 receded further and further into the background. There remained for January 6 only the scene of the adoration of the magi. As the meaning of the Jordan Baptism came to be forgotten, so too was the earlier vital understanding of the Christ. There remained only understanding of Jesus.

In contrast to the more abstract and intellectual Christianity of Rome, a more pictorial and vivid experience of Christianity has been preserved mainly in the Eastern orthodox churches of Greece and Russia. There, to this day, an understanding of the Baptism, through the heart, still survives. I can illustrate this with a single example. Monks of the monasteries on the holy peninsula of Mount Athos create many beautiful wood carvings which they sell to visitors. I brought back with me a small wooden crucifix, having reliefs carved on its back and front. On one side is the death scene on Golgotha, on the other the Baptism in the Jordan. It is not the manger in Bethlehem which is juxtaposed to the cross of Golgotha. The birth appropriate to the death on the cross is not the birth of Jesus, but the birth of the Christ. And that took place at the Baptism by John.

The being of Christ incarnated in Jesus of Nazareth, a human being. The physical and soul nature of a man, of the greatest of men, became the vessel of the Christ, the being who descended from out of the realms of spirit. This incarnation, this act of Christ becoming Man, is one of the most profound mysteries of all time. As understanding of this mystery re-enters humankind, so the way will be made free for a spiritual concept of the world, for religious life based on freedom. Here is the cardinal point for all things pertaining to the interrelationship of body, soul and spirit, to the penetration of the earthly and human by the heavenly and divine. Naturally, we cannot aspire to more than a faint preliminary pointer towards the mystery of the incarnation of Christ.

The teaching of Apollinaris of Laodicea was rejected as heresy at the second great ecumenical Council of Constantinople (AD 381.). He had formed the following view of the mystery of the Incarnation: He said that man was made up of body, soul and spirit; and that this was true of Jesus of Nazareth. But, at the Baptism in the Jordan, in place of the human spirit of Jesus, there entered the spirit of the Christ. After the Jordan Baptism, Jesus Christ possessed a human body, a human soul, but a divine ego, a divine spirit.

This view was no more than a formalized statement of what in early Christian times had held sway as a vital, self-evident tenet. But, the time had come for theologizing and dogmatizing; and so Apollinaris of Laodicea was condemned as a heretic.

Rudolf Steiner has enabled us to gaze, deeply moved, into what spiritual science has been able to tell us of the destinies of Jesus between his twelfth and his thirtieth year. Nothing has been handed down to us, exoterically or historically, about those years in the life of Jesus. Apocryphal accounts that are to be found here and there are in the main legendary, and were often written down very late.

According to Steiner, the ego alive in Jesus of Nazareth was the most mature and most all-embracing ego of all humankind. Spiritual science claims, as we have seen in an earlier study, that the ego of the earliest teacher of humankind, Zarathustra's ego, was incarnated in Jesus. The three wise men of the Orient bent the knee before him, who was the wise one among the wise. The three holy kings worshipped him who bore within himself the most royal of all human egos.

While this man Jesus of Nazareth was growing up in a humble and quite unpretentious environment, outwardly taking part in his father's trade, his great maturity and wisdom of soul influenced him in a twofold sense. Looking out upon the world of men, he felt the deepest, most shattering pain because of the impoverishment and desolation of soul not only among the Jews, but also in the cultic life of other people and in the worship of other gods. All the misery of humanity lodged in his soul; a humanity at that time deserted by God and in danger of falling a prey to the rapaciousness of demons.

As he gazed towards the spiritual world, he could feel the mighty approach of the being whom the people of Israel awaited as the Messiah; he could feel that being, the Christ, as he drew near — the Christ who alone would be able to heal the consuming need of soul. But, as time went on, the burning question inevitably occupied him more and more; where would the Christ being find a place in this world of human beings, sunk as they were in wretchedness? How would his spiritual nature be able to enter into a world alienated to spirit?

Questions such as these must have torn the soul of Jesus of Nazareth like a never-ceasing pain. As he felt the being of Christ draw nearer to himself, Jesus offered himself totally to the Christ being. Whoever thinks in terms of reincarnation, and especially in terms of the reincarnation of the first Zarathustra in Jesus of Nazareth, will be able to say to himself: There was a time when Zarathustra, the great teacher, had looked upward to the sun with profoundest reverence and devotion, seeking that spiritual being as the Light of the World behind the physical sun whom he called Ahura Mazdao, the mighty aura of the sun. Now, as Jesus of Nazareth, he perceived that same being whom he had seen in earlier times upon the sun. It is unimportant whether Jesus felt this consciously or in his soul emotionally.

Placed as he was midway between godforsaken humanity and the divine being drawing in strength nearer to earth, the soul of Jesus was overwhelmed. The very pinnacle of human spiritual struggle and pain must have come when Jesus of Nazareth, breaking beneath the burden of that hour and filled with the longing to sacrifice himself, to surrender himself, his endurance stretched to the limit, went down to Jordan to be baptized by John.

The desire to serve the approaching Christ, to help him towards incarnation — all this created that sacrificial state of mind which desired total self-surrender in order to become the vessel. We cannot describe what took place at the Baptism in Jordan better than the words of St Paul: 'So it is not I who live, but Christ lives in me.' (Gal.2:20).

The deed was done by Jesus of Nazareth before those words were spoken by St Paul. Jesus of Nazareth sacrificed his ego totally to become the vessel of the Christ. The ego of Jesus died, entered the world of spirit; the Christ being incarnated in the physical and spiritual sheaths of Jesus. As John the Baptist had made ready the way for the Christ into the world of men, so Jesus of Nazareth prepared the way for Christ into the human body.

We find wondrously realistic echoes of this, the mightiest spiritual event to which human history can point, in the legend of St Christopher. It is less difficult, and more appropriate, to speak of mysteries such as this one in images rather than in abstract words.

'Offerus, a pagan, lived in the land of Canaan. He was a man of very great strength and he was some twelve ells tall' — that is how the legend begins. The legend transports us to the site of the Baptism in the Jordan. Its earthy-sounding language sets before us the cosmic greatness of that soul. The name, Offerus, immediately reveals that the secret of the soul is based in sacrifice, in the *offertorium*, in the sacrificial offering of self. The giant looks for the most exalted master in order that he may serve him. First of all, he serves a mighty king; then the devil. But when he finds out that the devil is afraid of someone greater still, he sets out to find the one who is greatest of all — the Christ. A hermit bids him go to a certain great river — the Jordan — and there to become a ferryman. He builds himself a cabin by the river and carries people from one bank to the other. One night he hears his name called three times by a child. He takes the child on his shoulder and strides away with his burden. Half way over the river, the giant thinks he is drowning and says, 'I feel as if I were carrying the whole world upon me.' But the child replies 'It is not the world alone that you are bearing, but also him who created heaven and earth.' With those words the Child forces the giant down into the water, saying: 'I am Christ, and I baptize you, and change your name, Offerus, to Christophorus.'

These images give expression with the utmost beauty and purity to many of the truly spiritual processes of the Baptism in the Jordan. Through his sacrifice, Jesus became the real Christophorus. And, as Jesus became Christophorus, so was the Christ born on earth. We see Christ on the shoulders of Christophorus just as we see the child Jesus in the manger in Bethlehem.

Jesus stands before us as the consummation of humanity, and as the prototype of sacrifice. Man is the sacrificial chalice, Christ the content of the chalice. Thus the divine and the human unite in this stupendous and unique sacrificial scene. Similarly, if in a different way, they ought to unite in every human being; man ought to become Christophorus and make the words come true: 'So it is not I who live, but Christ lives in me.' John the Baptist says: 'He must increase, I must decrease.' Jesus of Nazareth makes real 'So it is not I who live, but Christ lives in me.' The Christ is able to enter into humanity by way of this twofold reality of sacrifice.

In order not to leave open to misunderstanding some utterances of spiritual science we have mentioned, let us enlarge upon them by means of what follows. Rudolf Steiner says that the Jesus ego passed through more incarnations after the Baptism in Jordan. The Jordan Baptism was for his ego the same as an earthly death. It is however a fundamental fact of the spiritual world order that the Christ being (not of course a human individuality) incarnated in a physical human body once only. It was this that compelled Rudolf Steiner in 1912 to protest to the leaders of the Theosophical Society, orientated as they were towards India, who were presenting an Indian boy, Krishnamurti, as a reincarnation of the Christ. The nature of Indian Theosophy became only too obvious in the estrangement from Christianity and the Christ. When those leaders, orientated towards India, brought about a parting of the ways, Rudolf Steiner continued his own spiritual scientific work in the form of anthroposophy, consistently revealing to all the world that anthroposophy was Christian through and through. It is a significant historical fact that Theosophy and anthroposophy separated over a question pertaining to the Christ.

Rudolf Steiner has given several informative indications concerning the further destiny and mission of the Zoroaster-Jesus ego, following the mystery of Golgotha. He tells how this exalted leader was incarnated in the fourteenth century, as teacher and inspiration behind the wonderfully inward writings of Middle High German mysticism, above all of the *Theologia Germanica* and of the writings of 'The Friend of God from the Highlands.' The recurring theme of the *Theologica Germanica* is that human nature must decline in order that the Christ may find room there, right up to the actual fulfilment of the words of St Paul. This was the book that so joyously inspired the young Luther, and which he saved from oblivion.

The nature of baptism

Pointing to that greater one, for whom he is preparing a path, John the Baptist speaks thus: 'I have baptized you with water, but he will baptize you with the Holy Spirit and with fire' (Mark 1:8). What is the nature of the baptism of John, and how does it differ from what John himself recognizes as the baptism of Christ? We shall offer a brief answer in anthroposophical terms and in terms of the history of religion.

In ancient times men had a clear idea of the inward and spiritual structure of the human being although they did not then formulate it as we do now. They saw in the external world of the senses the dominance of the four elements — of earth, water, air and fire. They were aware of the way in which these four elements participated in the nature of man — not alone in the body, but also in man as a whole, as in a being of physical body, soul and spirit. Earth's share in man is the physical body, but the element of water has its share too; it is active in the living, creative forces which stream through the physical body and shape it. They are described in anthroposophy as the etheric body. The sphere of air in man is in the soul; we associate it with breathing. Anthroposophy calls the sphere of air the astral body. In Greek the word *pneuma* covers 'a breath of air,' 'the wind,' but also 'spirit.' It implies spirit more in the sense of ensouled spirit, akin to air. Man perceived the fire element in the human being as existing more in what is individual to that person's spirit, to his ego. However, in those early days it was conceived of as soaring high above humanity, as not yet being incarnated.

The three higher elements are all named in the Baptist's utterances about the two kinds of baptism. We must keep in mind that the word for spirit also covers the element of air. John says 'I baptize with water, He will baptize with air (spirit) and fire.'

We shall understand something of the difference between the two baptisms if we are quite clear in our own minds that there were two possibilities for uniting man with the element of spirit at the time when the ego flame was still floating above him; either the spiritual part of a human being was lifted out of the body, or else the spiritual part was drawn down into the physical and soul sheaths. John's water baptism brought about the first. It freed man from his body. The person being baptized was plunged right under water until the same process was setting in as in dying. The three superior parts — etheric, astral and ego — were lifted out of the physical. The soul vivified the trinity of its own nature. It looked down upon the body, vehicle of the Father forces; it looked up to the spiritual ego which had been united with it in its earthly existence, seeing it in the form of a dove or of the tongue of fire. It felt itself to be at the centre — reborn through baptism — as the Son. The experience of the water baptism was associated with the experience which people describe who have been near death by drowning, or who have suffered a fall in the mountains, or been buried during the war; it is the experience of the memory tableau, when a whole life is recalled at one and the same moment as a vast and total scene containing all detail within itself. As the soul contemplated the totality of this scene, it became aware of all its errors and omissions. This is what happens after death in the first stages of soul consciousness. Here lies the reality behind the gospel words in which those who were baptized by John confessed their sins. As they came up out of the Jordan and regained the land, they could say that they had seen their sins and, having been reborn in very truth, they were beginning life anew.

All pre-Christian initiation consisted of lifting the human soul out of its earthly body, in a temporary transfer of the soul into the condition which normally sets in only at death. Freed of its body, the soul was united with its spirit ego, still hovering above it. The baptism which John celebrated in the Jordan was to some extent the last major drawing together of all pre-Christian religious and ritualistic life.

John's baptism was continued for a while in early Christian times in the form of baptism of adults. After that, however, man's nature changed. The ego drew further and further into physical and soul sheaths, the body became harder. The relationship to each other of the various component members of the body changed. It would be utterly contrary to nature nowadays to use a form of baptism such as John used. The soul-spirit element would not easily disengage itself from the hardened physicality; above all, it would not find its way back easily into incarnation. Had the baptismal ceremony not been weakened in Baptist circles to a mere pale token, the procedure would doubtless have called forth a good deal of mental illness as well as spiritual disturbance and disease.

John the Baptist himself points to quite another principle of baptism which he could see entering into humanity through the Christ. Baptism by air and fire, baptism by the Holy Spirit, would take the place of baptism by water. Baptism by water is a process of excarnation; baptism by the Holy Spirit and by fire is a process of incarnation. This kind of baptism, that of the Christ, occurred in its most potent form in human life at Pentecost, when tongues of fire of the Holy Spirit settled on the disciples. The human spirit-ego, full of the Christ, came down to man.

Pre-Christian baptism, the baptism celebrated by John, was baptism outside the body. Christian baptism which consists of an experience of the Christ, takes place within the body. Instead of the element of water in the human organism being lifted out of the earth element by the influence of external water and then being united with air and fire outside the body, air and fire are carried down into the body's elements of earth and water.

At the time when the ego was still evolving, humanity was in any case passing into those very elements. Because the Christ impulse was even then entering into humanity, human beings could in the Christian sense from then on become ego-beings. Since that time, man has been able to allow the Christian ego, the more exalted ego, rather than the lower ego, to descend into himself. In this way he accepts his ego within the meaning of that utterance, 'So it is not I who live, but Christ lives in me.'

Pre-Christian and Christian baptism married when Jesus of Nazareth received baptism in the Jordan. Baptism by water was accomplished externally; the etheric-astral body was lifted out of the physical. Outside the body the Christ-being flowed into the etheric-astral sacrificial vessel as an ego consisting wholly of love; then, as the etheric-astral returned into the physical body, so that new ego was also drawn into incarnation. Liberation of body and penetration of spirit met. Pre-Christian and Christian eras and paths intertwined. In that manner a transition was made ready from pre-Christian liberation of the body — which invariably contained within itself the reverse of freedom — to Christian penetration of the etheric-astral, the true path of freedom. The Holy Spirit, being pure spirituality, and the fire of the Christ-ego, is enabled to enter into a man without dulling his consciousness, let alone extinguishing it, but rather quickening consciousness so that it may awaken in the world of spirit although still alive in his earthly body.

Let us conclude our study of the Baptism in the Jordan with the following observation: There is beautiful significance in the fact that Christian tradition has placed the Three Kings Festival and also the Feast of Epiphany (that is, of the Manifestation of Christ to the magi) on the day of the Baptism in the Jordan, on January 6. Those were sacrifices that the magi brought to the Jesus child; it was sacrifice that Jesus brought to the Christ. The three kings carried the sum total of pre-Christian history. Jesus passed on that sacrifice to the Christ in that he sacrificed his ego and prepared himself to be the vessel for the reception of the Christ. We can state on the basis of spiritual cognition that the sacrifice of Zarathustra's disciples to Zarathustra became the sacrifice of Zarathustra to the Christ.

The threefold temptation

The first task to which the Christ being was destined was, according to the march of events in the first three gospels, the Temptation.

Although the story of the Temptation begins with the words, 'After this Jesus was driven by the Spirit into the loneliness of the desert to be tested by the Adversary' (Matt.4:1), we would be wrong to take the word 'wilderness' in its physical and topographical sense. The Baptist was spoken of as preacher in the wilderness and Jesus was led by the spirit into the wilderness. In both instances 'the wilderness' means loneliness of soul, the ego region, the physical solitude of a human being. The Greek word for 'desert' — *eremia* — is contained in words like 'hermit' which indicate one who lives in solitude, one who seeks out solitude for his soul's gradual unfolding.

As the being of Christ descended from spiritual worlds to incarnation, so he came to stand alone in human individuality. To be led into the wilderness means none other than incarnation, even if for Jesus, who had taken into himself the Christ being following the Jordan Baptism, a period of withdrawal to a lonely place in the desert may actually have taken place.

The three scenes of the Temptation should be understood spiritually as being three stages in the struggle to incarnate into a body.

Ever since primordial times, while still in spirit regions, the Christ being had been victorious over the powers of temptation. The Christ's heavenly hosts had long ago overcome Satan and his hordes, and had cast them into the depths. The Christ could say, 'I saw the satanic power fall like lightning from heaven into the depths.' (Luke 10:18). But whither did the hostile armies fall? They fell to earth. And now the Christ came down to earth. There he again met the adversaries. They were the first beings to confront the Christ on earth. He descended into the depths, and there he overcame the powers of the abyss. He met them within those members of the human organism in which he enveloped himself.

The Christ is like fire coming from heaven. This fiery ego sank into the three bodily members that correspond to earth, water and air, into the physical body, the etheric or life body, and the astral or soul body.

As he descended into the physical body, the Christ encountered the being whose desire it was to tempt him to turn stones into bread.

As he sank into the etheric or life body, he encountered the being who desired to tempt him to make light of life forces by casting himself down from a pinnacle of the temple.

As he sank down into the astral or soul body, he met the being who desired to tempt him to become Lord of the World instead of Saviour of the World.

A mighty being emanating from the highest regions of spirit found himself transferred to the world of earth, of the physical, of life body and soul, in which ordinarily only a human ego holds sway. To what extent is the being superior to those earthly sheaths, thanks to the cosmic powers indwelling in him? Could he not transmute the dead physicality which belongs to the mineral kingdom into something living? Could he not at will strengthen the feeble life forces present in the human organism, replace them with cosmic ones, like some great magician who plunges to his death before the eyes of the crowd and rises again immediately by drawing upon the treasure of cosmic life forces? Could he not immeasurably increase those weak human soul forces in such a way as to bind all human souls irresistibly under his own spell, force them into servitude?

The threefold temptation came at the Christ being as he sank into earthly sheaths out of his own divinely cosmic superiority over earthly human powers. It came to him out of human weakness, out of the earthly.

Doubtless the thought has struck many people: If it was indeed a god who walked the earth in the person of Christ, should not every stone he touched have burst into living blossoms? Should he not have been immortal even in his earthly physical existence? Ought he not to have made an irresistible impression on all men? A 'miraculous' conception of the miracles of Jesus — for example, of the Feeding of the Five Thousand — proceeds in fact from the assumption that the Christ did yield to the temptation to turn stones into bread. If, for example, one accepts Christ's walking on the waters in a physical sense, it would mean that the Christ had succumbed, at least at a later stage, to the second temptation, namely to trifle with the life forces. We shall be discussing the miracles of Jesus in a later study.

We must take more seriously the recognition that the Christ really did repel the threefold temptations, that he stripped himself of his cosmic superiority, that he did indeed pass inside human sheaths as a human being. For he did not come down from the pure heights of spirit in order to trifle with earthly corruption; He came to sow the seed of a new humanity and a new earthly existence into the putrefying world of creation. The process of becoming man was completed in the threefold temptations. In bodily, physical existence he wrested the state of being human from the forces of Ahriman, those forces which desire to draw everything dead towards themselves in order to endow it with a pseudo life (stones into bread). In the soul of man Christ wrested human life from the Luciferic powers who in their egotism desire to veil all existence in mist in order to dominate it (all kingdoms on earth). By his presence in the life forces of man, he wrested human existence from the Ahrimanic-Luciferic powers who desire to destroy the seriousness of life with magic trifling (the pinnacle of the temple).

If we wished to represent the progress of the Christ up to this point in pictures that are both true and simple, we could say: The Christ passed from sea to land as he descended out of the wide immensities of spirit to earth. This journey led him first into the dwelling place of the human body. We will find these metaphors to be very significant in our understanding of the gospels.

We must pause a moment to ask why the story of the Temptation is not contained in the Gospel of St John. The deeper we penetrate into spiritual understanding of the gospels, the more clearly do we see that certain spiritual and soul events, that certain steps, can be represented in the most varied pictorial forms according to the basic character of the particular gospel. We no longer regard as parallels in the different gospels only those passages which look the same on the surface or which quote the same words. There are hidden parallels in them that are all the more significant for being hidden. A clear parallel of the Temptation story in the first three gospels is lacking in John. There is, however, in John's Gospel a story which, while being an inward parallel, points to the same soul-spiritual event. Following the story of the Baptism in Jordan and of Christ's first deed, that of changing water into wine at the Marriage in Cana, the Gospel of John describes the cleansing of the Temple. The first three gospels only tell of it towards the end of Christ's life on earth when the story of the Passion opens. We will not go into the question of whether and when the scene of the cleansing of the Temple took place, that is, whether it occurred in Jerusalem externally, whether it was at the beginning or at the end of the Christ's ministry, or whether it happened both at its beginning and at its end. We only ask, what inward stage in Christ's destiny does John's Gospel intend to set forth in the cleansing of the Temple? It is the penetration of the dwelling, of the physical body, of man.

What it sets forth is the entry into man's dwelling place, into the physical body. And that reveals the interconnection between the Temptation story of the first three gospels and John's account of the cleansing of the Temple.

The being of Christ enters upon that dwelling, namely the temple of the body of Jesus. There he meets the adversaries whom he must first of all drive out with the scourge. He achieves entry into the dwelling, into that temple, by overcoming the adversaries. Here is the inwardness of that process. We shall not now decide the question whether this inward process of incarnation created an external manifestation at the Temple of Solomon in Jerusalem. We accept that it did happen. However, John's Gospel does lay stress on the incarnation aspect of this temple scene when it repeats the words of the Christ concerning the destruction and rebuilding of the Temple in three days, 'But he was speaking of the temple of his body.' (John 2:21).

Following on the story of the Temptation, St Matthew briefly gives the next step in the destiny of Christ. That step takes place externally as Christ passes from Nazareth to Capernaum. It is not unimportant that Capernaum was the 'city of Jesus' from the beginning of his ministry. Jesus' 'home' was in Nazareth. He was surrounded there by his blood relationships which reinforced the principle of his physical body. The dominance of the physical principle over the spiritual, the restrictions imposed by his physical environment, rendered work there impossible. 'And he was not able to do many deeds of the spirit there, for the hearts of the people were weak.' (Matt.13:58).

Capernaum is the town by the lake. It is where space takes over from confinement, where humankind takes the place of the family. In moving from Nazareth to Capernaum, the Christ completes the transition from house to water.

Matthew's Gospel lays great stress on this transition: 'He went from Nazareth and chose for his dwelling-place Capernaum, a town by the sea in the territory of the tribes Zebulun and Naphtali. The word of the prophet Isaiah was to be fulfilled: Land of Zebulun, land of Naphtali, towards the sea, across the Jordan, Galilee, land of the peoples: The people who dwell in darkness see a great light. And for those who dwell in the realm of death and shadows the sun rises.' (Matt.4:13–16).

This is where the Christ began his earthly ministry. In embarking upon it, he fulfilled three stages:

> From sea to land
>
> Into the house
>
> From house to the sea

And then, having himself passed along that way, he led his disciples along it. The situation in which the first disciples were called carries the very greatest creative forces. The Christ called to the land the first two pairs of disciples from the sea where they were either casting their nets from the boat, or mending nets. He then led them into the house, and finally out of the house to the sea. He caused them to find earth — the ego — humankind. That is the progression that we shall be following in the next chapter by drawing a detailed cross section through St Matthew's Gospel, as far as chapter 16.

CHAPTER FIVE

The Miracles in the Gospels

Superstition and disbelief

For centuries opinions have differed on the question of 'miracles' in the gospels. On the one side are those who believe in the miracles; on the other hand are those who argue against the miracles having actually taken place — stories of miracles could be legends by means of which the earliest Christian communities hoped to glorify Christ; alternatively, they could be explained rationally; or they could be interpreted as symbols. The end result was always a legend, be it the walking on the waters or the marriage in Cana. (Around 1800 the walking on the waters was accounted for by saying that Christ was standing on a floating log of wood invisible to the disciples. The miracle of Cana was interpreted thus: Christ changed the water of Jewish religion into the wine of the religion of Christ).

These two groups confront each other in hostility. The critics see the belief of those who cling to the miracles as superstition; on the other hand, these others see the critics as unbelievers. The split goes deeper than we admit or think. The opinions of those who reject the miracles are rapidly gaining ground, even into Catholic theology itself.

We can understand the anxiety of those who are trying to hold on to the familiar stories of miracles in the old way, and who feel that to touch them at all means disbelief. Indeed, he who loses any part of the gospel loses all of it. We have the 'good news' in its totality, or not at all. Whoever gives up part of it in fact gives up the whole. Nowadays, loss of the gospel and of the Bible has become a fact for a large part of the Christian community. Loss of the gospel is a symptom of the loss of Christian religion as a whole. The conclusion is justified in discerning an irreligious element and 'disbelief' in the critical approach to the gospels.

On the other hand it would be blindness to undervalue the inevitability of critical and intellectual thinking as 'disbelief,' to see no justification for it. It was, and still is, an essential transitional stage in the forward march of the human spirit, a stage when people feel themselves intellectually more bound to the laws of nature than to the stories of miracles in the Bible. Modern man has got to refuse having his religion measured by the number of miracles he believes in, even if he has to pay for freedom of thought by loss of the gospel. Just as we are right to see disbelief in those who, in line with modern critical thought, deny miracles, so we are right to see superstition in positive and uncritical belief in miracles.

If we are to find a way to understand the miracles through which a thinking person can win back the gospel he has lost, then we must embark upon a daring journey, one that will lead us midway between unbelief and superstition, as if between Scylla and Charybdis.

The reason for the conflict between the two interpretations of the miracles lies in the materialistic concept of the universe which evolved during the last centuries. Materialism lies hidden in both views of the miracles; it is the source of error in both conceptions, however different they may be. That being so, it is not surprising that an 'either-or' decision in favour of one against the other does not lead to a solution of the problem. Whoever decides in favour of faith in the miracles denies and foregoes thought. Whoever decides to deny faith in the miracles denies and loses the gospel.

A self-evident precondition to the basic question — are we to decide for or against miracles — is a very clear mental picture of what the gospel means by the sequence of events it describes.

People assume as a matter of course that in its descriptions the gospel has in mind a materially tangible course of events of which we become aware through the senses. The materialistic view of the world and its thought habits do not even raise the question whether the gospel means a process perceptible to the senses, or a supersensible one, or even one that is both sense perceptible and supersensible. This is because we have no notion of supersensible happenings and we are therefore unable to imagine ourselves in such a situation. Let us choose an example which will occupy us further in the present study. If we question Christ's walking on the

water, we think of the Christ in his physical body, normally obedient to the laws of gravity, walking on the water without sinking.
This concept, which was accepted quite as a matter of course in the
era of materialism, ignited the controversy between conflicting
opinions: what if a new misunderstanding was conceived in this
notion as well as an earlier error? In that case, the problem would go
like this: do you think that the question whether Jesus actually
walked on the sea was posed wrongly? Every answer to a question
put wrongly is wrong, whether we answer that question with 'yes'
or 'no.' The opposing viewpoints turns out to be like the fight for a
house which is not there at all.

A solution to the problem of the miracles is only possible today
because the question concerning them can be put correctly and the
problem carried to a deeper stage. The question no longer reads: did
the Christ walk upon the sea or didn't he, but how are we to represent
to ourselves the occurrence which the gospel describes as Christ's
walking on the water? Is that occurrence earthly and physical or is it
one in which the earthly and the supersensible meet?

The concept of actual spiritual events has to be mastered and
thought through if the gospel is to be won back as a living entity by a
solution of the problem of the miracles. The concept that brings victory
over materialism in relation to the understanding of the gospel is at the
same time a victory over the double danger of superstition — which
denies thinking — and of disbelief — which forfeits the gospel. It is the
bridge across the chasm that today separates people in the matter of
the gospel.

We can permit ourselves a few general remarks before we set out
to illustrate this through specific examples; for examples will find a
way out of the labyrinth of logical discussion better than all critical
expositions and theories.

Overcoming materialism is going to be more long-drawn out and
difficult in face of the traditional belief in miracles, than in face of modern biblical criticism. This is because criticism of the miracles corresponds to a more scientific outlook, while faith in the miracles
depends on a religious attitude of mind.

Materialism can hide and maintain itself more easily behind religious emotion of love of the Bible and perception of divine activity,
than behind scientific ideas of natural law. That is when it becomes

necessary now and again to point emphatically to the materialism lurking in the kind of biblical interpretation associated with accepted faith in miracles. In so doing, we risk now and then being ranged with the 'unbelievers.'

The Temptation as a key

The clearest and strongest defeat of the grossly material idea of the miraculous is the story of the Temptation of Christ. In it, the gospel itself provides a guide-line towards the spiritual solution of the problem of miracles. (We have already mentioned this in our last study, when discussing the story of the Temptation).

The Christ being descended into the weakness of earthly man from out of the fullness of divine and heavenly cosmic strength. Its indwelling creative power was too overwhelming for a human, earthly body. The cosmic life streams pulsing through him were too overwhelming for human life force. The majesty of soul raying out from him was too overwhelming for the soul nature of man. Body, life, soul — these were feeble sheaths for Christ, the holy one. Therein lay the threefold temptation that confronted the Christ at the beginning of his ministry.

The temptation to let loose his superior might over human and earthly physicality approached him with the invitation to turn stones into bread. The Christ repelled this temptation to reveal his cosmic creative powers; instead he submitted to the weakness of the human bodily nature. Here is the refutation of a materialistic notion of miracles such as that of the feeding of the five thousand. Had the Christ brought about the physical increase of loaves, he would have yielded to the first temptation. Not that he was unable to bring about a physical increase of the bread. He renounced his power because he came into the world not as a conjuror but as its redeemer. Herein lies the materialism and the superstition of a material and physical concept of the feeding; such a concept makes the Christ, had he succumbed to the temptation, into a magician.

The temptation to display his superiority over human life forces approached the Christ with the invitation to cast himself down from a pinnacle of the temple. He repelled it: instead of playing off divine immortality against earthly death, he submitted to human bondage, to the death of man's life force. Here is the refutation of a materialistic concept of miracles such as that of walking on the waters. Had the Christ literally strode over the waters he would have yielded to the second temptation which called on him to trifle with his own cosmic life forces. Not that he was unable to walk upon the physical sea. He renounced inexhaustible and deathless cosmic life forces because he came not to put mankind to shame with fakirs' tricks, but to die for men.

The temptation to let his own superiority have its way with the soul forces of humanity approached the Christ through Satan's promise on the mountain to give to him power over all the kingdoms of the world. The Christ repulsed this, the third temptation; instead he submitted to the struggle of the soul, the helplessness of man's soul nature. Here is the refutation of the materialistic view of, for example, miraculous healing, namely that the Christ healed by suggestion; it is also the refutation of the materialistic notion that he performed his miracles in order to prove to men his own overriding powers and thereby to force them into belief. Not that he lacked the power to let his radiantly divine powers of leadership shine forth; to reveal himself as Lord towards whom all men must be drawn, fascinated by that exalted light, and before whom all earthly powers would inevitably break down. But that was not what the Christ did. He let himself be scourged and mocked, he let himself be misunderstood and crucified. He stripped himself of that mastery that he could have exercised over human souls, for he came not to hypnotize and rule. He came to lead humanity to freedom and to serve them; the washing of the feet is the opposite of suggestion.

The significance of the story of the Temptation to an understanding of the Christ and of the gospel is felt and told with genius by Dostoyevsky in one of the classical passages of recent literature in 'The Legend of the Grand Inquisitor' which Dostoyevsky interpolated into his novel *The Brothers Karamazov*. What that story says is true: the account of the Temptation with its three questions of the tempter would be the most difficult of the stories to invent in the whole of the gospel. Had it disappeared from the gospels 'Do you think that the wisdom of all the Earth taken together could have invented anything to equal the three questions in power and depth?'

Here briefly is the content of the Legend of the Grand Inquisitor: Another one hundred heretics have just been burnt on the pyre in Seville *ad majorem dei gloriam* (the Jesuit motto, 'for the greater glory of God'). It is the time of the Inquisition. Then the Christ appears, walking through the streets in earthly human form. He has once more come down to earth, though only for a brief time, out of pity for suffering humanity. He heals the sick and blesses those who suffer. Along comes the Grand Inquisitor, an old man, cold, and ninety years old. The people have learnt obedience and fall back. At a sign from the old man the Christ is seized and thrown into prison. In prison, the old man confronts the Christ: 'Is it you — You? Make no answer — be silent. You have no right to add even one word to what you have said once upon a time. Why do you come to disturb us?'

And the old man expounded his grand inquisitorial views before the silent Christ:

It is good that your work has been passed over to us. We are more concerned than you are with the weakness of human nature and its humiliation. You would have given freedom to man, the most joyous gift in all the world. We know that man does not desire freedom; rather, man desires only to obey, to be a slave. You refused the fearsome and wise spirit when in the desert he spoke to you and called upon you to turn stones into bread. We know that man desires not spirit but bread. We can see that you made an error loaded with doom when you disobeyed the spirit who spoke thus to you. Therefore — we will follow him, and not you; and we will thus be better administrators of what you have done than you yourself can be. Otherwise what is to become of the millions and thousands of millions of those creatures who lack the strength to disdain earthly bread for the sake of the bread of heaven? Or, do you love only the ten thousand who are strong and great? You refused the call to perform the miracle because of your notion of freedom. You hoped that man, following your own example, would keep his faith in God, even without miracles. You did not know that man rejects God as soon as he rejects miracles, for man seeks the miracle rather than God. And since man cannot do without miracles, he will create new miracles aplenty for himself, miracles of his own, and he will adore every kind of magic and witches' trick. You did not descend from the cross when they were calling out at you, mocking you, 'Come down from the cross and we will believe that you are he!' You did not descend because, once again, you would not enslave men with a miracle, you craved faith given freely, not faith given in response to a miracle. You craved love freely given, and not servile rapture of the slaves of that force which once and for all terrified men. There again you overestimated humankind, for indeed, men are but slaves ... That is our secret! We have not been with you for a long time, we are with him! We have accepted from him what you rejected in anger, the gift he offered you at the last when he showed you all the kingdoms on earth; we accepted Rome from him and the sword of Caesar. Why did you reject this, his last gift? Had you accepted the third piece of advice of the mighty spirit, you would have fulfilled all towards which man strives on Earth.

Dostoyevsky does indeed touch on the greatest riddles of the Christ nature and of historical Christianity. The Grand Inquisitor traverses every era of historical Christianity, more openly here, in a more concealed way there. His desire is to proclaim to men a Christ who meets human weakness halfway. That is why in place of the Christ who rejects the threefold temptation, he sets a Christ who performs miracles in the domain of the senses. Carefully he blends materialism into concepts of the gospel which men devise for themselves, and in particular of the miracles of the gospel. The Christ does not meet human weakness halfway; instead, he takes human weakness upon himself — 'Rather, he emptied himself in offering and took on the form of a servant. In human form he took on body, and he showed himself in the form of a man throughout his whole life.' (Phil.2:7f).

We have not said all this without being aware of the consequences of what we have said. Many will see a chasm yawning between the traditional way of understanding the gospel and the arguments brought forward here. Many will feel 'If all of this is right and the Christ performed no miracles at all, then the whole gospel has been wrenched from my hand.'

At this point we have to ask for patience. We would not have written down these views were it not for the conviction that they could help regain the gospel. Many, many people have in fact lost their hold on the gospel. Intellectualism took it from them. But there are many who think they still have it yet, because of the way in which they understand the gospel, what they are holding onto is the gospel through which the spirit of the Grand Inquisitor breathes. Nowadays, people must have the courage to lose all that if they want the gospel of Christ to speak to them in purity. Romanism, and what pertains to the Grand Inquisitor, survives in every form of historical Christianity, even when men oppose Rome and think themselves free of Rome. This is not the fault of the gospel, but the fault of an imperfect understanding of it. Inmost liberation from Rome and from the cold spirit of the Grand Inquisitor presupposes the attainment of spiritual understanding of the gospel, the conquest of materialism applied to the gospel. We would like to think of these studies of ours as being of service in that task. It is not enough today to say that 'we take our stand on the basis of the gospel.' Actually, each of us takes a stand on whatever basis of understanding he or she has. To place oneself upon the basis of the gospel means to undertake a never-ending task of realization, that is, of working one's way through the mire of human concepts of the gospel, ever nearer to the gospel itself. That is the task facing our own era, the era of the consciousness soul in relation to the gospel. True reverence towards the gospels can only exist in our service to this task. Where this task is not recognized, there credulity and reverence turn all too easily to adoration of the Grand Inquisitor.

We are most unwilling to give utterance to generalized ideas and principles such as have appeared in this study up to this point, because at bottom they can be little more than a plan of our affirmations. It is essential nowadays constantly to render account of the methods and principles of spiritual endeavour and that is why we have initiated these discussions of principles. But now we must examine the actuality of all the miracle stories in the gospels. In so doing we shall gradually neutralize those seemingly negative arguments by building up positive considerations. The negative applies not to miracles in the gospel, but to the materialistic way of thinking about them. The Christ performed no miracles in the material sense. In so saying, we do not in the least belittle the grandeur of Christ; on the contrary. That Christ became man is and will remain the greatest miracle of all creation. And it is this central miracle that meets us in every story of Christ's ministry on earth. There is no need to believe in isolated miraculous deeds provided we gain a view of the miracle of the Christ being himself.

There are remarkable sources available today from whence a materialistic view of the Bible's miracles gains support. We are being fairly flooded with a pseudo-occult literature. We need mention just one example: *The Life and Teaching of Masters of the Far East,* by Basil Spalding. The book tells of Masters of the Himalayan region who, through a form of magic, are able to create bread, money, and so on, from nothingness, to walk on the water of rivers, to heal the sick, to pass in a moment of time over great geographical distances, to appear in closed up rooms and so on. These things are always clothed in Christian terminology and covered by 'the faith that moves mountains.' The miracles of Christ are referred to all along, as are his words that 'You shall perform greater deeds than these.' The book further claims that John the Baptist received instruction from these Masters in the Himalayan regions. We are not concerned whether the book depends for its detail on delusion or on confusion between the supersensible and the material. There is without a doubt plenty of both in it. We do not however get rid of books such as this one by declaring them to be a swindle. We are only entitled to condemn them if we can recognize how much there is of what is relatively factual in what they set forth. In the near future, we will assuredly have to concede that magical deeds of the kind described are actually possible. It is going to be possible by magical means physically to walk on water and the like. But even should we ever be able to admit that these things are possible, we shall see how far removed from them are the deeds of Christ and the gospel; indeed, how different they are altogether. There is a big difference between questioning the physical course of events (for example, Christ's walking on the water) because we consider anything of the kind impossible, and questioning them even though we know they are possible if magical arts are used such as those known in Central Asia.

The Christ did not physically walk on the water but this was not because he was unable to do so; he did not do it because he was not a magician. He was the true Redeemer, become Man. Our presentation of the walking on the waters as a spiritual act does not flow from any effort on our part to 'rescue' the miracle by an interpretation that would make it seem possible after all. A concept of the universe such as we have tried to present here, one which is aware of actual spiritual processes like that of walking on water, admits that magic is possible. But there is a gulf between the truly spiritual events of the gospels and the magical processes assumed by materialistic views of them. That gulf separates Christianity from paganism. By sweeping away materialism in the understanding of the gospel, we can (if we can put it so) overcome paganism and attain to true Christianity in our concept of the gospel. That sounds ambitious but we must say it in face of the torrent of Orientalism and Americanisms, tainted with magic, that threaten to flood Christian life. We say this fully aware that these studies, owing as they do their existence entirely to Rudolf Steiner's spiritual achievements, could be a very modest beginning to the fulfilment of tasks we have suggested.

The walking on the water

We shall now pass on to discuss specific examples. For this purpose we have chosen the walking on the waters and the appearances of the Risen Christ, since the clearest idea of the actuality of spiritual processes can be gained in these portions of the gospel.

The walking on the water in St John's Gospel is the fifth of the seven miracles, and it is the stage leading from the feeding of the five thousand to the healing of the man born blind. In St Matthew's Gospel this scene comes between the miracle of the feeding and Peter's confession at Caesarea Philippi: 'You are the Christ, the Son of the living God.' Having experienced in the feeding Christ's power of bestowal, the disciples are being prepared to recognize the true nature of the Christ. They were being made ready for the removal of the blindness which still kept their eyes from seeing the true nature of the Christ. For the present we can only touch here on these secrets of gospel composition. A fundamental feature of the event brought to us as the walking on the waters is this: the disciples learned to recognize the true nature of the Christ.

The true nature of Christ is not earthly but heavenly. Jesus was the Son of Man, born of earthly origin. The Christ is the Son of God, born of heaven. The nature of Christ must be understood as being not of this earthly world but of the world of spirit. That is what was borne in upon their souls in the image of Christ walking upon the water. The juxtaposition between land and sea is an earthly image of the difference between the world of the senses and a world of spirit. For the present we can ignore the question of how we are to imagine the situation and the course of events of the scene beside the lake. Referring to the spiritual significance of this experience for the disciples we can now say: He who walked on land was the Christ become altogether Man, become altogether Jesus; He who revealed himself to the disciples as walking on water was the divine Christ himself, within his own being, as one who in essence belonged to the world of spirit.

As the image of him who walked upon the water imprinted itself upon their souls, so the disciples knew, although not as yet in full awareness, a divine being is walking this earth with us in the person of Jesus. After this experience Peter could say: 'You are the Christ, the Son of the living God.'

No matter how many processes, external or spiritual, we may yet have to recognize in the scene of the walking on the water, a significant spiritual experience on the part of the disciples is here clearly revealed to us. We could even claim that in it we have before us a kind of protophenomenon of an actual spiritual experience.

This is the first step: the disciples behold a figure whom they do not recognize. The vision fills them with terror. Their experience is the stage of Imagination. Everything is in heaving motion, eager to tear the soul from its foundation.

Here is the next step: the disciples hear the figure speak and the words they hear tell them who it is coming to meet them. Hearing and recognition calm their fears. 'Fear not, it is I.' This is the stage of experiencing the Word. Here the meaning is revealed of an image that is at first only frightening. Realization associated with vision brings confidence.

The third step is this: Christ comes to the disciples and enters into the boat. The disciples take him up, unite themselves to him. They let his being touch them, giving them strength. That is the step at which they experience the being of Christ.

Every actual spiritual experience follows the same sequence of image, word and being. There are many examples of this in the gospel. When Mary Magdalene sees the Risen Christ, she sees him first as a vision of the gardener. She recognizes him in the tone of his word, when he speaks her name. And then she stretches out her hands actually to touch, to feel him.

Progress through vision, sound and essential being is, as we noted in the first chapter, the same as the progress through which the Revelation to John guides us in turn by way of seals, trumpets and vials of wrath. This is the same sequence as that which anthroposophy calls the three stages of supersensible cognition: Imagination (cognition in the form of pictures), Inspiration (cognition in word), and Intuition (union with the essence of being).

Under just what conditions did the disciples have that spiritual experience when the Christ revealed himself to them in his spiritual nature? What is the significance of the sea, of the storm whipping up the waves, or of the ship in which the disciples journey, or of the hour of the night as it merges into dawn?

Many a passage in the gospels presents events entirely in pictures of external life, and yet they are to be seen as taking place wholly in the realm of spirit. For things spiritual have to be set forth through pictures drawn from the world of the senses. In that situation things external, drawn from space and time, are merely pictures standing in for the spiritual. Such an event is the walking on the waters.

Conventional commentaries often point to inconsistencies in two of the stories with regard to the time frame:

> And he left the crowd and went up on the mountain by himself to pray. Late in the evening he was still there alone. The ship was already many stadia from the land and was being beaten by the waves, for the wind was against them. And in the fourth watch of the night he came to them, walking on the sea. And when the disciples saw him walking on the sea they were frightened and cried out with fear: 'It is a ghost!' But at once he spoke to them: 'Take heart, it is I; have no fear!' (Matt.14:23–27).

Johannes Weiss *(Writings of the New Testament)* sees in these contradictions proof that the two stories, the one of the feeding of the five thousand, the other of the walking on the waters, were originally separate and had nothing to do with each other. 'The inconsistency in the time references seem to suggest that the scene that now follows must once have been narrated independently. Mark 6:47 first mentions that it was evening (sunset) and that Jesus saw the ship tossed about in the middle of the sea. Suddenly we are transported in verse forty-eight to the fourth watch of the night. This indication must have been associated with the second story. The evangelist was only able to connect the two with difficulty.'

Obviously, an externalized, materialistic concept of what happened can only stumble along until the only way out is to push the blame onto the evangelist for being an incompetent writer.

A detail such as the wide difference in the time indication (sunset and dawn) which frames the walking upon the waters, can, if properly understood, guide us beyond materialistic conceptions and point to the more spiritual phenomena, which are really intended.

A materialistic era cannot understand sleep. People could not accept that in sleep the human soul and spirit are able to pass through actual experiences. They said: 'If a human soul really does experience something in sleep, then it is only dreams.' In fact, the worlds where soul and spirit tarry are at least as actual as the world of the senses; but human beings do not bring memories back from sleep. As for dreams, they are indeed echoes of the waking state and of the body, rather than memories of the soul's experiences in spiritual regions. In sleep humanity meets many a spiritual being. It can often happen that someone is inconsolable over the death of a loved one, and yet in sleep at night meets the soul of the person who has passed on and is spiritually reunited with them. As the materialistic centuries that lie behind us pass away, so the prejudices will slowly pass by which only daytime experiences are taken seriously, while experiences of the night are totally disregarded.

Materialistic habits of thinking explain why the knowledge is being lost which survived as tradition from earlier, more spiritually aware times, and which found expression in the generally accepted customs of morning and evening prayer — knowledge of quite special significance regarding the holiness of falling asleep and awakening as a two-way transition across the threshold, as a passage from land to sea, from sea to land. Evening prayer saved one from entering the world of spirit empty handed — to put it metaphorically. Morning enabled one to carry the treasures of night into the next day. Whatever dominates thoughts on falling asleep and on waking has nowadays turned into sheer barbarism. Those able to observe know that at the moment of waking most wonderful spiritual feelings and experiences of soul slip and sparkle through the soul, whether or not they are associated with dreams of which one is conscious. Those who, by their presence of mind, can grasp and hold onto them, are able to feed on them for days and feel themselves borne along by them. Through those dreams of awakening, the soul is able to salvage echoes of night time encounters and to carry them into the daytime.

The great feeding of the five thousand had brought the disciples' souls into especially intimate closeness to the spiritual. Something happened to them when they were honoured by the task of distributing the bread that Christ had blessed. They had become a community through the bestowal of the food of Christ.

This became even more evident when the disciples entered for the first time after the miracle of the feeding upon the world of sleep. The night that followed the miracle of the feeding of the five thousand was for the spiritual community of the disciples especially blessed. It was then that the Christ was able to reveal himself in the region of spirit walking upon the sea as Lord of the spirit region. The Christ met those souls cleansed and uplifted by their exalted experience — although admittedly the waves beat high because of the mighty impression they had received; the Christ did indeed encounter them as a spirit being.

While day reigned, having laid aside his cosmic and divine powers, his life revolved on the process of becoming Man. In the realm of night he lived as Lord of the elements and of the cosmos, and he was able to reveal himself thus to his own.

It would be an elementary misunderstanding if the concept set forth here were to be interpreted like this: that the disciples dreamed that the Christ had walked upon the sea. The dream would have gained considerably in credibility since the disciples had all dreamed the same thing. But this was no dream — it was an actual Christ event brought about by Christ himself. The image which appeared of the Christ walking on the waters was, in a most marvellous manner, and in the clearest way, carried over into the full consciousness of day.

If the detail of the gospel story is carefully noted, then it is not difficult to recognize, in the account given in the gospel itself, what we have been saying here. St John's Gospel expressly says: 'Now when they wanted to take him into the ship, immediately the ship was at the land, at the place to which they wanted to go.' (John 6:21). Even as their meeting with Christ begins to merge into essential communication, they wake and suddenly they have touched land. They wake in communion with Christ.

The appearance of the Risen One at the lake

Maybe the idea here expressed can best be clarified if we bring that scene of walking on the water together with another scene which in some ways resembles it, that is, the appearance of the Risen Christ by the Sea of Galilee. There are a number of things that become evident when truths bear each other out in different passages of the gospels.

The two stories bear a strong pictorial relationship to each other when we are told in both of them that Peter wanted to set forth to meet the Christ. St Matthew describes how Peter climbed from the ship in order to stride over the waves towards the Christ as he was walking on the sea (Matt.14). St John tells how Simon Peter threw himself out of the ship the more quickly to gain the shore where the Risen Christ was standing (John 21:7).

These two stories concerning the personality of Christ, when placed side by side, give us a tremendous opportunity to comprehend pictorially the nature of Christ. Before his death on Golgotha, Christ was in an earthly body, even though his true nature belongs to the world of spirit. If he was to be recognized, he had to reveal himself as the one who walked upon the sea.

After his death and resurrection, Christ passed over into the spirit world. Since then, though a heavenly being, he has in very truth united himself with earthly existence. In order not to go unrecognized, he had to reveal himself standing on the shore.

These two stories, wherein the disciples twice behold the Christ, add the spiritual element of true Christianity to what the eye sees. The walking on the sea is like a call: 'I am alive on earth with you as a human being; but you must seek my true nature in the realms of spirit.'

The appearance of the Risen Christ on the shore is like this call: 'I died, and went from you. But you must seek my true nature in earthly existence, which I shall from now on penetrate through and through, and transform by the powers of Resurrection.'

> Christ upon the Sea before Golgotha
> Christ upon dry Land after Golgotha.

These are pictures from which can flow recognition of the divine nature of the Christ.

In the scene of the walking upon the waters we find a hint of the experience of waking in the sudden transference of the ship to the land; similarly in the story set at the lake-side we find a hint that the disciples' spiritual experience is by night, and on the threshold of awakening. The disciples see Christ but do not recognize him. Only the disciple John recognizes him: 'Then that disciple whom Jesus loved said to Peter, "It is the Lord!" When Peter heard: It is the Lord, he flung on his cloak and tied it round himself, for he was naked, and threw himself into the sea.' (John 21:7). We should not overlook particular details such as this. A practical view of such an action is immediately confronted by contradictory indications averse to common sense; it does not make sense to clothe oneself when one is about to cast oneself into the water. The reverse would make sense.

In this instance, too, what appears contrary to sensible behaviour can and must point to another and more spiritual interpretation. A human being asleep is — pictorially speaking — 'naked'; he has left behind his earthly sheath. When he wakes he slips back into his body, that being his garment. When we wake up and dress, that is no more than a kind of doubling of clothing the self with a body. The disciples are returning from the sea and are drawing near the shore. They come from the realm of sleep and are approaching their awakening. The vision of Christ is vouchsafed to them there on the shore. As they behold him they become aware of the transformation that earthly existence is passing into. In the Risen Christ they see the beginning of the new earth and the new incorruptible bodily nature.

We assume that views like the one before us can afford only scant pointers and suggestions in describing the actual spiritual events we have in mind. These events we must assume to be in fact richer by far. Many questions will of course remain open; they will be clarified, step by step, in the course of our study. It is important to realize the pointers towards real spiritual events — such as in the present case actual experience of the soul in sleep and in waking up — are not intended as a new schematic model according to which from now on all miracles can similarly be explained. The more we gain access to spiritual truths as we overcome materialistic habits of thought, the more impossible it will be to set up schematic models.

With every new miracle story we come across new and altogether different phenomena; this makes it necessary to start all over again trying to understand each of them. It would be wrong to follow a 'schema' and to imagine that all stories of miracles should now be presented as being wholly spiritual. All we can say is that throughout events in the gospels, spiritual facts and happenings play their part in and reach into all of them. Whether events are perceived supersensibly or physically as well at the same through earthly senses, this we have to decide from one case to the next.

We chose the example of walking on the waters because in it the spiritual process as such, relatively speaking, predominates most clearly. However, not even here should the possibility of an earthly, physical scene be excluded, because of what we have said. We could ask: whereabouts in earthly space were the disciples when the Christ revealed himself to them on the lake? And we could answer, perhaps they really were crossing the lake by night, in a condition resembling sleep; they may have been spiritually transported by the mighty impressions made upon them by the miraculous feeding; they could even have been asleep when, as day dawned, Christ appeared before their souls' eyes, walking on the billows of the spiritual sea. The physical sea, nocturnal and storm tossed, would have been in harmony with that inward sea where the disciples met the Christ. In that case, outward and inward would have wholly interpenetrated one another in the disciples' consciousness — their bodies crossing the physical sea, their souls traversing the spiritual one. Nevertheless, questions concerning the external and physical garb of the spiritual event is in the case of this story irrelevant and, moreover, difficult to decide.

As for the religious significance and power of the images as they concern the walking upon the waters, it will easily be seen that they will emerge not weakened, but all the stronger for the present conception of it.

Clearly, the conception of liberal theology, of so-called scientific religion, loses the religious substance of this portion of the gospel. The scene becomes merely a legend. The picture persists, but it has no power because the weight of truth is lacking. I quote a passage from the commentary by Johannes Weiss, mentioned earlier (Mark 6):

> To seek for an historical kernel to this legend would be vain. The Emperor Julian (the Apostate) makes this comment in the course of his speech against Herakles the Cynic: 'Herakles undertook that journey across the sea upon a golden bowl; but I believe that for the gods there was no bowl; I am firmly convinced that he walked upon the sea on foot, as if it had been dry land.'

Johannes Weiss seems to be of the opinion that to the Emperor Julian the 'miracle' of Herakles was made possible through the purity of his sacred body and by his immaculate spirit: 'For Zeus the Mighty and Athene Pronoia had created Herakles to be the Redeemer of the World.' Would not the miracle of the walking upon the waters have emerged from similar reflections on the personality of Jesus? We can see quite clearly from the comparison how little we have of the real basis of the gospel as far as he is concerned.

The above quotation shows us clearly enough the way in which we have to relinquish the gospel piecemeal as a result of accepted thought patterns. This account shows us the walking upon the waters as the product of pagan fantasy; it comes from the reflection that at the very least Jesus must have been capable of what the pagan gods could do.

The fact that we can find echoes of and parallels to portions of the gospels in pre-Christian (for example, Greek) mythology should really lead us on to the trail of spiritual concepts. But we still fail to understand that element of truth which lies at the basis of pre-Christian religions and mythologies. For example, the myth of Herakles is a pictorial essence of ancient initiation experience. The true spiritual sequence of events depicted in the image presented by walking on water was known in the supersensible experiences of Greek mysteries.

The disciples underwent, thanks to the Christ, what human souls in primeval times underwent in the divine world when the Greek mysteries were still sacred. This the disciples passed through far, far more purely, more spiritually, because, following the miracles of the feeding, the Christ revealed himself to them in spirit.

The uncritical, orthodox conception of the walking on the waters does not lead to pure, clear-sighted religious experience of that walk. This is because dread of the marvellous thrusts itself between the soul and the religious experience. The event accordingly remains a unique miracle which took place in the distant past. (To consider that dread a true religious experience is most certainly not Christian. It is associated with pagan magic, for it has nothing to do with the fully awake ego of a human being striving after inward freedom. It is associated rather with a spiritual condition devoid of freedom and subject to suggestion).

The view sketched here assumes the event to be eternal and therefore ever present. Human souls, in our own time especially, can accept that we are voyaging on the stormy sea of soul and destiny. It is the same sea upon which the disciples saw the Christ walking. Can there be a greater hope for our own time than that the Christ may become evident even today walking upon that water and speaking to fear-ridden humanity: 'Fear not, it is I.' The Christ desires to reveal himself in future to humanity spiritually (on the sea) even as two thousand years ago he sojourned among men physically (on land). What the disciples went through two thousand years ago in the night after the feeding was a preview and an assurance of Christ's return. The scene, including that of Peter's sinking, becomes an image of the soul, a reflection of what is going on spiritually in our time, in preparation for the future; it does not however cease to be a uniquely important event in the historical life of Jesus and the apostles. We can take a step further in our religiously practical application of our spiritual concept: if human souls were to win back the proper rhythm in relation to the spiritual world, a rhythm enabling them reverently to take note of the experience of waking up, then there could be many who, through this picture of meeting him who walked upon the waters, would become vividly aware of encounters with the Christ of which their souls may be deemed worthy.

The whole of the poetic work of a man typical of our time — August Strindberg — culminates in his presentation of Christ walking upon the water. The poet, together with Indra's daughter, are inside Fingal's Cave where sunken ships, destiny's relics, are being washed ashore. The two human beings can hear the men's suffering in the song of waves and wind and they become aware that the crew of a stranded ship are terrified at the sight of Christ upon the water. They are casting themselves into the sea for they cannot hear those words, 'Fear not; it is I.'

Heinrich Heine, whom we know mostly as a mocker, creates the scene in a beautiful poem entitled Freedom:

> Half in sleep and half awake
> I beheld the Christ
> Redeemer of the World,
> In billowing robe of white –
> He passes, immense,
> O'er land and sea.

Emmaus and the Risen One eating

In order not to stop at a single example, which could easily result in a certain one-sidedness, let us look at two appearances of the Risen Christ, described in the last chapter of Luke:
— Christ and the disciples at Emmaus
— The Risen Christ eating in the presence of the disciples.

Stories of the Resurrection can easily be taken, like the story of the walking on the waters, as an example of miracles to be accepted as being purely spiritual. A spiritual concept of the Resurrection of Christ, ranking as it does among the gospel miracles, was established earlier; however, we can find no convincing or truthful view of the cosmic scene. It is a fact today that modern humanity has to a large extent lost the reality of Christ's Resurrection.

During Easter, the Resurrection is preached from countless pulpits as if it were the same as immortality. But resurrection is more than immortality. It is a mystery of the body, not of the soul. The last of the two scenes which close the Gospel of Luke inexorably establish as much. Christ appears to the disciples. They are terrified, for they take him for a ghost, a spirit. But, in order to prove to them that he is no mere spirit, Christ asks: 'Have you anything to eat?' He eats fish and honey before their eyes.

We have now to say something fundamental about reading the gospel, and in particular about reading this passage. We are wrong if we read any gospel story and fail to take into account the place and the stage in the gospel where it occurs; nowhere is such an error so fatal as in stories of the appearances of the Risen Christ. Nearly always people read excerpts from the gospels as if nothing preceded them. But whether a story comes at the beginning, in the middle or at the end of the gospel is not immaterial. Every chapter carries the 'good news' to a higher, more holy stage of revelation and experience. There can be no way of looking at the sequence of stories more banal than treating them as though they were arbitrary, unconnected episodes. The gospel always carries within itself the character of the path. Every passage in it presupposes that those who desire to understand it have faithfully passed through all that went before. Every account has a level of its own, determined by what precedes it. It occurs at a height which depends upon the passages ahead of it.

As we have said, nowhere is it so fatal as in the case of the Easter stories to treat them as if they lacked altitude, as if they had occurred on a flat plain, at ground level. Only those can hope to understand the Resurrection stories who have passed reverently through the whole of the gospel but especially through accounts of the Passion and of Golgotha. This they must have done in such a way as to have been transformed themselves, step by step.

Those who approach the Easter stories in that spirit cannot possibly arrive at a grossly materialistic conception or a mere abstraction. They will find that the stories about Easter have their habitation on a mountain peak, exalted and holy, a peak that must be scaled. It should gradually be accepted as an inevitable principle in every study of the gospel; each story must be sought upon its own mountain.

Passion and Resurrection are preceded significantly by the scene of the Last Supper. It is the portal to death and to Resurrection. Both take their actual beginning from there. For the death of Christ, as well as his Resurrection, is a process, an event that the Christ did not pass through in a moment of time passively — but a deed occupying a whole span of time. The death of a human being is a moment to be suffered, not a deed to be carried out.

A mystery confronts us in the institution of the Last Supper, which lays upon all who would enter the temple of the great mystery of Golgotha the trial of their lives. If, while passing through the scene of the Last Supper, any fail to realize within themselves at least a breath of sacrifice, and of transformation — to them Golgotha, and especially the Resurrection, will remain a sealed book.

When the words were spoken that inaugurated the Last Supper, the physicality of Christ expanded; no longer was it confined to the physicality of Jesus; no longer did it renounce its overflowing cosmic abundance; it began now to stream forth in sacrifice, to flow into the nature of the earth itself. Earth was represented here by the bread and the wine lying in his hands. From then on, the soul and spirit of the Christ were to live not alone in the body of Jesus; they bestowed themselves sacrificially on earth in the bread and wine. Accordingly, the bread did indeed become the body of Christ, and wine his blood. The Christ had lifted up bread and wine in blessing, uniting his soul with them, as the Act of Consecration of Man expresses it. The Supper was the true beginning of the Passion and of the death of Christ insofar as it was also the beginning of a sacrifice, of the great offertory.

At the same time, and by the same sign, it was also the beginning of the event that led into the Resurrection. If Goethe's utterance is right that 'the place where a righteous man has trodden is made holy ground,' then it most certainly is true to say 'where the Christ has trodden is holy ground.' Bread and wine became the place where the Christ has trodden; more, they became the sheath for his soul, for his spirit, they became the vessel of heavenly powers on earth. They were thereby transmuted from within outward, transubstantiated. The light of the spirit alive in them shone through them. Spiritual eyes could have seen them shining like the sun from the monstrance.

The process of transubstantiation reached its full development in the Resurrection. Resurrection and transubstantiation are one and the same riddle. Whoever can understand transubstantiation — the transformation of bread and wine — can also understand the Resurrection of Christ, and vice-versa. The loss of true understanding of transubstantiation as a real, spiritual process is one of the most fateful events in man's development. As men began to waver between coarsely materialistic views of the Eucharist, so they passed into the era of materialism and abstraction. Today, renewed understanding of transubstantiation and resurrection is still the means for overcoming materialism with the greatest power; it will break open the way to a new comprehension of the gospel and of spiritual Christianity in general.

The resurrection of Christ was the transubstantiation of his physical body, wherein the spiritual being of Christ and his soul-body had dwelt for three years. What rayed out towards the disciples from the bread and wine as the light body of the Christ created by transubstantiation, was the same as he who appeared before them when they beheld the Risen Christ. The material part that filled out the physical body which the Christ had borne succumbed to corruption and was taken in by earth as are all earthly things. This resembles the bread and the wine, after their transforming, being eaten and drunk at the Last Supper. We can in fact say that the transforming process, the light body's origin, was completed only after the destruction of the purely physical. The earthly body perished: the body of the Resurrection came into being.

Ever since the transmuting process, which was the other aspect of the Christ's great sacrifice and which led from the Eucharist right up to the Resurrection, there has been something spiritual happening, something growing and alive in the world of earth, invisible to earthly eyes. The body of Christ's Resurrection, the light body of the new earth, is building up from all those human souls, permeated by the Christ, into which the soul of Christ is able to discharge itself.

Anyone who can pass through the gospel scene of the Last Supper as if he were part of it, draws into himself the power to understand the passion and death of Christ. He becomes able to do this for he can feel within himself the sacrifice of Christ, the dying of Christ into the essential being of earth. By experiencing transubstantiation, the enkindling of the light body of Christ, we draw into ourselves the power to understand the Resurrection of Christ.

The meaning of the Eucharist, as a Christian religious service, is this: the human soul is given the chance in the sacrifice and transubstantiation — the middle two of its four parts — to approach the mighty cosmic event as it marches on through the centuries. The sacrifice of the Eucharist in the ritual of the Act of Consecration of Man is one of the most magnificent opportunities for meeting the Christ as he offers himself for sacrifice. The transformation that follows the Offering is among the most glorious opportunities to meet the Risen Christ.

Here lies the key to the two Easter stories at the end of St Luke's Gospel. A brief look at them may suffice, since we shall be discussing here only what is basic to the question of miracles. We shall reserve consideration of detail for later studies.

A third figure joins the two disciples along the way to Emmaus; they hear him and see him, but do not recognize him. As evening draws near, they enter a house. The third figure follows them in at their request, having been about to pass on. What now takes place inside the house is a celebration of the Eucharist. The bread is lifted on high with words of blessing, the same as those uttered by the Christ over the bread while he was still with the disciples. Fulfilling the sacred ritual, the disciples' experience is just as if the ritual were being celebrated by Christ himself. And when they experience the transubstantiation, they suddenly recognize that third figure who has joined them. If we wish to gain a more accurate impression of the recognition, we could perhaps say, the physical sun had gone down outside; its setting was the reason why the travellers entered the house. Now the disciples lift up their piece of bread in simple, holy ceremony. A spiritual sun thereupon shines on them from the bread, and in its rays they behold the face, the body of the Risen Christ. Now, in communion with Christ, in essential union with him, it becomes clear to them that he whom they saw and heard along the way was already the Christ. The two disciples meet the Risen Christ in their experience of the Last Supper and of Transubstantiation. The first of the two Easter jewels is set into the mystery of the Eucharist.

A certain insensitivity has become current because the usual translation of the passage where the two disciples tell the others of their experience is 'And how he was known to them in the breaking of bread' (Luke 24:35). This creates the erroneous idea that the one who is later recognized, was a human being identified by his gestures and by the movements of his hands in the breaking of bread. But the third one was present in the bread rather than in the hand that broke the bread. Correctly translated, the passage should read: 'He revealed himself to them spiritually in the act [in the sacrament] of the breaking of bread.'

The sentence, which remains somewhat lacking in content if interpreted in physical terms, points clearly to the nature of the whole scene as being a spiritual event and experience (Luke 24:28): 'And he made as if to go on.' We find ourselves here before a parallel with the scene of the walking upon the waters that is highly relevant to our present consideration: 'He comes to them, walking on the sea. And he wanted to pass by them.' (Mark 6:48). Such detail is important, if I may put it that way, for the 'technique' of becoming aware of the order of supersensible happening. When a soul encounters a spiritual being, then that spirit will be found in flowing movement appropriate to the soul. The extent to which the soul can achieve a true personal meeting and union with the spirit depends entirely on the vitality of the soul passing through the experience; in other words it is vital to the extent to which it may be possible to hold that experience. How often does the figure of Christ pass by the soul of men, and men lack the strength to meet him? We can recognize the same theme in the two stories — in that of the walking upon the waters and that of the appearance at Emmaus. If mankind is incapable of taking Christ into the boat, or of bringing him into the house, then Christ passes by humanity. A fundamental law of every supersensible experience is revealed to us.

The second of the two Easter stories at the end of St Luke is probably one of the passages in the gospel which have thrown up the greatest number of queries. The idea of the Risen Christ eating fish and honey before the disciples has confused many a person struggling towards a spiritual understanding of the Resurrection; it may even have made such a one despair of ever entering into a relationship with it.

The whole scene becomes clear if it also is understood to be an aspect of the Eucharist, as a Eucharistic experience of the disciples.

Eating takes place twice in the course of every true celebration of the Last Supper; it is carried out once in the physical, sensory sphere by those taking the Communion, and once earlier, in a spiritually physical sphere, by the Christ in Transubstantiation. The Christ is present at the Eucharist in a body of light, in the body of Resurrection. As bread and wine, those earthly gifts are offered; the Christ accepts them into his light body. Bread and wine become body and blood of Christ because he makes them part of his own light body, and in so doing brings them to a point of spiritual luminescence, as from an inward sun. Just as a human being takes in food and drink when he eats and drinks, so does the Christ in transubstantiation.

The transformation — transubstantiation — is eating and drinking by Christ; Christ takes bread and wine into his own body and into his blood. Thinking pictorially, Christ's eating is a reversal of human eating. When a human being eats, we see the food pass into the person eating. When it is Christ who is eating we can imagine how he who eats passes as a being of light, a spiritual sun, into the food. But, when Christ's eating is perceived in the image which we see through imaginative sight, as the disciples were able to perceive it in the scenes set forth in the last chapter of Luke's Gospel — then it looks the same as human eating. The disciples experience the transformation of the food they offer him, as Christ eating; the change which they actually perceive taking place in the food, they experience in such a way that the food actually was *in* the Christ.

We can imagine the food that the disciples offered Christ which he consumed before their eyes was then accepted and eaten by them in holiest communion. This can only be a contradiction for a materialistic point of view. As a true and vital experience of the Eucharist revives among us through the renewal of religious life, through the life of the sacrament, so the gospel, when it speaks of the Risen Christ eating, will become more familiar and trustworthy. A resurrection story could seem puzzling, even repelling, only to an age devoid of ritual such as were the last centuries. There was then only the ritual of the Petrine church, a ritual unsubtly materialistic and therefore not really understood. In every Eucharist, the Transubstantiation of bread and wine is Christ's eating; and this takes place before man's eating of the bread and wine in the Communion.

A mystery stands in front of every miracle, every time a different mystery. The mystery of sleep (if we are to try to define it in a single word) stands before the miracle of the walking on the waters. The mystery of transubstantiation is before the miracle of the Easter stories at the end of St Luke's Gospel.

We shall find our way back to the gospel if we can regain a cosmic view in which mysteries like those of sleep and of transubstantiation again become known to humanity. The gospel's cosmic view and the current world-view are split far apart. It is not surprising that with today's conception of the world, the gospel is misunderstood. A cosmic view will only become clear when the detritus of materialism obliterating the gospel is cleared away. These studies are meant as a contribution towards clearing up the detritus, and towards fathoming the gospel's cosmic view.

A scene such as this one has again and again frightened off and rendered uncertain attempts to comprehend the Resurrection in spiritual terms. We shall only be sure when a spiritually realistic idea is found, rather than a non-material abstraction. Spiritual comprehension must prove itself in relation to that scene of the Risen Christ, eating.

CHAPTER SIX

Personal Christianity in the Gospels

Goethe's drama, *Faust,* contains a brief passage that is deeply symbolic of the spiritual situation in which civilized people of our day find themselves. Faust has just taken an Eastertide walk through the world of spring. What he found there has not satisfied the urge and the yearning of his nature. He turns back to his study. After disappointment in the outside world he seeks the world within. Having entered upon that inward world, which way does he turn?

> I have left behind me the fields and meadows shrouded now
> in deep night. Alas! When the lamp in our own small study
> sheds its friendly light we long for the springs of life. Ah me!
> No longer do I feel satisfaction welling up in my bosom. Why
> should the river dry up so soon and we be left again prostrate
> in our thirst? I have experienced so much of that. But the lack
> can be made good! We are coming to treasure things that are
> exalted above this earth. *The longed for revelation burns nowhere*
> *in greater majesty and beauty than in the New Testament.*

But Faust cannot find the springs of life any more, not even in the gospel which offers itself to him. He opens the Gospel of St John but he is brought up short at the first word.

We have ourselves passed through the walk at Eastertide in the final phases of our cultural evolution. The external world became the scene for science, for the achievements of civilization in general. But then, in recent years — especially since the experiences of war — we have come to feel more and more clearly that people had unjustly let themselves be seduced one-sidedly by the external world of the senses. The external world, having become powerful and demanding, was beginning to taste stale. The soul was turning back to the inner world; the springs of life could perhaps be found there after all. The human soul is now looking everywhere, groping uncertainly for the way into that world within. One thing is certain: the inner world will have to be at least as rich in images as is the external world. We seek riches within because we have after all sought for them in vain outside.

It is in the nature of external evolution that humanity is being alienated from the garden of nature and now lives predominantly in urban environments. People themselves are bringing that about by building factories where previously inviolate nature had refreshed and vivified them. The world of cities is the outward sign of the ever more urgent withdrawal from the outside world into the world within.

How should the inner world be equipped in order to bestow greater satisfaction than the outer world was able to give? In recent centuries men sought and created for themselves an externalized world image. In it they sought and will go on seeking more and more the image of an inward world.

In our time the yearning for images is very strong without people being keenly aware of it. Symptoms of every kind point in this direction. Cinema and television respond to a need of modern man. The present era is forgetting the way to read books. People seize upon pictures to look at; they want to look, not think.

The approaching supersensible world nowadays manifests itself in the urge to look at pictures. The feeling for images, the ability to look, will be the beginning, the first stratum in experiencing a spiritual world that is drawing nearer to us all the time. When someone longs for a world of images, for the picture, that person is longing for the supersensible world, even though he may not know it. He is entering into the hidden recesses of his own personality. Is a rich world of pictures unfolding even upon the walls of the soul's dwelling place? As Faust says, we are coming to treasure the things that are exalted above this earth; we long for revelation. So, Faust reaches for the gospel. It remains arid, shut against his perceptions. No springs of life well up from it towards him. The reason for that does not lie in the New Testament, but in Faust. As long as the pictorial sense is not awake, just so long will the gospel remain closed to modern humanity. In the external world people have acquired the ability to think. They enter the inner recesses with that power. Thought is not the key to the world of images where slumbers revelation of an exalted region. Modern man is in the same situation as Faust. He has deserted the outer world; the inner world has not yet been unlocked.

If mankind does find the gospel, then people will find the rich content of the inner world. And they can find the gospel when they come to love the image and understand it. Pictures, images, are letters of the writings in which revelation speaks to us of things beyond this earth. To understand the gospel is the need of the present hour. When intellectual thought fails, the picture is the key. A general attitude of mind such as this is needed all the time if, later on, a new understanding of the gospel is actually to bear its fruits towards reshaping life.

The calling of the first disciples

Linking up with the end of our fourth study, let us once again place before us the scene of the calling of the first disciples.

As Jesus is passing along the shores of the sea of Galilee, he sees two ships. One of them is further out from land, the other is close in shore. There are two brothers in the first of the ships, namely Simon Peter and Andrew, and they have cast their nets into the sea. In the other ship are two other brothers mending their nets, James and John, the sons of Zebedee. The call to follow Jesus reaches both pairs of brothers. They set out to obey it.

Let us not treat a single line in that picture as being of little significance. Both ships have to be rowed ashore. The first step towards following Jesus is to leave the sea and come on land.

The scene already contains the most important basic principles of Christianity and of its history. Jesus not only spoke to people in parables and pictures — his life also speaks to us in parables. Those are not verbal parables but parables enacted. They are not mere symbols, they are actual destinies. We can approach them if we recognize that there were no coincidences in the life of Jesus: right down to its seemingly least important feature, it is a picture language of the revelation inscribed into the earthly world.

In taking a trivial externalized view unconnected as yet with any pictorial sense for the scene we have sketched of the call of the first disciples, we shall find nothing to it beyond this idea that the disciples of Jesus were only simple fishermen.

Modern understanding rather belittles Jesus' disciples as 'just ordinary men of the people.' We say 'ordinary' but mean 'uneducated.' It is most important if we are to grasp the significance of the gospel as a whole to get the right idea concerning the life of the disciples before they were called.

Even a few decades ago, people felt differently towards the simple, unpretentious fishermen whom Jesus called to be his disciples, just as they did towards the shepherds who, in the night of Christmas, beheld and heard the angels. Back in the early nineteenth century there were those among the people who, while living remote from the schooling of their time, were the bearers of treasures of profound wisdom; and they were acknowledged as such. Some of them may have been old shepherds, quietly tending their flocks, dreaming and gazing into nature and into its cloud pictures: into the colours of stones, of plants and of the atmosphere. No book learning was theirs. If education is to be judged by the number of books a man has studied, then these men were 'uneducated.' Yet, when people were in trouble or sick and when the learned doctor or priest failed them, then it was that people knew they could find help from those shepherds and herb gatherers, help that stemmed from a more profound education and wisdom than books convey.

We have only to turn to the autobiography of Friedrich Christoph Oetinger, a Würtemberg prelate, to find how he owed his life to one such sage of the people — Mark Völker, a Thuringian peasant. Having read about him we shall see for ourselves the effectiveness of simple, uncultured men like Mark Völker. Oetinger is describing him:

> My way took me via Erfurt. Not far from there, I made the acquaintance of a peasant who was supposed to have second sight. This peasant, named Mark Völker, was an extraordinary person. His father having died early, Mark, the youngest child, was neglected; he learned neither to write nor to read. He served in the army as a stable boy. Second sight was revealed to him while serving in the field. By means of it, he saw first of all the destinies of his brothers and sisters, just as Joseph had seen those of his own. He saw them not in sleep in the way a sleeper sees images, but while awake. I tried out Völker, and thought it worth my while to spend a good deal of time with him and enquire into his second sight. There was about him

much of nature, but also a graciousness, an unusual humility and modest courtesy; added to this, great powers of insight, and all of it beneath the roughest peasant exterior; essential wisdom was his to a high degree. He understood the most exalted order of the birth of things.

By way of a further example we can mention the herb gatherer of whom Rudolf Steiner speaks in his autobiography in relating his own school days:

It so happened that I got to know a simple man of the people. He travelled to Vienna every week by the same train that I used to take. He collected medicinal herbs in the countryside and sold them to the apothecaries in Vienna. We became friends. You could speak with him about the world of spirit as to someone with experience. He was a deeply pious person. He had had no schooling. Although he had read many books on mysticism, whatever he said was not influenced at all by such reading. His was the outpouring of a life of the soul, imbued with elemental creative wisdom. One soon realized that he read those books because he wanted to find in others what he knew of his own accord. In his company you gained deep insight into nature. On his back he carried his bundle of medicinal herbs but he bore in his heart the results won from the spirituality of nature while out collecting herbs.

I have cited these examples in so much detail because it seems important to make the picture of those fishermen of the Sea of Galilee more true and lifelike than is usually the case. Much talk of those 'simple evangelists' will fall silent when people gain a clearer view of the 'simplicity' of the first of the disciples.

Their work as fishermen kept the men described as two pairs of brothers on the waters of the sea. But at sea a certain elemental and natural spirituality influenced human souls more in those days than it does now. The soul of the spiritual world was nearer while one lingered in thought on the waters, than it was on land, so that the sea itself was felt to be a quiet, living image of the world of spirit in contrast to the dry land, a likeness of the earthly world of the senses.

Something of what people once used to feel at sea by way of visions of spirits and of dim perception of them has survived to this day. It survives in the so-called superstitions of men of the sea who can tell us all manner of things about seeing spirits, and about the revelations of the stars. We should realize that the first disciples were not set for the first time upon the beginning of a spiritual path by having been called; they had been plunged already into an element of spirit. This emerges quite clearly if we compare St John's account of the call with the story in the Gospel of St Matthew. John's presentation is quite different from those of the other gospels. We are confronted by so-called contradictions in the gospels. John tells how John the Baptist stood beside the way along which Jesus was passing. He pointed to Jesus, saying: 'Behold the Lamb of God.' The Baptist's two disciples became disciples of Jesus through these words from their master. Who were the two whom St John's Gospel indicates as having been the two earliest disciples? We learn the name of one of them. 'Andrew, the brother of Simon Peter, was one of the two who had followed him because of what John had said.' (John 1:40). The next thing said is that Andrew immediately fetched his brother Simon so that Jesus was able to accept him as a disciple under the name of Peter. So here we have one pair of brothers together, whom the other evangelists name at the scene of the calling. We may therefore suppose that one of the other pair of brothers — James or John — was the unnamed disciple of John the Baptist. This is the first of many passages in St John where a disciple is spoken of without being named. The name of John's disciple is not given anywhere in the whole of the gospel. It is never mere chance if someone in the gospel is not named. That silence is often speech of a very special kind.

So we can deduce that the second disciple of the Baptist was the disciple John; just as Andrew brought Peter to Jesus, so John could have led his brother James to Christ. So there we have the second pair of brothers.

With that we gain some insight into links between the earlier disciples and their calling. They were led and taught by the Baptist; in any case, they would have been as brothers to those who were the direct pupils of John. Even though they were 'simple men,' they were knit into a close spiritual community with those who were gathered about the Baptist and cultivated an exalted spiritual content. The two Johns may in time come to life very vividly to the pictorial sense; John the Baptist as the teacher, the apostle John as pupil.

Andrew and John found their way to Jesus, the true Master, being themselves disciples of the Baptist; Peter and James found their way to him, being brothers of Andrew and John.

How are we to reconcile the divergent presentations in Matthew and John? Did the Christ call the two pairs of brothers from sea to the land, or did he accept the other two who came to him, following in the wake of the two disciples of John?

There remains an insoluble contradiction here so long as gospel scenes go on being presented as no more than external. The contradiction disappears with a more spiritualized, more truthfully pictorial, acceptance of them.

Those two brothers actually were at sea as to their souls and spirit, that is, they were engrossed in definite spiritual interconnections in a particular kind of spiritual experience. They had to sacrifice and forsake the old, rich spiritual experience if they desired to become disciples of Christ. They had to come ashore and start at the very beginning so far as life in the spirit was concerned. The first step those who follow the Christ must take is to plant their feet firmly on land, giving up bliss of the spirit — 'from sea to land' is the first call and also the first step in Christ's school. The follower cannot smuggle in extraneous things no matter how precious some spiritual treasure may be. 'Those who follow me must deny themselves.'

The sea the disciples must forsake is, in spiritual terms, the life spent up to that time in spiritual communities whether in the group of John's disciples or in other similar groups. And in St John's Gospel we see how the two to be called first do bring a sacrifice in leaving their revered and beloved master. The pictures of the disciples' calling are not at variance with each other in the spirit world. We must keep in mind that actual vision in spirit (that is, imagination) and word experiences within the spirit (inspiration) played their part when the gospels were coming into being. The scene of the calling of the disciples was not drawn for the evangelists from external sense recollection; it stood out before their souls as spiritual, pictorial vision: Matthew beholds the two ships, with two brothers in each, who then come ashore; but John sees the Baptist standing by the wayside with his pupils. We could ask: which of these two scenes gives us the outward historical course of events? We are constrained to look upon John's account as the one most in keeping with outward reality because he was a disciple in John's group; this was the factual, external form of 'being at sea.' If we are right that the second unnamed pupil of John the Baptist was John, the disciple who wrote the gospel, then the account in that gospel is in fact drawn from the memory of someone who was a participant, whereas the account of Matthew (also of Luke and Mark) is derived from the visions of people who were not personal participants.

It is however quite possible that the scene in which the two ships approach land did at some time assume physical reality. Is a scene to be taken as being only of the spirit, or can it be accepted as being external and earthly as well? We should learn to consider this question as being less crucial. It could become part of our soul's content if we can recognize the spiritual truth and keep it in our hearts, as did Mary the words of the shepherds.

Just to render more flexible our habits of thought to date, I should like to say this: it is still a question whether the fraternal relationship between Peter and Andrew, and between James and John, was a physical one. Crudely put, it really is doubtful whether Zebedee was the physical father of the sons of Zebedee. It is certain that Peter and John, and also the sons of Zebedee, were adherents in a spiritual sense of certain groups; adherents of monasteries and fraternities address each other as 'brother.' Whether a physical brotherhood existed as well as that fraternity cannot really be deduced for certain from the gospels. In older traditions, such brotherhood was a strongly felt emotion. I shall quote one of many examples, the opening of the legend of James, taken from the 'Golden Legend,' the *Legenda Aurea*.

> James was called the Son of Zebedee not only according to the flesh, but also because of the meaning of this name, for Zebedee, being translated, means 'one who gives' or 'one who is given.' But James gave himself to God for martyrdom and was in turn given to us to be our spiritual guardian. He was called the brother of John because he was his brother according to the flesh, but also because he was like him in his habits, for they were alike in their eagerness, their passion for holy knowledge, in their desire for the same promises from the Lord.

We could perhaps represent the matter to ourselves by saying that there were groups where a certain wisdom of the common people was cultivated and passed on. The central figure of such a group was someone who could have been looked on as a father, as was Zebedee and indeed John the Baptist. If we remember how important a part the image of the fish (Christ as the Fish) played among early Christian communities in the catacombs, then we realize that the disciples could well have been drawn towards some such group whose 'coat of arms' — to call it so — contained the fish. Even if there were groups made up of professional fishermen, then this would have been only the external aspect of the fact that within those groups a life of the spirit was mutually cultivated dependent on the 'sea' and the 'fish.' Let us look back again at St John's account of the calling of the disciples. The call of Philip is told after that of Peter and then comes: 'Philip was from Bethsaida, the town of Andrew and Peter' (John 1:44).

If we try to identify Bethsaida geographically from biblical books we come up against difficulties. The difficulties arise from maps of the Holy Land usually printed in bibles, where Bethsaida is marked twice — once north of the Sea of Galilee and once west. 'Bethsaida' means 'The House of Fish' just as 'Bethlehem' means 'The House of Bread.' So we can think of Bethsaida as being the name and seat of some such 'fish' group. The brethren assembled in the house of the fish. One of the brethren of Bethsaida, Andrew, was at the same time a disciple of John the Baptist. The Baptist led him to Christ. Andrew fetched Peter who was his brother in the house of fish. Then Andrew and Peter having preceded him, Philip also found his way from the Bethsaida group to Christ.

Andrew called Peter saying: 'We have found the Messiah.' Are we not looking right into the secret of the Bethsaida group? A band of simple fishermen is assembled — the 'quiet ones in the land,' who know about the coming of the Messiah and are bound together in expectation. The 'fish' tells them the secret of the Messiah as he tells them many other things that are not known to ordinary folk. Bethsaida, the house of fish, was more than a geographical place. It was a centre of wisdom where wise but unassuming men of the people met. There were 'Bethsaidas' everywhere. We could assert that there were probably several more, definite places about the sea of Galilee having the same name. They took their name from the communities who lived there.

We have then brought together all kinds of elements to enable us to picture the life of the disciples before they were called. Everyone is free to fill out that life with more detail. A rich life of the soul, a rich unfolding of destinies opens out before us. The disciples were indeed 'upon the sea' when Christ called them. And they had to leave everything; they had to emerge out onto land as the Christ himself had done when he descended from heaven to earth, when he came from the sea to land for humanity's salvation. The calling of the disciples has become for us a picture and thereby a part of the 'living gospel,' the *evangelium aeternum*, which speaks not only of the past but also of the eternal present.

All must come out on land if they desire to become Christians. Personal life begins only on land, but so also does personal destiny and personal relationship to God. Christianity always begins by bestowing the courage on human beings to accept personality. It says to humankind, 'Just as long as you are richly endowed with the uplifting soul and spiritual content of life, just so long will you be delayed in the forecourt of Christianity. You will pass through the gate of Christianity only when you have become poor and when you set forth in the poverty of individual earthly existence.'

Why could the Christ not make use of spiritual powers within which the disciples had hitherto been living? Those were powers of life and of vision that emanated from nature, from winds, from the waves of the sea; they were inspired by life-forces of external nature bestowed on them from outside. They had not been achieved from within. Only spirituality won inwardly, from out of the ego, counted for the Christ. He looked to his followers not for the spirituality of nature, but for the spirituality of the ego. Between them lies poverty, like death between life and resurrection. As man strides from sea to land, his decision is made to accept poverty, to accept death; but at the same time this is the beginning of resurrection.

With the beginning of the Reformation a feeling for true Christianity spread among the people, a feeling that begins with the stride to the land, with the courage to take up personal destiny. People sought personal Christianity, even if its price was impoverishment. They felt that Roman Catholicism was pagan, un-Christian, not willing to refrain from bedding down the individual in old communal and spiritual forces, desiring to protect men from the impoverishment of personal destiny. Here is a fact: Catholicism is still upon the sea; Protestantism is on land. Ancient nature forces influence Catholicism through ritual, through the uniformity of dogmatic thought. There men still exist in the blissful treasures of soul which precede a man's becoming an ego, an individual, at the same stage as the disciples were before their calling. Protestantism has at least begun to come ashore. But there too we find everywhere the tendency to hold on to the old instinctive religious and communal forces that people bring with them naturally. People try to delude themselves about the loss of the old childlike religiosity which is overtaking humanity in a big way. Anyone who is naturally very religious in the sense that he is able to swim along readily with some communal stream, has not yet scaled the harsh shores of following Christ. Those, however, who have lost the simple-hearted religious energies, and today they include the great majority of people if they would only admit it to themselves — those can assure themselves that 'human destiny has cast me up onto parched shores, whereas earlier I had been upon the sea. And it is the will of Christ himself that those who wish to follow him should leave the sea.' At first loneliness and impoverishment rule the land. But for those who persevere in the path of Christ, that path opens into a new richness of soul, a new experience of religion and of community. It is inevitable that impoverishment should lie between the old religiosity on the sea, and the new devotion of the ego. Blessed is he who is a poor man for he shall be rich. Woe to the man of wealth for he is menaced by poverty.

To all those who desire to become followers of the Christ, the answer sounds: 'Foxes have their holes and the birds of heaven have their nests, but the Son of Man has nowhere to lay his head' (Matt.8:20). No man can truly become a Christian without the home-lessness of becoming an ego.

The marriage at Cana

We have paused to consider in detail scenes of the disciples' calling in order to thoroughly clarify the nature of gospel images. We can now study some further images more briefly.

The first deed of Christ in which the disciples participated was, according to St John, the changing of water into wine at the marriage at Cana.

Every incident in the life of Christ can be seen from two sides. We can in the first place concentrate on the historical sequence of events and try to understand them. In the second place we can ask what went on in the disciples' souls through taking part in the event, what did it do to them? All the deeds of Christ, such as the healings, are twofold: on the one hand they happened externally in relation to this or that sick person who was healed. On the other hand they happened in a more inward way to the disciples who were present. It is only when we also look at the deeds which the Christ directed outward, performing them at the same time upon the disciples — only then do we possess the living 'good tidings,' eternal, and yet belonging to our own day.

Just as the disciples were there when those deeds were done by the Christ, and just as they were transformed and led by them to higher stages along the path of the soul — so, by reading the gospels aright, we are also there when the Christ is performing those deeds; we too are transformed by them and are led by them to higher stages along the soul's path. The deeds of Christ become deeds done to us when we begin to realize that they are deeds done to the disciples.

Every gospel story becomes a step that follows the Christ, a step along the way of the disciples' souls, if we can conceive of them as images.

Let us then look at the story of the marriage in Cana as if it were the picture of an episode in the disciples' souls.

The change of water to wine is akin to that step taken from the sea to land. It is the same, but it takes place even deeper in the human heart. The transformation of water to wine takes place within a human being, within a disciple of Christ. It is the transformation from consciousness of the natural to the spiritual, to ego awareness of the inmost soul. Before the evolution of the ego and of personality, man still lived on the watery element, in the sea, and the sea was within him. Nature's cosmic life, the life that unites all things, also supported man. Man was still a drop in the sea, part and parcel of cosmic life, related to nature as well as to the human community. Man was still a member of the whole. Once the ego was born in him, he became an individual; he saw himself as being someone apart, he freed himself from the all-penetrating whole. Instead of existing in universal waters, he began from then on to live within his own self, in his own blood, the vehicle of human personality. Water is changed into blood. The same process takes place in the plant world when watery sap rises from the roots and is transformed into aromatic wine by the power of the autumn sun. Those forces that transform water into wine are cosmic ego forces. The Greeks knew them as Dionysus Zagreus. Human ego forces turned water into blood. These the Greeks knew as Dionysus Bacchus. The Christ brought about at the marriage in Cana the process ordinarily activated by cosmic ego forces, namely by forces which the sun's Dionysian qualities bring about in the vine; even so did the Christ bring about among those present — and especially among his own disciples — what ego forces would ordinarily bring about in human beings. The deed in Cana stimulated and fortified what pertained to the ego in man. It was a charter for human personality. It meant not only: 'You humans are not merely permitted to be ego beings'; it meant also 'If you wish to follow in my way, then you are to become ego-people. You are to find your way from the cosmic principle, from the water, to human individuality, to the wine.'

So much for the deed of Christ within the disciples' souls. But what of the historical course of events which happened at a specified place at a specific time?

We must take note of the way in which St John's Gospel stresses the location of Cana and of Galilee: 'And on the third day a wedding was celebrated at Cana in Galilee' (John 2:1) — 'This, the very beginning of his signs, Jesus fulfilled at Cana in Galilee' (John 2:11) — 'After the two days he went on to Galilee' (John 4:43) — 'And he came again to Cana in Galilee, where he had made the water wine. There was a courtier whose son was lying ill in Capernaum.' (John 4:46). Doubtless the Gospel of John would not stress these particulars of the location of Cana of Galilee — 'out from' Judea 'to' Galilee — so frequently or with so much emphasis had it all been coincidental. Unquestionably, just where the first miracle and also the second one took place was not without significance.

Judea, whose centre is the hill upon which Jerusalem and the Temple are situated, is the opposite of Galilee, whose centre is the Sea of Galilee.

Judea is the land of sternly Judaic folk culture. The law of marriage within the tribe is everywhere associated with the bonds of close blood relationships. The people as a whole was dedicated to the task of producing a physical body eminently suited to receive ego-intellectuality and the ego impulse itself; this aim was to be achieved through the highest degree of inherited uniformity.

Galilee is the land of diverse, racial intermingling. Rudolf Steiner has often explained that Galilee was in ancient times a region of transit for many migrating peoples; in contrast to Judea the people of Galilee drew their strength from a thorough-going mixture of blood and races. Impulses of humanity in Galilee confronted the folk impulses of Judea. People in Galilee still lived upon the sea, in the watery element, and were filled with an all enveloping natural spirituality. Judea, on the other hand, was situated on land; there, water has become wine.

People in Galilee were nearer to the spiritual world, even though in an ancient, elemental fashion. The word 'Galilee' is associated with the Old Testament name of Gilgal. Gilgal is not an earthly place name. Rather, it is a spiritual region. Gilgal means: 'The wheel of overthrowing'; it is the indication of a primal rune common to all humanity, of the wheel-rune which is nowadays often misunderstood and abused; it originally meant the transition from consciousness based on the senses to supersensible consciousness.

It used to be experienced as a mighty turning round of the soul's wheel. Very important stories of the Old Testament are enacted at Gilgal, such as Joshua's crossing of the Jordan, and the choosing of Saul as King.

It is important to the New Testament that Jesus called his first disciples from among the people of Galilee, that is, people who had something spiritual to sacrifice. It is also significant that he took up his abode there. It was there that he performed his first miracles, the first of them being the transformation of water into wine.

The name of Cana is associated with Canaan, with the land as a whole, in an original and elemental way. But it is also associated with Cain. Cana was no Abel-city, but a Cain-city. The name Cain means something like 'he who can.' So Cana was a city where the creative forces of action were dominant. It was 'the city of those who can,' the city of doing. And that is where Christ performed his first deed. He linked that deed to the nature forces of Galilee, but he changed them even as he used them. He drew nature forces from man's past into his own service, and thereby conferred on them his own ego and his own personality.

Speaking pictorially, Christ himself had but recently passed from water to land. The overflowing cosmic power streaming down from the newly incarnated Christ was all-powerful in Jesus of Nazareth. The Christ was himself like unto Galilee, like Cana, and not yet like Judea. Creative powers of nature were still active in him. The forces beaming forth from him, exercising their strength, were still akin to the powers of the sun which ripens water in the grape to wine. At the Cana celebration Christ was the cosmic king.

As we shall see later, the miracle of Cana is the only event in the life of Jesus that stands out as an actual miracle, an intervention by higher natural forces. Miracles occur not at the end but at the beginning of Christ's ministry. We really have to take note how the miraculous work of Christ ceases at a definite stage in the life of Jesus. The last healing took place before the gates of Jericho when Christ was setting out for the last time for Jerusalem. The Passion took the place of miracles. The last miraculous deed in John comes in chapter eleven, that is, half way through the gospel. There are no more miraculous deeds in the second half. But even before the miracles cease, we can observe an advance towards inwardness in the deeds of Christ. We have so far only observed it in the example of the Christ walking on the water and we have yet to prove it by studying other deeds of his. The first sign given by Jesus, the miracle of Cana, was external. Christ actually began externally and passed further and further inward. It was progress towards becoming man, of the Logos becoming flesh, of the incarnation of the cosmic power coming down to us from the cosmos. We may call it the great passage from sea to land, from Galilee to Judea.

We should not however imagine the first sign in terms too materialistic. The account in the gospel is very delicately accurate. We are told how at the very moment the master of the feast tasted the water, that water became wine. The water in the pitchers would probably still have been apprehended as water, but the human organism experienced it as wine. The change of water into wine was in a sense a spiritual penetration of the water by ego forces of the cosmos. Once that penetration had reached through to the physical, the water changed in colour and odour and communicated itself to the outward senses as wine. But if spiritual penetration had taken place mainly in the region of the soul, then it could only have been apprehended in the region of what pertains to the human soul. The sense of taste, being more inward than the sense of sight or of smell, is closer to the soul. Soul recognizes soul. As the ruler of the feast tasted and drank the costly wine drawn from the water pitchers, the human ego in the blood recognized the cosmic ego nature of the transformed water. As water is changed to blood within the human body so the water in the water pitchers was changed to wine. The inward aspect of the miracle touched the external.

But we must now point out another feature of the story in which a traditional error has become established. By uncovering that error, Rudolf Steiner has opened whole worlds overlaid in the gospels. When Mary spoke to Jesus because the people had no one, Jesus answered her in words translated as 'Woman, what have I to do with thee? My hour is not yet come.' That sounds like a harsh and heartless rebuff. Yet the miracle does take place and the shortage is overcome. Rudolf Steiner showed up in this passage a sinister far-reaching error of translation. The Greek text includes a mystery term which says something like this: 'what is it that flows between me and you?' Jesus is indicating a current of spiritual power, a power of the soul, keeping him in touch with his mother. It was inevitable that words such as these should be misunderstood in an era which recognized only what was perceptible to the senses.

'My hour is not yet come' here means 'I am not yet fully ego; the hour when I shall have to act wholly from out of my own ego is not yet come. But I am still one with thee; I am permitted to act through the forces which are flowing between you and me.' The change of water to wine proceeds from those forces. The Christ had not yet passed altogether from sea to land. He was still connected to the sea of the spiritual world, as if by a navel cord. That is why cosmic forces were still actively coming from him. In earthly terms this continued communion is expressed in what was passing between the Christ and Mary.

We are here facing one of the primal phenomena of man's existence. When a child is born, a significant change takes place in its organism. As long as the child remained in the body of its mother, it lived entirely in the watery element. The watery element pulsated right through the infant organism in its embryonic state. When the child's organism is freed from that of the mother at birth, the mother's blood goes on flowing for a time into the child's organism along the navel cord, which still connects mother and baby. Water is changed to blood in the child. The child actually passes through the miracle of Cana.

The primal phenomenon of birth is before us in the image of the first miracle. But it was preceded by another birth, the incarnation of the Christ in Jesus of Nazareth. This birth was also followed by a period during which the newborn being was tied to the mother by a navel cord, but spiritually. Its mother was the world of spirit, the world mother herself. Mary actually mirrored the spiritual world in that she was in a sense the vehicle of eternal womanhood, of cosmic motherhood. Jesus was referring to that cosmic blood that palpitated through the navel cord, in his mystic utterance: 'Pay heed to the forces flowing between me and you.'

Antecedents of that world are revealed in the simple and unpretentious event in Cana which we may be sure passed quite unnoticed and unremarked by most of those present. Here before us is the primal phenomenon of birth, of becoming a human being, of becoming a personality. Christ himself, striving towards 'his hour,' towards his own assumption of humanity, introduced a deed into the realms of earth whereby he hallowed all striving after personality.

The miracle of Cana is told only in the Gospel of St John. Do not the other gospels contain that step along the way which involves the birth of personality? That step is present in them, but is experienced differently. The Sermon on the Mount in St Matthew is the disciples' inmost experience; it is the same step as the transmutation of water into wine of St John. That will become clear in later studies fully concerned with the Sermon on the Mount. For the present we shall only note a common kind of allegorical interpretation of the miracle of Cana. The water is assumed to be the Jewish religion, the wine is Christianity, while the story of the marriage in Cana is a metaphor for the transition from Judaism to Christianity. In face of the story of Cana such an explanation is nothing but a denial of it. It is however relevant to the Sermon on the Mount. Where it says, 'You have heard it said to *your fathers* ... but *I* say to you' we do indeed have the change of the waters of Judaism into the wine of Christianity. The law was given to the fathers, the same for all men, making them one people. That was the water. But now it is the ego, Christ's ego, the essential 'I' speaking in the true sense. There is no common pattern. Each utterance is personal to every individual. That is the wine.

We shall see in the structure of the Sermon on the Mount how it leads us from holiest, highest heaven (the Beatitudes) right down to earth in the picture of the house to be built not on sand but on solid rock. The Sermon on the Mount is a pilgrimage of personal Christianity. We shall not for the present further anticipate discussion of the Sermon on the Mount.

Three healings

The step from sea to land was sealed by the first miracle, the changing of water into wine. Whither does the path of the soul, along which the Christ takes his disciples, now lead? *It leads into the house.* The house is the scene of personal destiny and of personal Christianity. Our human bodies, that separate one human body from another, are our houses, the seat of our personality. If we look at the part of the gospel that follows what we have so far studied, we shall find the image of the house more often and find it more distinctly. In John the cleansing of the Temple follows immediately on the wedding in Cana. Christ entered the edifice of the Temple — he meant the temple of the body (John 2:21) — and there he wrestled the powers of his adversary to their downfall. In Matthew we can clearly discern three stages of existence in the house:

> Christ heals the centurion's son (Matt.8:5–13)
> Christ heals the man sick of the palsy (Matt.9:1–8)
> Christ reawakens Jairus' daughter (Matt.9:18–26)

In the first of these scenes, the image of the house is present but — as it were — remote. The sick man is in the house. The centurion says 'Lord, I am not worthy to have you enter my house.' (Matt.8:8). In the healing of the man sick of the palsy, the house plays a bigger, deeply pictorial part — especially in St Mark (2:1–12). From inside the house Christ speaks to the people who are outside pressing about him. Four men bring up the man sick of the palsy on a stretcher, but they are unable to reach Jesus except by climbing to the roof, stretcher and all, then making a hole in the roof and lowering the stretcher through it.

The house dominates the third scene. Jesus enters the chamber in Jairus' house where the young girl is lying. He takes with him into the house only the parents and three of the closest of his disciples.

It is the house that separates a group of people, or an event, from all other people and from whatever is going on in the world. An inward event is thereby made possible.

As we bring the three scenes before us as pictures, let us look first of all at what they meant as stages in the disciples' path, at the deeds that Christ did to the disciples as he healed and awakened.

The steps to be experienced in these scenes are these: If we, as personalities, have courageously set out on life, we have to scale three cliffs. The first danger lies in our environment that influences us; powers of the past are dominant there. The next danger is that of the immediate present. It grows from a person's inmost self. The third danger threatens us in relation to our own part in building the future. It questions the very things which we, as witnesses, would bring forth from out of ourselves. We could set down the threats that peer out of the past, present and future as: weakness, sickness, death.

Weakness threatens people out of their own environment. Old usages and customs surround us; they result from what our predecessors created, and they carry one along just so long as one is not yet awake as a person in one's own right. One can still hold on to them. If we adjust to transmitted customs and usages we find protection from moral insecurity and deviation. But should we set out to shape our lives on the strength of our own individuality then, all too soon, the deficiencies and corruption of the prevailing forms begin to reveal themselves. Acceptance of usages and customs once made a moral style of life easy. But to live in righteousness on the strength of one's own morality is difficult. One is left entirely to oneself, all alone. One can go wrong, and it is not easy to find the way back.

Infirmities and lack of control become especially evident in life when a boy reaches puberty and starts looking about for a career. All too soon he can find no support in his father's world that now surrounds him, nor can he place any reliance in it. The relationship of the growing lad to the older generation is determined more and more often by disillusionment because of the deficiencies in the manners and customs of the ancestral world from which he has received his body. And this becomes all the more evident as personal character asserts itself. As individuality matures so the world leaves people to themselves. The more their life blood pulsates through them, the more they become aware of their own deficiencies. Experiences associated with puberty in young people are becoming a general feature of our time. It is almost as if a kind of 'pubescent experience' were passing right through humanity. People are becoming emancipated from the usages and customs of the world about them. Justifiably, they are finding 'bourgeois morality' boring and effete. But, just because those habits and formalities did hitherto provide some sort of support, human failings are now coming to light. The ego becomes aware of its failings even when compared with the body-orientated inadequacies of the fathers. As a result people now find themselves up against the second cliff as individuals, that is, sickness. We have set out on the path of becoming individuals, but the ego in us is still feeble. Desire, sin, burns within the soul unbridled by its enfeebled 'I.' The fire burning within the region of the soul dries up the living, creating streams that keep the body healthy. The body becomes sick. Sickness is the consequence of weakness, of sin.

And so we have before us, man distorted in the process of becoming an individuality:

The 'I'	weak
The soul	burning
Life	drying up
The body	sick.

There are undoubtedly illnesses conditioned by outer factors. Nevertheless, sickness, as an archetypal phenomenon, emanates from within the human being and is caused by weakness at the core of soul and spirit, by sin. In this area, humankind is at the present time struggling against itself.

Now comes the third cliff of personal destiny; the death of the living forces of procreation, of creativity. A person labours but no 'work' results. A person speaks, but no viable seed sinks through the word into the soul of the other. They can create no future, try as they may. They could say: 'The eternally feminine, the original motherhood within my self, is dying.' As long as that eternally feminine, that holy principle of future potential, is still alive in souls, then a conversation is to the speaker a living witness, a seed sinking into the soul of the other; from that seed a new living creature will spring up. For the listeners, the dialogue is pure, unblemished conception. In the soul's womb a seed ripens, but the soul that conceived it is virginally pure. When the virgin in us is dead, then speech becomes hollow and empty, while listening turns hard, shut in on itself. In our own time people

have in large measure lost the ability to speak and to listen. Death of
the soul has set in, the death of the soul's virginity.

In healing the nobleman's son, Jesus healed *weakness*. Let us watch
the course of events on that occasion. St John's Gospel emphasizes that
Jesus did this 'when he had come from Judea to Galilee' (John 4:54). In
Judea, a lad entering on puberty found unbroken strength in his
father's world. The soul is at work upon the body up to the time of
puberty. Once the body is mature, then the house is ready, and that is
the way in which the soul experiences the body. At birth the soul
invariably enters upon an incomplete dwelling; from fourteen years
the soul itself co-operates in building its own body. The soul wakens
to itself. But now begins the see-saw between sensuality emanating
from the body and spirituality stirring in the awakening soul. If the
body integrates to become a related whole, then the youth will have
something to hold on to. In Judea, family but more especially the
father, gave a boy such a hold. Did not a boy's soul, because of the
close blood ties, in a sense perceive his parents, his brothers and sisters, but most of all his father, as the multiplication of his own body?
In Galilee, land of strangers, of mixed races, a youth waking up in his
own body felt himself surrounded by strangers in whom he could find
no support. The father, hitherto close and dear to him, now seemed
unfamiliar. The lad, left to himself in his house, was shaken by a fever.
The father in his helplessness — for he could not help — hurried off to
the Christ. He found him in Cana. The lad was sick through weakness
in his father. Here we see an illness of puberty. In giving strength to the
father, who clung to Jesus in faith, Christ also cured the boy. It was the
healing of weakness, of weakness of the house, of body, of the paternal principle. The cause of weakness was the body. This was overcome.

During the Act of Consecration of Man words addressed to Christ
speak of the sickness of the body — 'the dwelling' — and of the healing of the soul through Christ's word. In a way, this utterance is a
translation of words spoken by the centurion to Christ: 'Lord, I am not
worthy to have you enter my house. Speak just one word, then my boy
will be healed.' (Matt.8:8). If we examine the logic of the utterance, we
find apparent discrepancies. It is the body that is sick, but the soul is
cured through the word. It corresponds to the story: the father is sick
but the son is cured for the father joins the Christ. The boy, whom an

earthly physical environment cannot help, is helped even as the Christ finds a place in that environment. Here is the essence of Confirmation. The young man is permitted to enter into Christ's environment, where the earthly environment reveals to him its own weakness as well as his. Following the first miracle, the primal phenomenon of birth is thrown open. The second miracle is followed by the primal phenomenon of puberty and of its sequel, Confirmation.

In healing the man sick of the palsy, Christ helps us to overcome the second cliff of individual life. This is no externally miraculous healing. The cure took place from within, even as the illness originates within. First of all the Christ addressed the patient: 'Your sins are taken from you.' Strength was enabled to flow again into the man's soul and spirit because of his inward relationship with the Christ. The fire was silent. The waters of life could flow again and could once more restore the body to health. The word of absolution had so intensified the fortifying effect on the 'I,' it had so heightened the harmonizing of the soul, that the strength of it passed on directly to the physical body. The Christ united himself with the ego of the sick man, thus making it possible for the man himself to overcome his illness (Matt.9:1–8).

The third miracle in John corresponds to the healing of the man sick of the palsy: that is, the healing of the impotent man at the Pool of Bethesda. The pool, alternating between arid stillness and lively movement brought about by the angel, is nothing but an outwardly visible representation of invisible vital currents in the human organism. Those patients who were not yet awake to their own individuality were vouchsafed the experience of witnessing the water of life in the pool, but also within themselves, when moved by the angel who brought about recovery. Their illness did not emanate from their ego; accordingly they could be cured by helpers from above and outside. The man sick for thirty-eight years was, however, infirm because of his ego. He could therefore only get well through his own ego. The Christ asked him, 'Have you the will to become whole?' (John 5:6). He appealed to his will, to his 'I,' to move the waters himself, not however externally in the pool, but within his own nature.

> The 'I' is strengthened by the Christ.
> That which pertains to the soul is bridled.
> Life streams are enabled to move again.
> The body is restored to health.

The Christ accomplished the first miracle through the bond with his mother; the second through links with the boy's father; the third by means of links with the patient's ego.

The third scene, the raising of the little girl, leads into deep secrets of life. Rudolf Steiner has pointed to the key to this story in his *Background to the Gospel of St Mark* and one marvels that these interconnections, so wide open to the light of day, have not been perceived before. In telling the story of the raising of Jairus' daughter, each of the gospels also weaves into it the story of the woman with the issue of blood. The woman had been ill for twelve years; the little girl was twelve years old. The woman became ill when the child was born. That points to some kind of bond between the two of them and their sickness. Just as the scene of the centurion in Capernaum indicates the phenomenon of male puberty, so the scene in the house of Jairus indicates the phenomenon of female puberty. The little girl became sick and died because the maternal forces did not waken in her. Death of the womb stretches out to grasp the whole of the human being. But the woman with the issue of blood had too much of the force that the girl lacked at a time when those forces could have saved her. Maternal blood, lack of which killed the young girl, but excess of which made the woman ill, is the bearer of the future of humanity. A part of humanity's future died with the girl. Her death was humankind becoming sterile. In curing the child, in restoring the balance between the girl and the woman with the issue of blood, the Christ restored the future of humanity. He nullified the third cliff along the way of becoming an ego.

So here we have an especially beautiful example of the ways in which the appreciation of a picture reveals the living gospel. Let us visualize the scene in Jairus' house.

The Christ is standing between two groups of three people in each group: on one side, by the girl's bed, are her parents; these three are related by blood. On the other side are Peter, James and John, three men related in the spirit. The Christ, the seventh, is between them, carrying out a priestly rite in those solemn words, *Talitha Kumi*. The girl raises herself on the side to those related to her by blood. Nothing external happens to those related in spirit. What happens inwardly? In them, too, the virgin is called awake. The virginally-maternal, the eternal woman, was dead in all humanity. From now on, it is to come to life again through the labour of the apostles. The disciples are made the vehicle of the re-awakened eternal feminine. From now on their ministry among humankind will be able to engender life.

The raising of Jairus' daughter carries us beyond the stages of personal Christianity. It points into the future of humanity. The Christ had led his disciples from the sea to the land and, once on land, into the house. Now we can sense how he sets about to guide them from the limitations of the house out into space. Personal Christianity is not the whole of Christianity. It is one step, to be followed by a further step. That step, which we may call cosmic Christianity, proclaims itself for instance in Matt.13:1–3: 'On that day Jesus went out of the house to the sea and there he sat down. Then a great crowd of people streamed towards him, until he eventually had to get into a boat and sit down in it; and the whole crowd stood on the shore. And he said many things to them in parables.'

The journey from personal to cosmic Christianity in the gospels will be the subject of the next chapter.

CHAPTER SEVEN

The Miracle of the Feeding

The feeding of the five thousand and of the four thousand

It lies in the nature of the gospels that artists have understood them a great deal more profoundly, more truly, than have those who think along theological lines. And we have to admit that particularly in the case of the feeding of the five thousand, the very best theology, right down to many a detail, is contained in this poem by Conrad Ferdinand Meyer:

> The Spirit spoke: Look up! I saw it in a dream.
> I lifted up my eyes. In luminous cloud-filled regions
> I saw the Lord break bread for the Twelve,
> And heard him speak words of love.
> Reaching far out, above their heads, his all-embracing gesture
> Included earth itself in the ritual.
>
> The spirit spoke: Look up! And I beheld a linen cloth
> Floating on high; a meal was provided for many;
> Tables there were, spread under a thousand hands;
> But the far limits of those tables
> Paled into grey mist. And in the mist
> There sat on the dim steps pitiful figures, uncalled.
>
> The spirit spoke: Look up! The blue mist bathed
> A measureless banquet stretching as far as I could see.
> There life-giving fountains sprang high and bountiful;
> There no hand reached out a cup in vain;
> There all the people lay on ample sheaves.
> No seat was empty and no-one was allowed to perish.

The conventional view which sees the story of the feeding as nothing more than an externalized historical event that took place, or is supposed to have taken place, two thousand years ago — this is how such a view feels about that story. One would be entering upon empty symbolism were one to try and interpret it within the meaning of C.F. Meyer's poem.

The kind of symbolism which considers actual historical events as mere allegory, and in so doing loses touch with the ground beneath our feet, is quite alien to our method of study. The gospels recount for us real historical happenings. But events of this kind are events in the world of external sense perception and at the same time in the world of the supersensible, the world of the spiritual and of the soul. There is a small part of heaven in every gospel story. A spiritual image, a supersensible form, a divine deed, slumbers in the detail that belongs to what is perceptible to the senses. To see only the external is materialism; to see only the spiritual is abstract symbolism.

Conventional theology looks only at the external event; the artist is prone to look at its soul, at what is visionary, at its image. A new kind of theology seeks to open a way to the image, to conjure the image out of matter. Our gospel studies set out to create this new kind of theology but without losing sight of historical actuality. To the extent that this aim is attained, theologian and artist will again become one, just as they were one in early Christian times. This kind of theology will become in the best sense 'popular.' Gospel scenes, freed from bewitchment, will surround the human soul like a gallery of living pictures. Seeing them, the soul will understand, and it will find religious nourishment. Some parts of these studies may seem hard to understand, for it is obvious that they contain unfamiliar and strange ideas. Yet I write them convinced that, within a matter of years, results of this new approach will become the accepted possession of souls in far flung communities. These views are through and through due to Rudolf Steiner's life work and we must be thankful for them. In earlier times, men could exist in legends of the saints as if in a world of buoyant emotion; so, in time to come, people will find the way back again to the gospel; they will be able to live in it as in a world of portrayals of life's true wisdom.

Two stories of feeding are recounted in the Gospels of Matthew and Mark; the feeding of the five thousand and the feeding of the four thousand, whereas the other two gospels, these of Luke and John, tell only of the feeding of the five thousand.

The duplication of the stories of the feeding conveys virtually nothing to conventional theology. For some it means that Jesus accomplished the miracle of increasing the bread not once but several times. For others it is a case of a 'doubling up' — retelling the same event twice. For a time some very curious literary and historical constructions appeared. For example, this is how Adolf von Harnack has explained why the second feeding, and whatever occurs between the two feedings, is lacking in St Luke. He relies on a common assumption that Luke, like Matthew, copied from Mark, and he suggests that, while copying, Luke's ink or maybe paper gave out just when he had completed the feeding of the five thousand. Later on, Luke confused the two stories in the original; so, instead of going straight on to the feeding of the four thousand after that of the five thousand, Luke had, while copying, missed out that part by mistake.

We shall see however that there are cogent spiritual reasons why the two first evangelists have both feedings while the two latter have only the feeding of the five thousand.

Let us concentrate on the difference between the numbers governing the two stories of the feeding. First, five thousand men are fed with five loaves and two fishes, and twelve baskets of fragments remain. Next, four thousand are fed on seven loaves and a few fish, and there are seven baskets over. Close observation of the relationship of these figures will give us much to think about. Seen externally, the miraculous power diminishes in every way from the first to the second feeding.

We have now reached a point at which it will be necessary to say something about number in the Bible. Modern man knows numbers only by counting them. The unit is the starting point. Every number expresses a certain sum of units. With the rise of the materialistic era, number became quantitative. But number was at one time qualitative. Every number was a qualitative unity, a 'configuration.' The difference between size and quantity which two different numbers express was less essential, if at the same time one felt the difference in the nature of each. The essential qualitative significance of individual numbers played an especially important role in the philosophy of Pythagoras. We shall try to set out, in connection with the explanations that Rudolf Steiner often gave, the difference between quantitative and qualitative number.

Let us consider the number three. If I think of it quantitatively, then I can start with a unit. I must then combine units such as that one in order to express the number three. To the qualitative view 'three' is in its own right a unity, an entity complete in itself. In this case the number indicates internal organization and the vitality of that unit, not external cumulativeness. If we wish to distinguish numbers qualitatively, then one number is not greater than another. In every number unity is present, conferring identity upon it. But the higher number has richer internal organization, it possesses a different configuration:

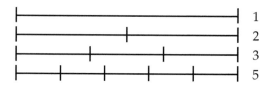

We feel ourselves constrained to represent the number not simply in lengths but in figures. Every number is a different entity, it expresses a different world secret. Numbers are the names of beings, they are not the mere indices of quantity.

A merely external, quantitative sense of number has made itself very much at home at the present time when money rules everything. To feel one's way into earlier, truer perceptions of number is going to be difficult for some people. But the Bible, like all ancient documents, rests on just such a basic understanding of numbers. Those five thousand and four thousand do not stand for so many people counted.

This, briefly, is its meaning. In the biblical view of the world man feels himself to be, as it were, set within a vast world week, consisting of seven world days. This does not mean the kind of day contained in modern thinking between sunrise and sunset; this is clear from the fact that the creation of the sun — ruler of the world of what we now call 'day' — takes place on the fourth day (Gen.1:14–19). The creation of the world, and the march of world history, each occupies seven vast world days. What happens on the third day is represented by the sign 3000. People of the fourth day are the 4000; those of the fifth day are the 5000. Of the seven world days, the fourth, being the middle one, plays an especially important part. There is an ancient tradition which we can still read about in the world's calendars. Christ is said to have been born four thousand years after the creation of the world. Enlightened people of our own time have thrown this tradition overboard as childish superstition. Modern people know from the findings of geology and archaeology that the age of the earth, and of the old cultures which preceded the rise of Christianity, is incalculable and that it exceeds the span of four thousand years more than a thousand times. And yet that old tradition is nevertheless right because the Christ became man in the year four thousand of world history. But that number has to be read differently, qualitatively and not quantitatively. It then means: the Christ became man at the very midpoint of time, on the world's middle day.

That kind of interpretation of number can be proved neither by mathematics nor by logic. We have to accept it as an hypothesis, to be tested against as many examples as possible. We should use it as a key to help us as we try to unlock closed doors. We could instance many an example from the books of the Bible where the fruitfulness of the interpretation of number expounded here is preserved. We shall confine ourselves to a few especially instructive passages from the Old Testament.

We should add that each of the seven world days had its own symbol from the starry heavens; this was because ever since the most ancient times the 'days' were calculated according to the passage of the sun in spring through one of the twelve constellations of the zodiac. The sun takes 2160 years to move from one constellation of the zodiac into the next. (We are speaking of the vernal equinox of the sun, that is, that part of the heavens at which the sun rises when spring begins. That vernal point moves from year to year. It moves into a different constellation at the end of every 2160 year span. After 12 × 2160 years, that is, a Platonic Year, the vernal point will have moved right around the heavens). So a world 'day' lasts 2160 years. The last move of the sun into a new constellation took place in AD 1413; the one before that was in 747 BC. The year 4000 lasted from 747 BC to AD 1413 and was the world's Middle Day. At that time the sun stood in the constellation

of Aries, otherwise the Lamb. The third day (3000) was in the sign of
the Taurus (the Bull), the fifth (5000), the one in which we are now living, is the sign of the Pisces (Fishes).

First day (1000) *c.* 7200–5000 BC   Sign of Cancer
Second day (2000) *c.* 5000–3000 BC   Sign of Gemini
Third day (3000) *c.* 3000–747 BC   Sign of Taurus
Fourth day (4000) *c.* 747 BC – AD 1413   Sign of Ram
Fifth Day (5000) *c.* AD 1413 – 3500   Sign of Pisces

Anthroposophy names these eras after the cultures that in each
case were the cultural bearers for humanity.

1. Ancient Indian Civilization   Cancer
2. Ancient Persian Civilization   Gemini
3. Egypto-Babylonian-Chaldean Civilization   Taurus
4. Graeco-Roman Civilization   Aries
5. Present Civilization   Pisces

Now for some examples.

While the children of Israel were wandering in the desert and while
Moses was on Mount Sinai receiving the inspiration of the law, the
people reverted to the worship of Egyptian idols; they set up the rites
of the Golden Calf (that is, Taurus). Egypt had led humankind
throughout the third world day, the era of the Bull. Its time had
expired. Moses had led the people of Israel out of Egypt under the sign
of the Ram, the sacrificial lamb, in order to prepare for the fourth day.
The people betrayed the lamb and turned back to the bull. They
should have belonged to the 4000, but they fell back to the 3000. So
Moses had to punish their guilt. And we are told (Exod.32:28): 'And
there fell of the people that day about three thousand men.' That three
thousand is what belonged to Egypt. No matter how we picture to ourselves the outward form of the punishment decreed by Moses, we can
in any case assume that the extermination of those three thousand to
be the extermination of Egypt among the people of Israel. The number
does not indicate how many were killed; it does indicate what Moses'
punishment destroyed.

A strangely uncompromising order was at one time given to Elijah.
He was to confirm three men in their offices: Hazael as king of Syria,
Jehu as king over Israel, and Elisha as his own successor as prophet.
'And him who escapes from the sword of Hazael shall Jehu slay; and
him who escapes from the sword of Jehu shall Elisha slay. Yet I will

leave seven thousand in Israel, all the knees that have not bowed to Baal, and every mouth that has not kissed him.' (1Kings 19:17f). At such words as these there rise before us all the bloody scenes of the Elisha and Jehu stories which it is so difficult to make sense of in the context of the sacred writings of the Old Testament.

A deeper understanding of the number seven thousand gives us the key. The seven thousand are people who belong to the end of time, those who have endured the judgment of the world which is world history itself. Much of humanity will fail to press on to the last hour and will perish earlier because it cannot keep pace with world history. Elijah the prophet is enjoined to prepare for the last hour of the world's course, to whip up humanity's most radical, most ineluctable will directed towards the future; on the other hand, those who fail to keep pace will fall into and suffer the abyss. Whosoever serves the future must oppose everything belonging to the past with undeviating and ruthless determination. Elijah's three successors are to root out the past from Israel because concern is for the seven thousand, who are the goal of earth's evolution. Once again we stress how externalized the gruesome death scenes are of the Jehu stories in the form in which they have evolved; also the way in which they should be understood.

Moses' task lies within the number four thousand; that of Elijah in the number seven thousand. Moses is to make ready the near future, Elijah the most distant future.

If we turn from there to the two stories of the feeding in the gospels, then a light is suddenly shed on the difference between the two events. The four thousand are contemporaries of the life of Christ. The five thousand were at the time not yet alive on earth; like the fifth world day, these were still at rest in the womb of the future. The spiritual world is the womb of the future from which flows all earthly destiny. The feeding of the five thousand is, then, a form of sowing for the future, a deed of Christ through which the germ is laid of something which is to come; of something to do with the future. In saying that, we perceptively touch the spiritual, the supersensible nature of the first story of the feeding. The Christ fulfils a mystery in the womb of the future, of the spiritual and divine world, in order thereby to provide in advance for humanity what is yet to come.

Who are the five thousand? What was at that time future has in our time become the present. *We*, the people of the present day, are living in the fifth world day. *We* are the five thousand!

Those mighty events of the midpoint of time, of the midpoint of world history and the mystery of Golgotha itself, have all of them become for us the past. We must look back into the past, into the world day that is now yesterday, in order to find the earthly life of Christ. The Christ who lived in an earthly body is not among us, is not our contemporary for we are not the four thousand; we are the five thousand. But it was for us that the Christ, while he still walked this earth, consummated a mystery; he introduced refreshment for the journey into our nature while we still sojourned unborn in the spiritual world, were still moving towards our earthly destiny. The treasure which the Christ at that time buried in us, we have now to raise from the depths of our own souls. The feeding of the five thousand has in our time to be proved true, to be justified.

There lies the profound truth of Conrad Ferdinand Meyer's poem; modern man experiences the miracle of the feeding as an immediately contemporary spiritual fact. What was once made to sink like a sun into the world's womb 'in luminous cloud-filled regions' is rising now.

What is the key to the question, why should the feeding of the bigger multitude be described first, and the feeding of the lesser one second? The key is linked to a general impression of ours that the feeding of the five thousand is more a supersensible event, while the feeding of the four thousand is an earthly contemporary one. We have here a growth of power, progress in the movement from the first to the second feeding. The feeding begins in heaven; it ends on earth. The mystery of that meal is fulfilled in heaven first, and then on earth; it incarnates, it passes along the same way as did the Christ when he became man. Light is shed at the same time on the circumstances that the last two evangelists (Luke and John) tell only of the feeding of the five thousand. From first to last the gospels lead upward, to higher and higher spheres. Luke and John tell only of the feeding which took place as a spiritual event in a spiritual world that contains the future.

We have so far disregarded details in the stories of the feeding. Anyone approaching us from the conventional view of the gospel stories will muster all the earthly detail in order to attack what we have so far advocated. He will feel that what we have been saying about the first feeding is an empty assertion, an interpretation derived from nothing more than a rather abstruse theory of number. And yet, just because of this example of a particular point of view, we must take special pains to see that individual features of the story are treated with scrupulous care, free from prejudice.

Now, there is one detail of vital importance which is clearly expressed in the gospel: the feeding of the five thousand took place as night was falling (Matt.14:15; Mark 6:31–35; Luke 9:12).

The feeding of the five thousand was an event of the night. The feeding of the four thousand was an event of day. How are we to imagine the night event? It is significant that all the gospels begin the story of the five thousand by telling how Jesus and his disciples withdraw from life's daytime pressures. The term 'desert' or 'desert place' indicates a withdrawn solitude of soul. Those indications are not to be taken as referring merely to externals, as becomes clear from contradictions arising when we really try to follow through such superficial interpretations. The disciples say, 'This is a desert place,' and that is followed immediately by, 'And he told the crowd to sit down on the grass' (Matt.14:19), and St John expressly adds, 'Now there was much green grass in that place' (John 6:10). The contradiction between desert and grass points from a merely earthly interpretation to a more inward one. Its meaning is withdrawal by Jesus and his disciples into the peace of their inmost souls.

St Mark's Gospel tells with special emphasis at the beginning of the story how Jesus and his disciples go into the desert. 'Come with me now to an intimate gathering in a lonely place where you can come to rest a little. For there were many coming and going, and they could not even find time to eat. So they went by ship to a lonely place by themselves.' (Mark 6:31). If we are to understand this aright, then we must conceive of it as a kind of transition into another form of consciousness, a form of meditative sleep. We could also read the same verses in this way: 'Jesus said to the disciples: Let us enter into the inmost places of our souls and let us leave the physical world behind us, and enter into the world of spirit in which you sojourn in sleep.' And even Jesus himself sought solitude of soul; he too left behind the shores of physicality in order to voyage forth onto the seas of spirit.

St John's Gospel seems to tell the story of the feeding quite differently: 'And Jesus went up on a mountain, and there he sat down with his disciples' (John 6:3). Once again we must admit that so long as we stay with the physical interpretation the scenes in St John and St Mark are totally at variance with each other. The contradiction falls away as we learn that the scenes are letters of a language describing things spiritual, things pertaining to the soul. The summit that Jesus and his disciples ascend is the summit of a state of consciousness that thrusts into the world of the spirit. It is night. The souls of Jesus and of the twelve rise in reverential unity and meditation into spiritual immensity.

The people who stream in crowds after the souls of Jesus and his disciples do not do so in clear consciousness; they follow with their faculties still earthbound. Jesus sets out in a boat '... but many saw and recognized them as they set off, and they hurried there on foot from all the towns, and even overtook them' (Mark 6:33). Jesus and the disciples are surrounded by the whole of humanity. 'And as he disembarked he saw a great crowd, and he was moved by compassion at the sight; for they were like sheep who have no shepherd, and he began to teach them many things' (Mark 6:34). That takes place in spiritual regions. Jesus sees the crowds pressing around him and the disciples, and he sees in them something to be fully realized only in the future, on earth. Humanity is to be leaderless, having no priests. Those souls pressing forward are the very people who are to be alive in the future, during the fifth world day, and as the five thousand they are to be a flock without a shepherd.

The spirituality of that moment is very clearly brought out by St John's Gospel in a few words: 'Now when Jesus lifted up his eyes ... (he) beheld a great crowd of people streaming towards him ...' (John 6:5). Lifting up the eyes is an act of transference to a higher state of consciousness, into spiritual vision.

But how are we to imagine that introductory earthly scene as being part of the whole? Jesus is in the company of his disciples away from the confusion of massed crowds, perhaps on some mountain top, at night, asleep. Not asleep perhaps in the accepted sense of loss of consciousness, rather in a kind of visionary sleep when souls, set free from the body, hold communion one with another, when they feel they are surrounded by the souls of future humanity.

Someone however may object: could not a detail so obviously of this earth as 'there was much grass in the place' be the refutation of a glib transference of the scene into spiritual regions? He could ask, why so detailed and vivid a description of the environment if all this is happening in the spirit?

This is the very detail that once again confirms our presentation. For as we have said, to the contradiction in the external scenery between desert and grass, we should also add the following: A person awake is full of destructive processes brought about by the activity of spirit and soul taking place in the waking body. While asleep, soul and spirit are outside the body; nevertheless, they play their part from without in its regeneration and refreshment; the body itself is taken over by processes of revitalizing growth. Life withers in the body of one who is awake; it blooms and sprouts in that of a sleeper. Rudolf Steiner has often told how, in the clairvoyant's supersensible vision, the body of a waking person resembles a parched field; that of a sleeper is like a green meadow. There is much grass in the place. There, the fruitfulness of night, restoring all that has been wasted during the day, reigns supreme.

The enigma of numbers

We come now to the secrets of numerology still present in the feeding stories, apart from the numbers four thousand and five thousand. In the case of the five thousand there are five loaves and two fishes available; in that of the four thousand there are seven loaves and some small fish. There are twelve baskets of fragments left after the first feeding and seven baskets after the second. In this connection literature has often pointed to the correspondence between these numbers and those of the starry heavens. The conclusion has been drawn — as it has been by Arthur Drews in his book on St Mark — that the gospel stories actually describe episodes among the constellations and stars; that is, the events in Jesus' life never really took place in history, that they are no more than legend — events which disguise astrological truths. It is true that right through the gospels distinct scenes in their proper sequence can be seen to correspond with the sun's repeated passage through the zodiac. Only a spiritual concept of the cosmos is able correctly to assess this without falling into Arthur Drew's error of judgment. Christ's life on earth was shared by the stars. It does not follow because stellar events are basic to the gospels that the Christ never lived. It does follow that the life of Jesus was unique, a cosmic portent, which took its course in perfect harmony with the world of stars and with the cosmos.

The heavenly belt of the zodiac comprises twelve constellations. Of these, seven invisibly rule the daytime sky; five are visible by night. The twelve constellations are the heavenly baskets, the heavenly loaves. A blessing of nourishment streams from them to earth. While the five thousand are being fed by night there are five loaves in the heavens, that is, the five night-time constellations. For the feeding of the four thousand there are seven loaves in the heavens, the seven constellations of day.

At the time of the mystery of Golgotha the sun rose in the constellation of Aries, the Ram. The constellation of Aries was the first one of that day. Pisces, the Fishes, was the last of the five constellations of night. The constellation of Pisces was slowly drawing near to the horizon. The era of Pisces was approaching, although it was as yet the time of the Lamb. Christ, the Lamb of God, was represented in the catacombs by early Christians by the sign of the Fish — in anticipation of the future. The Greek word for 'Fish' Ἰχθυς *(Ichthus)* stood for the name of Christ, since every letter of that word formed an initial of the title of the Christ:

Ἰησους Χριστος Θεου ʽυιος σωτηρ *(Iésous Christos Theou huios, sótér)*
Jesus Christ of God the Son, Saviour

The constellation of Pisces (Fishes) was, at the time of Christ, embarking on its era; it was moving slowly from the constellations of the night into those of the day. Among the five night pictures there were the two fishes, but of these already a small part was already with the seven 'loaves.' The five thousand were fed by night; there were 'two fishes.' But for the second feeding, there were seven loaves and 'a few small fishes.'

Twelve full baskets of fragments were left after feeding the five thousand. Those twelve starry baskets that are never emptied, no matter how much they give, reveal all their riches by night. There are of course no more than five to be seen shining in the heavens. But then, by night, human souls are outside their bodies by means of whose eyes one sees the external splendour of the stars; the souls are themselves part of the sphere, of the realm of stars. Nor are they deprived of the seven daytime constellations, even though those five are below the horizon. All twelve starry baskets are open, all twelve of them are brimful, even after the meal is over.

Seven baskets remain after the four thousand have been fed; as many baskets as there were loaves. Seven constellations send down their blessing from heaven even though their brilliance is outshone by the sun. The seven baskets that by day are above the horizon will not be emptied; they will remain as seven filled baskets.

We are going to leave a more detailed discussion of the course of events in the feeding of the four thousand for the present. As for the five thousand, events from the opening scene to the feeding itself are not hard to follow. Christ creates a new link between earthly humanity and the starry world. People are sheep without a shepherd; they are leaderless, they have no priests. That is why they lack the bread of the stars. Earth and heaven have lost their connection. The flock without any shepherds has to feed itself on earthly food because there is no-one any more to give them bread of the stars. The Christ makes it possible again for heavenly bread to be given them in the future. Here we reach a very significant aspect of the miracle of the loaves and fishes. That feeding is regarded as a rule in far too primitive a light as a deed of the Christ alone. But the story is in fact told as being in a sense a deed of the twelve apostles. When the disciples say 'They have nothing to eat' the Christ replies, 'You give them something to eat' (Matt.14:16; Mark 6:37; Luke 9:13). Having broken the bread and blessed it, he gives it to the disciples, and it is they who feed the multitude. By feeding the five thousand Christ inaugurated Christian priesthood and in so doing he saved the flock without a shepherd; he rebuilt for earthly man the heavenly life; he opened the starry baskets.

At the same time, the meaning of that number, of the 'twelve,' comes to life in a marvellous way. There are twelve baskets of bread standing open among the stars. Twelve filled baskets remain after the meal. Twelve apostles surround the Christ, forming a closer ring inside the wider circle of the satisfied multitude. The Christ, surrounded by his apostles, is an earthly reflection of the sun at the centre of the zodiac. And, after the feeding, are not the twelve apostles in a sense the twelve baskets of bread that are left over? It is they who bear the bread of Christ through space and time in inexhaustible fullness of blessing. They carry the blessing of the deeds of Christ out of the fourth world day, when the Christ walked earth himself, into the fifth day, the era of the five thousand and, beyond that, into the most distant future. Humanity is no longer a flock without a shepherd. Apostolic priesthood had its beginning in that night of the feeding.

A third feeding with the Risen One

Let us turn to another story of a meal, one that the disciples celebrated with the Risen Christ. It took place on the shores of the lake, after the disciples' fishing expedition, and it is told in John 21. One way of verifying the ideas we are setting forth here would be to show the way in which those truths confirm each other, the way in which most relationships become apparent between passages of the gospel that have hitherto seemed quite disparate.

Seven of the disciples are together. At Peter's instigation they set out by night onto the Sea of Tiberias, but they fail to catch even one single fish. Towards morning the Risen Christ is standing on the shore. He asks the disciples, who have not recognized him, 'Children, have you nothing to eat?' They have to admit that they have none. But at the word of Christ they cast their nets once more. Immediately the net is filled with fish, so that they are unable to draw it in. It is then that John recognizes Christ and he communicates that recognition to Peter. Peter can restrain himself no longer; he wraps his cloak about himself and plunges into the water in order to reach the shore and his Lord the more quickly. The others run their little ships right up the beach. There they see fish and bread laid out on glowing coals ready for the meal. To this they add the fish which their latest catch has yielded. These number one hundred and fifty three. Christ calls them to the meal. Recognizing him, they obey the summons. From the hand of Christ they receive the communion of bread and fish.

In chapter 5 we considered the experience of the disciples of the miracle of walking on the sea as an experience of awakening. As they return from the sea of the spiritual world, on which their souls were voyaging in sleep, and as they approach the shore of the physical and the sense perceptible, the disciples become aware of the Risen Christ. Peter hastens towards the Lord, just as he did at the walking on the waves; this time it is because he is quicker than the others to pass back into his own body and to reach the shore. He is awake sooner. For now the Christ has changed the scene of revelation. He no longer walks on water; instead he stands on land. While he was still in the body and with the disciples on earth, his true being was in the spirit, that is, on the sea. Now that the Christ is no longer in the body, after his death on the cross, a normal person would sensibly seek him in the spiritual world. But in fact the essential being of Christ is more than ever to be sought on that earth for which he sacrificed himself and which he has begun to illumine from within.

Ever since Good Friday, Christ left the daily life of the disciples. He went from them because of his own death. Would they find him in the life of night? Would their souls in sleep, free of their bodies, encounter Christ, who had been freed from his own body by death? That is the question that presents itself to the souls of the disciples, as they join Peter in his night time fishing. But even out there, on the sea, they are left all alone. The Christ does not come to them walking on the waves, and they catch nothing in their nets. By themselves they lack the strength to carry any achievements from the realm of night into that of day. With Christ dead, they are impoverished both by land and sea. The portal of awakening will reveal that their poverty is to persist on the water. And then, as day dawns and as they approach land, Christ appears to them on the shore.

That question 'Have you nothing to eat?' makes them aware of their own condition. They have no food for the spiritual infant in their own being, no food for their higher nature, still so frail, whose desire it is to get back from water to land. Christ had been the food for their inward being, for the child within them. He had left them. The child within them had no food. The tender young spirit-self of man was in danger. It was not yet able to draw nourishment for itself from the nocturnal sea. The fishing nets remained empty. But then, from the earthly world of the physical, a light shone out towards those souls that were about to wake up. Those souls were making ready to re-enter the physical world. It was the light that the Christ had kindled in all earthly existence by his activity on earth, by his deed of death-in-life on Golgotha. They did not recognize the vision of light shining for them on the shore in the half-light of daybreak. But that light enkindled in them the strength to cast their nets once more. And now there is plenty to eat for the little children. The vision of the shining earth enables souls, their weakness notwithstanding, to accept treasure of the spirit world. Sleep becomes fruitful thanks to the transformation wrought by Christ on earth. Those able to unite themselves with Christ receive strength from him to bring back to the shores of daytime life treasures of the world of spirit. Christianity will in future justify itself for many people by the manner of waking up. The morning hour will have Christ-gold in its mouth in a very deep and spiritual sense.

There are one hundred and fifty three fish. The disciples find a meal prepared on land. They add to it what they have brought along in their nets. The Risen Christ shares food between them. The child within, the higher man, accepts the sacrament.

What does the number one hundred and fifty three have to tell us? Old theology, associated with the archaic experience of number, has attempted some strange and varied interpretations. We read in Thomas Aquinas' *Catena Aurea* (the Golden Chain) his explanation of the gospels, linking up with the early Christian church fathers. The number one hundred and fifty three is the sum of all the numbers from one to seventeen. The number seventeen is made up of ten and seven, the numbers of perfection and revelation. I quote this interpretation here as an example of an earlier kind of thinking about number, quite different from today's concepts of it. For Thomas Aquinas and his contemporaries, that interpretation was wholly satisfying, whereas to modern people it is rather a hieroglyph which only deepens the puzzle of that number one hundred and fifty three.

The spiritual significance of a number such as this one can undoubtedly be expressed in many different ways. However, the inward link between the feeding of the five thousand and the disciples' draught of fishes after the Resurrection enables us quite clearly to discern one aspect of what the number means.

The starry heavens, regarded as a night time spiritual sea, can be divided into twelve constellations, just as the year is divided into twelve months. As each month is divided into a number of days, the year totalling 365 days, so the twelve constellations of the zodiac can be divided into a total of 365 aeons. Five constellations belong to the night. We can see that these are the five loaves of the feeding of the five thousand. Between them, they have one hundred and fifty three aeons, with three constellations having thirty one aeons, and two constellations having thirty aeons, or days, ascribed to them. The constellation of Pisces (the Fishes) had at the time not yet dawned. It was potent just below the threshold of waking, daytime consciousness. The constellation of the Fishes was the starry gateway that leads from night to day. It imprinted its own character upon the night's achievement. The Christ was to enable humanity to carry that over into day on waking. This converts the one hundred and fifty three aeon-powers contained in the five bread-baskets of the night into the same number of 'little fish.' The one hundred and fifty three fishes are the same to the hour of dawn, of waking up, as what the five loaves and the two fishes are in the story of the feeding of the five thousand.

The ideas developed here will be of great religious importance when people no longer feel that those ideas are unfamiliar and strange, and when humanity begins again to take account naturally of supersensible and invisible cosmic forces. People of our own time will be struck by the feeding of the five thousand and by the draught of the one hundred and fifty three fish, feeling that it concerns us intimately. Is the starry bread, is the power of the fishes, to remain buried in us? The miracle of the feeding will rise from the depths of oblivion as an experience of the immediate present. The fullness of grace of the spiritual bread will replace the frailty and the lack of direction in present day souls, in the flock without a shepherd. The child within the human being will be made strong. The sacrament of the five thousand will be vouchsafed to them; the Christ is passing through our era, bestowing gifts. There will be those who from their own experience will say:

> The Spirit spoke: Look up! ... In luminous cloud-filled regions
> I saw the Lord break bread for the Twelve,
> And heard him speak words of love.
> Reaching far out, above their heads, his all-embracing gesture ...
> There all the people lay on ample sheaves.
> No seat was empty and no-one was allowed to perish.

The feeding of the four thousand

The feeding of the four thousand compared with that of the five thousand has occupied a rather unimportant place in peoples' awareness. Concepts commonly associated with the feeding of the five thousand are more justified than they would be if applied to the other episode. If we imagine the Christ surrounded by his disciples, physically present before an actual crowd of people, bestowing upon them supersensible food — then such a scene would be appropriate to the feeding of the four thousand. There was no head count of the four thousand present; these made up a multitude of the contemporaries of Christ and were fed by him. The actual number of that crowd may have been greater or less; the question arises how are we to understand the miracle of the increase of loaves? In our fifth study we touched on the fact that we are not concerned here with a physical increase. Not that the Christ would have been unable to bring about such a thing. But it lay neither in the intention nor in the guiding principles of the Christ to perform tricks bordering on black magic. If the materialistic view of the miracle of the loaves and fishes is right, then the Christ must have succumbed, at least subsequently, to the temptation to turn stones into bread.

We are indeed concerned with an actual, a truly earthly scene in the feeding of the four thousand; but there is no question of feeding with physical bread, of which more is left over than there was at the beginning. We have already suggested that we are to read into those numbers — the seven loaves and the seven baskets of fragments — that the four thousand were fed in broad daylight on the bread of starry forces. In order to bring the scene of that meal quite vividly before us, we shall have to follow up the nature of that bread.

What kind of bread was it that the Christ, through the disciples, used to feed the people? We find a clear answer if we make use of a key which has hitherto been virtually unknown but which has several times been of service to us, and which has led us to significant solutions: the key of composition.

We shall look into the Gospel of St Mark and there study the passages that occur between the feeding of the five thousand and the four thousand. There are three scenes for us:

1. Jesus and the Pharisees
2. Jesus and the Syrophoenician Woman
3. Jesus and the deaf and dumb man.

The Pharisees see Jesus' disciples eating bread without first carrying out the ritual washing of hands prescribed by the law. Jesus says to them: 'It's splendid the way that you nullify the commandment of

God in order to enforce your own traditions! ... In this way you make the tradition which you have received superior to the divine word.' (Mark 7:9–13). This scene leads us into a Judaism of the fourth world day, a Judaism that has lost the word during the era of the four thousand. We could entitle the story 'The Lost Word.'

We next see Jesus in a pagan region, in the borderlands of Tyre and Sidon, the land of Baal and Astarte; here the divine word was perverted to the use of black magic. Jesus was still able to converse with those who had lost the word, the *Logos*, but he had to avoid those among whom the *Logos* was being misused. He declines to act on behalf of the 'dogs.' He wishes to act for the 'children.' The Christ is able to speak to the Syrophoenician woman only because she turns with all her heart towards the true Word. 'For the sake of this word, go your way; the demon has left your daughter.' (Mark 7:29). He heals possession due to perversion of the *Logos* by that race. We could call the story 'Of the Perversion of the Word.'

Finally, the healing of the deaf and dumb man sets forth in an externalized picture the recovery of the Word. The external healing of deafness and dumbness corresponds to an inner recovery of the Word as heard and spoken by the disciples within their souls. In restoring the outer word to the sick man, Christ restores the inward Word to the disciples. The external process of healing is reflected in the souls of the disciples as an inward healing process. Just as the Christ restored life by the solemn mantric words, *Talitha Kumi*, to Jairus' daughter and at the same time to his disciples, so he gave back the Word to the deaf and dumb man by the solemn mantric word, *Ephphatha*, and in so doing also gave it back to the disciples.

The feeding of the four thousand follows on directly from the scene of the deaf and dumb man. The bread that feeds the people is revealed by the inward structure of the stories as being the sequel of the story that precedes it. The bread is the Word that Christ and his disciples speak to the people. And so the nourishing power of the Word unfolds. The healing of the deaf and dumb man opened not his ears alone, but also the ears of all people. The conclusion of the story of the healing of the deaf and dumb man, leading as it does into the story of the loaves and fishes, is especially obvious: 'And he told them to say nothing to anyone about it. But the more he forbade it, the more they proclaimed it. They were beside themselves beyond all measure and said, "He has done great deeds; to the deaf he gives their hearing, to the dumb he gives their speech".' (Mark 7:36f).

We can see a wildfire of the Word, of hunger for the Word, passing through the people. It is like a 'word wave' emanating from the healing of the deaf and dumb man. Jesus forbids talk about that cure, and the word wave spreads out all the more. In order to understand how that is we only need to follow the healed deaf and dumb man himself: he was quite unable to obey Christ's command since, even if he is silent about the cure, every word he speaks and every word he hears are living testimony to the deed of Christ. The new word, the Word of Christ, speaks out of him no matter what he is saying. On every side human souls perceive the new word's currents of strength. They can feel the dryness, the aridity and hunger of their own souls all the more keenly as they compare their own old, dried up words with the new enkindling Word. The people feel — we are deaf, we are the speechless ones. But the Christ makes the deaf to hear and the dumb to speak. And so the people come streaming towards the Christ, their souls wide open to the Word. Christ sinks into the open souls his Word, his own *Logos* being and World Word; he unites them all.

The people are satisfied, right down into the physical, by the Word wherein the baskets of star bread open up for them. The Word becomes bread for them. That is the meaning of the feeding of the four thousand.

Christ and the Pharisees: The lost word
Christ and the Syrophoenician woman: The perverted word.
The healing of the deaf and dumb man: The word returned.
The feeding of the four thousand: The new word becomes bread

The feeding of the five thousand

The feeding of the five thousand is a kind of central point of the gospel insofar as it represents the activity of the Christ among humankind. It is the middle one of the seven miracles in St John's Gospel and it reveals an inexhaustible wealth of mysteries. We shall be referring many times to the place occupied by the story in the gospel as a whole. For the present we shall indicate one absolutely central mystery which finds expression very clearly in the wordless gesture of composition.

The sequence of events has now passed from the phase of personal Christianity towards the community (in John the three miracles of Cana, of the nobleman's son, the cure of the man at the pool of Bethesda; in Matthew, the centurion's servant, the healing of the man sick of the palsy in Capernaum, and Jairus' daughter). That feeding is the sacred meal, the sacrament of community. The individual is led out beyond himself in that he is accepted as part of the great body of Christ, through the bread of life. What in fact is 'community?'

The gospel reveals the answer to this question: it is a mystery. It does this in the passage where it leads into the temple of the sacrament, into the miracle:

1. Jesus in Nazareth
2. The mission of the twelve
3. The beheading of John the Baptist
4. The return of the twelve and the feeding of the five thousand.

In Nazareth Christ can do no 'mighty' works among people who are related to him by blood. The step has got to be taken from family to community, from the community of blood to the community of the spirit. The circle of the twelve disciples is the beginning of the community of spirit taking shape around the Christ. It is the original nucleus of the Christian Church. The brotherhood of the twelve takes the place of the ancestral city of Nazareth. 'Then he called the twelve to him and began to send them out in pairs; he gave them authority over the unclean spirits ... And they went out and by their proclamation they called on the people to change their hearts and minds, and they drove out many demons and anointed many sick people with oil and healed them.' (Mark 6:7–13). Blood relationships in Nazareth render it impossible for Christ himself to achieve mighty deeds. Those related to him in the spirit are able from that time on to do deeds together with Christ. They can now do what hitherto only Christ could do.

But now, the gospel having spoken of the complete powers of the apostles, we have simply to go on reading what follows in the gospel. The art of continuity is reading with a deep sense for the sequences of composition.

And King Herod [Antipas] heard of it, for Jesus' name had become known, and he said, 'John the Baptist has risen from the dead, that is why such world-powers work through him.'

> Others said, 'He is Elijah;' yet others said that he was a
> prophet or like one of the prophets. But when Herod heard
> that he said, 'He whom I beheaded, John, has risen.'
> (Mark 6:14–16).

There follows the detailed account of the drama of John the
Baptist's death, of the blood-soaked head in the charger. The gospel
goes on:

> And the apostles gathered around Jesus again and told him
> everything that they had done and taught. And he said to
> them, 'Come with me now to an intimate gathering in a lonely
> place where you can come to rest a little.' (Mark 6:30f).

There follows the feeding of the five thousand. It is of the utmost
importance that at this juncture it is the disciples who accomplish the
feeding:

> And he took the five loaves and the two fish, lifted up his soul
> to the Spirit, blessed and broke the loaves and gave them to
> the disciples, so that they should share them out to the people
> (Mark 6:41).

There is hardly another passage in the gospel in which the language of composition rises to a gesture so exalted: why should the
drama of John's death be inserted between the mission of the twelve
and their return, between deeds of healing by the twelve out in the
world and their deed of feeding as they gather round the Christ? What
has John the Baptist to do so intimately in the circle of the twelve?
When Herod hears about the activity of Christ's disciples he says, John
is risen from the dead. That is why the Christ, together with his disciples, is doing what he does. It can often happen in the gospels that
opposing characters such as Herod utter very deep truths.

Here we have shown to us one of the most momentous events in
the history of heavenly regions, interwoven with the story of earth. It
is shown us by the gospel in its own chaste language. While John the
Baptist lay bound in prison, his soul felt cut off in endless yearning
from what was going on in the neighbourhood of the Christ. He felt he
had to send messengers. Nothing on this earth drew his soul as did the
mystery of the Christ become man, and of what was happening
around him. And then the hand of Herodias the Sorceress reached out
for his soul. But the devotion and longing of John's soul for the company surrounding the Christ was far mightier than the powers of

Herodias. As Herodias held in her hands the charger with the blood-soaked head, she was powerless to bind to herself her victim's soul. The soul of John was where no prison could restrain him; it was in the group around Christ. Twelve men formed that group about the Christ. A thirteenth was present in spiritual form, invisible, freed from the body; it was the Baptist. He no longer had a human body, and had to take part in earthly life through the circle of the twelve around Christ, of whom some were deeply devoted to him for they had once been his disciples. Instead of being served by a single body — that body which Herodias had destroyed — a whole community of human beings now ministered to him; the group of twelve became the vessel for his participation in earth's destiny.

The circle of twelve from then on gained a protector, a helper, an angel to hover above them in spiritual regions. A significant change for them took place on that account. A link was created between them and the world above. They began to live from out of the spirit. That made them a spiritual community, able to achieve more than the sum of its individual members could have done.

If nowadays a group of people were to experience the mystery of community, they would probably say, 'A good spirit watched over us on this day.' We may say such things without thinking much about them. What do we mean by 'spirit' in these days of abstractions? We are putting into words a truth more profound than we ourselves realize. For wherever there is indeed a sense of community, it can come about only because a good spirit, a beneficent genius, has come from heaven in order to raise a human group to be his vessel and body. It is impossible to experience a sense of community except when we have been fed and nourished from above, from out of the spirit. Communities do not originate from below; they invariably originate by way of an exalted mystery. There is always a miracle, an instance of the spirit world sinking into the world of earth. There is community wherever a group of people become the body of some exalted spiritual being.

When Christ sent forth his disciples he linked them to the world of spirit, making of them a community. In giving them authority to do his deeds, he bestowed on them 'his own angel,' that is, John the Baptist. He gave them John to be their leader, a helper on high, the soul within their group. The drama of John belongs to the mission and spiritual arming of the disciples by the Christ. That is why the story stands between their being sent out and their return. Above the feeding of the five thousand hovers the helping angelic being of John the Baptist, as if he were holding the basket of loaves from which the apostles served the people. The presence of John turns that meal into a sacrament of community, a celebration of the Holy Grail.

The proximity of those two stories to each other — the beheading of John and the feeding of the five thousand — becomes a splendid revelation of the most profound world symbols. Herodias, with the charger in which lies the blood-soaked head of John, is the black magician lusting to compel the spirit of John into serving that power; it is the power of the Antichrist mystery. The dish with the severed head is the black grail, the Anti-Grail.

The disciples — the circle around Christ with John hovering above them while they feed the people with the bread of life — these are the true company of the Grail. The white Grail, the luminous bread of Christ, is sown in the soul of all humankind as seed for the future. The two confront each other: the lust for personal powers (Herodias) and the mystery of Christian community (the Twelve); the Anti-Grail and the Grail of Christ.

By pointing to an Old Testament story of feeding, liberal theology has often sought to unmask the story of the feeding of the five thousand as legend. After the death of Elijah, his disciple Elisha feeds a large number of men with a small amount of bread. 'A man came from Baal-shalishah, bringing the man of God bread of the first fruits, twenty loaves of barley, and fresh ears of grain in his sack. And Elisha said, "Give to the men, that they might eat." But his servant said, "How am I to set this before a hundred men?" So he repeated, "Give them to the men, that they may eat, for thus says the Lord, They shall eat and have some left".' (2Kings 4:42f). The idea was to show up the New Testament story as an imitation of the one in the Old Testament and thereby to reveal its legendary character.

Actually, we are here touching on profound depths of interdependence between the Old and the New Testament. We shall indicate them here only briefly in order to enlarge upon them on later occasions.

In the Old Testament, Elijah is what John the Baptist is in the New. Elijah falls victim to Jezebel and her assistant, King Ahab. John the Baptist is the victim of Herodias and of her assistant, Herod. Forces of the anti-Grail bestir themselves and reach for the angel in man. Outwardly, success is theirs. Elijah, identical in his earthly form with Naboth, is destroyed by Jezebel, just as John the Baptist is destroyed by Herodias. But the spirit of Elijah and the spirit of John continue in their spheres of activity — the bestowal of spirituality. In ascending to heaven, Elijah casts his mantle on Elisha; he gives him his own soul's strength; he continues his world task through his disciple. John the Baptist hovers above the group of twelve messengers of Christ. He continues his activity through them. Elijah makes possible the feeding through Elisha; John brings about the feeding of the five thousand through the twelve apostles. Anti-Grail powers reach out for the Grail, but the Grail is victorious and opens its gift-bestowing fullness to starving humanity; it is the Bread of Life. Here is no case of the New Testament miracle of feeding being rendered insignificant; on the contrary, we are gazing right into the story of the Grail, of that Holy Supper which continues through all time. We learn to recognize the character — both eternal and present — of the sacrament of bread.

CHAPTER EIGHT

The Parables in the Gospels

The words of the *Chorus Mysticus* in which Goethe's *Faust* ends are like a heavenly stairway. They enable earth's soul to rise into the opened heavens — earth, revealed in the light of heaven, makes known its meaning; all things that fade are only parables; heaven reveals its own upliftingly-loving soul:

> Eternal womanhood draws us to the heights
>
> All things that pass are no more than parables
>
> The unattainable becomes achievement here
>
> The indescribable is here fulfilled,
>
> Eternal womanhood draws us to the heights.

There can only be true parables beneath a heaven revealed. The lettering of earthly creation lights up, becomes legible in the down-streaming rays of exalted worlds. If we know nothing of the supersensible world, then we cannot really know the parables; we cannot understand true parables such as those of the gospels.

As long as we know only the world of thoughts and ideas, rather than that of actual supersensible beings and forces — just so long are we able to advance only as far as allegory, as far as simile, or even to pictorial representation of a thought. We cannot attain to the true parable. Adolf Jülicher's two-volume work on the parables of Jesus has been accepted in the course of the last few decades by Protestant theology as epoch-making. Jülicher declared himself opposed to that 'allegorical interpretation' of the parables which he discerned in all earlier theology. He found one major thought rendered visible in each parable. This idea made the task of the student that of finding the intermediate point of comparison. To Jülicher, individual features of a parable recede, being insignificant compared to the idea which he asserts is going to illustrate, to bring home, the parable. This accounts for discrepancies in details. He considers the parable of the treasure hidden in a field and the parable of the pearl of great price to be paired; they are supposed to illustrate the inestimable value of the kingdom of heaven. There are objections and discrepancies in the detail, but the details are not important. The parables illustrate one and the same idea: just as any man will gladly, joyously, renounce all lesser things, in fact all he has, for the sake of some fortunate possession (for example, a buried treasure, or a pearl), even so must everyone give up all in return for the kingdom of heaven, that is, in order to enter it. 'In the drastic form of these paired parables Jesus sought not so much to create a polemic against Jewish national expectations, as to spur his own followers to realize through utter and joyous sacrifice, the immeasurable worth of the kingdom of heaven.'

An interpretation such as this one does not attain to the true character of the parables any more than did the allegorical one; it makes no advance on it. Its deficiency becomes apparent because there is no perceptible difference between these two parables to which we have referred, that is, between the parable of the hidden treasure and that of the pearl. The allegorical interpretation sets out to deduce from the picture a sum total of thoughts and ideas. What we have presented as the Jülicher concept is concerned to discover a single idea, a single thought. The pictures in this way retain several options. You can build up at will quite a number of pictorial disguises and similes. Jülicher is of the opinion that Jesus' intention was to impress the same idea on people over and over again but in ever new parables.

But, no sooner are the gospel parables read 'beneath an open sky,' that is, within the context of a view of the universe that acknowledges a supersensible world — than their essential divinity reveals itself, right down into the smallest detail. The picture is, generally speaking, a letter of the script in which the supersensible can be expressed. The problem is to learn to understand this pictorial language, just as one learns to read and understand any unfamiliar language. A child learns letters at school. The task of reading the pictorial language of the parables is a task for a theology aware of the supersensible. Those who can stay 'in the picture' while reading the parables will advance the furthest. They will be able to do without any interpretation which only leads right out of the picture into abstract thinking. The 'picture' is not an illustration, nor is it a 'clarification' of some thought; it is the name and expression of a supersensible fact; and that means it is a parable. All things that pass are only parables. He who knows supersensible reality recognizes in the lettering of evanescent existence the forms and figures of the spiritual.

There is, however, one more key required to the gospel's parables, as well as a feeling for the picture itself; namely, a feeling for the sequence of those pictures. Pictures that are transparencies to spiritual reality, together with the sequences of pictures that lead towards spiritual experience — these are the two keys to understanding the parables of Jesus. They are the pictorial alphabet of a heavenly language. The composition of those pictures, the way in which they follow one another, show us the rungs of a ladder.

To begin with, it is good to turn our attention to the second of our two keys, that of the composition of the parables. It is easy to see that for the most part the parables of the gospels are grouped together or at least that they belong together, even when they are distributed through a larger portion of the gospels. They are grouped so as to go forward step by step. If we can recognize the group and the series of parables, then it becomes easier to read the pictorial script.

We are going to discuss three such groupings or series, but without entering upon the details. We hope to contribute to the creation of a general view of the parables and in that way to a feeling for their nature.

There are seven parables altogether in Matthew 13:

1. The sower
2. The tares and the wheat
3. The grain of mustard seed
4. The leaven
5. The treasure hid in a field
6. The pearl of great price
7. The net cast into the sea

The next series consists of seven important and interconnected parables which wind their way through the second half of the Gospel of St Matthew. These are going to be the point of departure for a later study of the structure in Matthew between the Transfiguration and the beginning of the Passion:

    1. The greater debt and the lesser debt (18:23–35)

    2. Equal wages for unequal labour in the vineyard
       (20:1–16)

    3. The two sons in the vineyard (21:28–31)

    4. The messengers of the lord of the vineyard (21:33–44)

    5. The royal wedding (22:1–14)

    6. The wise virgins and the foolish virgins (25:1–13)

    7. The talents (25:14–30).

Last of all we shall look at the five parables which stand side by side in chapters 15 and 16 of St Luke:

    1. The Lost Sheep (15:1–7)

    2. The Piece of Silver (15:8–10)

    3. The Prodigal Son (15:11–32)

    4. The Unjust Steward (16:1–12)

    5. Dives and Lazarus (16:19–31)

The first seven parables in Matthew

Chapter 13 of Matthew's Gospel comes at an important stage in the course of the gospel as a whole. It leads on to the feeding of the five thousand in chapter fourteen, to the founding of the spiritual fellowship, to the mystery of communion. To that end, humankind must have outgrown the narrowly personal stance which is the region of egotism. Human beings must have grown beyond personal ties with blood relationship if they are to mature to membership of the fellowship of the spirit.

The seven parables form a whole, and as such they are held together by a framework which renders clearly recognizable the theme of the group. We pass from blood relationship to a spiritual relationship. The chapter of parables is directly preceded by this scene:

> While he was still speaking to the crowd, see, his mother and
> his brothers stood outside and wished to speak to him. And
> someone said to him, 'See, your mother and your brothers are
> standing outside and wish to speak to you.' And he replied to
> the man who was speaking to him, 'Who is my mother and
> who are my brothers?' And he stretched out his hand
> towards his disciples and said, 'See, my mother and my
> brothers. Whoever acts out of the will of my Father in the

heavens is my brother and my sister and my mother.'
(Matt.12:46–50).

The seven parables are introduced by the words, 'On that day Jesus went out of the house ...' (13:1). They are therefore closely linked with those words of Jesus concerning right relationship. After the last of the parables, the gospel goes on:

And it happened: When Jesus had finished his series of parables he went on and came to his home town. There he taught
in the synagogue in such a way that the people were beside
themselves with amazement and said, 'From where does he
get this wisdom and the power for such deeds? Is he not the
carpenter's son, and is not his mother called Mary? Are not
James and Joseph and Simon and Judas his brothers, and are
not his sisters all well known to us? From where does he get
the power for all this?' His way of being caused confusion
amongst the people. (Matt.13:53–57).

Jesus could find no understanding in the city of his own tribe, of his own blood relationship. What was his to bestow called for might-ier souls, for souls more open than those to be found in the confined circles of family and tribe. Bitter words are forced from him: 'A prophet is nowhere less accepted than in his home town and in his own house. And he was not able to do many deeds of the spirit there, for the hearts of the people were weak' (Matt.13:57f).

The same things that are put into words by the two scenes that introduce the parables are also presented in a different way by the sit-uation at the beginning of the chapter:

On that day Jesus went out of the house to the sea and there he
sat down. Then a great crowd of people streamed towards
him, until he eventually had to get into a boat and sit down in
it; and the whole crowd stood on the shore. And he said many
things to them in parables. (Matt.13:1–3).

The gospel contains not only the verbal parables, as Jesus spoke them, but also those enacted in the life of Jesus. Novalis says: 'The life of a truly saintly person should be consistently symbolical.' This is a truth, a key, essential to understanding the life of Jesus. That unassum-ing scene, when Jesus passed from house to sea, was a parable which by its exalted gesture speaks of destiny and providence. The Christ was leading people from the sea to the land and so into the house (see

Chapter 6) as he pointed them from the generalities of pre-individual existence to ego-life; a life rich in challenge. But then came the step when he would lead the human being, who had in solitude become an individuality, out beyond himself into the spiritual community which embraces all humanity. He moves from the constriction of the house out to sea. The people on land see him seated in the boat against the background of sea, and are enlarged by that sight. The parables told by Christ from the boat were to widen their sensibilities, to carry men and women away from ties that had bound men of old. The parables were able to do this while he spoke from the boat, and later on to his disciples within the house. The motto of the seven parables could well be 'out of the house to the sea.'

Let us now approach the parable images themselves. We will then recognize that those pictures portray a journey that leads to the sea. From the first to the fifth parable we are in a field, on land. The sower casts his seed upon the land; the treasure seeker digs deep down into the field. We have the land in the second last parable, the pearl of great price has been raised from the depths of the sea; the net full of fish is drawn from sea to shore. We become aware of progress from land to sea even in the sequence of scenes.

It is important to perceive the distinction between the first four and the three last parables. The separation is brought about in the thirteenth chapter by these words: 'And he dismissed the crowd and went into the house. And his disciples came to him ...' (Matt.13:36). Jesus then gives his disciples the interpretation of the second parable, that of the tares and the wheat, just as he had previously done with the parable of the sower. The three last parables are directed to the disciples and he speaks to them within the house.

The first four parables he gives the people speaking from the sea. The last three he gives his disciples speaking inside the house. It is of paramount importance to the understanding of the gospel to make that distinction. What Christ says within the circle of the twelve must be understood differently from the way in which we understand what he says to the people. We will have to consider this in greater depth when we discuss the Sermon on the Mount. Hitherto that difference has virtually never been made or understood and this led to many distortions and misunderstandings of the religious message and of its feeling.

Perhaps no two parables have been chosen so often as texts of sermons as have those which Jülicher designates as a pair, that is, the treasure in the field, and the pearl of great price. But, if you take them out of the context of all seven of the parables, if you overlook the fact that they, together with the seventh (the fish net) represent teaching bestowed exclusively within the intimate circle of the disciples — then all too easily they can bring about the very reverse of what is their intention in the gospel itself: They could inculcate egoism (for religious egoists do exist!) whereas their purpose is to lead to movement from house to sea, to that step away from egoism towards the conquest of egoism. Parables that occupy fifth or sixth places in a group or series should not be treated as if they came first or second. Parables told to the disciples should not be treated in the same way as parables addressed to the people at large.

Let us now take a look for a moment at the two parables, that of the treasure, and that of the pearl, as if they formed the two lowest rungs of a ladder, the two nearest the ground. A man is digging in a field and as he digs he comes upon a treasure of gold. He hastily covers it up again with earth and sets off to the owner of the field in order to buy it; but he remains discretely silent on his motive for buying. The owner of the field is probably induced to sell at a figure that he could no doubt have increased many times because of the treasure of gold, which after all belonged to him as did the field. If we accept the parable at its earthly face value, then what it tells is the story of a swindle. Even if the religious feeling of the notion of the kingdom of heaven does lift the story a little above the merely earthly, yet a certain flavour of selfishness passes over to our souls from the treasure seeker such as we usually see him. If nowadays religious feeling has been largely misrepresented through the egoistic note implied in 'grace only' and 'entry into the kingdom of heaven' then this has in some small degree been caused by misunderstanding and misuse through the centuries of the parable of the treasure hidden in a field; not that misunderstanding and misuse have been due to ill will, but rather to superficial and inaccurate reading of the gospel.

The problem of the next parable, that of the pearl of great price, is similar. Unless the picture is seen as a stage — an advanced stage, namely the sixth — along a way where the soul should already have experienced many a change within itself, then that verse about a merchant who sold all he had to buy a pearl could all too easily turn into a source of religious selfishness. With his own soul's salvation in mind, a man forsakes life's obligations, forgets the needs of others, and those of his environment; he becomes deaf while 'the whole of creation suffers and sighs ...' (Rom.8:22). Literally or metaphorically, he enters a cloister where he can place his life's centre of gravity on his own soul's struggle and upon the acquisition of the pearl of great price; for that is how he has understood it.

Why was the series of parables, begun on the shore of the sea before a crowd, continued inside the house before the disciples? It was because the disciples should already have reached the sea by reason of what they had experienced while with Christ. Although the last parables were spoken in the house, they were nevertheless spoken on the shores of the sea because they were heard by the disciples. The disciples were no longer in the house of the soul; they had matured as far as the apostleship, and in this calling they are to be privileged to live and labour for others, for humankind. One stage further and we see them carrying out the feeding of the five thousand as priests of Christ. This fact, that inwardly the disciples had left both land and house behind and attained to the sea, we can put thus: They had grown out of the earthly sense world into a world of spiritual images. The sense world is the land, the field; the spiritual world is the sea. This must not be understood as an abstract allegory which says, 'the field means the world of the senses, the earthly sea means the supersensible world.' No! The field is the sense world in spiritual language, that is, regarded from above; the supersensible world is the sea. The earthly sea is 'no more than a parable,' the same as all things evanescent; it is an earthly reflection of the actual supersensible world, to which man, through his ego, belongs.

When a human being dies, he sets forth from the land to the sea. He sinks down into the world of images where he needs no interpretation of true parables any more; he can understand the language of parables, for he has left behind the language of earthly thinking together with his own decaying brain. So, when we say that the disciples, through their discourse with the Christ, had inwardly reached the sea, we mean that they had outgrown material and bodily life, expanding in the same direction as the soul moves at death. They experienced the last three of the seven parables, not as on earth below, but on the three uppermost rungs of the heavenly ladder where picture language becomes the unmistakable expression of specific spiritual experiences and circumstances. There, in the spiritual realm to which their master's intimate teaching had lifted them, the disciples heard and recognized the parables of the treasure, of the pearl and of the net.

We are going to permit ourselves a bold attempt at pointing out how, under an open sky, upon the heights of spiritual regions revealed, these three parables become real and transparent to the spiritual gaze. Perhaps we can gain the clearest and most powerful impression of living in true spiritual spheres, where life is free of the body, if we think of those who have died and of their destinies. We are therefore going to try to draw nearer to the last three parables, to try to understand them by asking, what can those three scenes tell us of the region in the heavenly kingdom where sojourn the souls of those who have passed on. There can be no perplexity, no confusion, at those heights between what is of earth and what is of heaven.

When the link between body, soul and spirit, in which a man finds himself in life, is loosened by death, it is then that the essential being sets forth upon a three-stage pilgrimage. In the first stage, he is still close to earth, and to his body, looking back on them. Then earth sinks and the human being plunges utterly into the region of souls; that region resembles the sea, compared with the firm land of the region of the body. At last the human being enters upon the true spirit world; it is like the furthermost shores of that sea of which earth is the nearer shore. This journey from land to the bottom of the sea and thence to the shores of existence on the far side can become visible to us from these three parables.

First of all, the soul peers back at the body's sphere on earth. It looks like a dark field. Earth has been the site of earthly life, of earthly activity. Was not all work, all experience in the flesh, a digging in the field? What is it the soul is seeking now? It asks of what use was it all, what are the fruits of this, my whole life? Black darkness of an earth sinking enfolds the soul like terrifying night. Is this darkness in fact the only result of all the effort and affliction? The vision of the dissolving soul yearns to penetrate into the depths of the field and in so doing it turns into the treasure seeker. Liberation shines to greet souls, fearful and oppressed, if even a single ray of light can find its way to them from the black earthiness. Whence comes that ray of light? In the same measure that the life one has left behind on earth enkindled spirit in earthly matter, so a golden treasure lies in the field, a treasure whose consoling light reaches upward to the passing soul. The light-filled treasure will be the greater the more a human being has found of goodness, of the Christ in the earthly sphere, the more he has made them real.

If the field remains dark then that soul sinks into the oppressive night of death — the second death. The soul dies, the body being dead already. But if the treasure glows from out of the earth, then the soul comes to love earth, even though in life the soul may have groaned beneath the burden of existence. To dig the field was worth while for the sake of that treasure of light. It is worth keeping on digging to exert oneself for the sake of the treasure. Burning desire awakens in the soul, desire to reach the field once more as a sphere of activity, to get to work again for the sake of the golden light of the world. The field that the treasure seeker is trying to acquire, having caught sight of the treasure, is not heaven but earth.

But earth can also be a parable for the kingdom of heaven. If we think of the field with the treasure in it as heaven, then we become religiously selfish if, in overlooking our earth, we follow the parable through. But if, gazing down from the region of spirit, one sees earth as the field with the treasure, then to cherish in one's heart that longing for the field brings liberation from egoism. It is the desire to take upon oneself toil, sacrifice, burdens, in order to serve the light of the world. If we limit that parable to earth, then it depicts a swindle. If we recognize that it runs its course upon the heights, then it inspires us to sacrifice our lower nature to a strong desire to serve. What we have described here in connection with scenes that we can create for ourselves of life after death, applies to the lives of those human souls who are mature enough to look back from the heights to earthly life. It applies to souls who can, as it were, rise above the common run of things. The parable liberates them from themselves, while it entangles more than ever in hidden egoism anyone who is not above the common run of things. The words do come true: 'To him who has shall be given, and he shall have in abundance; from him who has not, even what he has will be taken' (Matt.25:29). Christ gave this parable and the next to the disciples as to people who 'had.' Had Christ given it to the people at large he would have taken from those who had even what they did have. The Christian interpretation has in large measure made the very mistake that Christ avoided. Instead of conferring freedom and unselfishness it inflicted, without wishing to do so, bondage and egoism.

The next step after death that the human soul must pass through when the field of earth has sunk right away is the passage through the sea of souls. Memories of earthly life are no more: the soul has traversed the river of Lethe, the river of forgetting. All that is left now of earthly life is the surge of joys and pains. The sea of souls, which in earthly life surged through this soul, now washes about it. Again the question arises: What is the eternal value of what has passed through my life on earth? Has it all blown away, or does my part of it survive? The soul plunges into the depths of the sea that is its own being, now poured out. But it can only find peace and an answer if it succeeds in bringing up the pearl of great price. What is that priceless pearl? In nature the origin of the pearl tells us an eloquent story. The pearl is formed in the shell when the pain of some injury, the suffering induced by the intrusion of some foreign body, penetrates the mollusc. Pain is mother to the pearl.

Just as a pearl lies on the floor of the material ocean, so a pearl rests at the bottom of the sea of souls. It is life's tear, transformed. A life devoid of pain and of suffering results after death in a pearl shell with no pearl. In that other world free of the body, the soul can expect to find the costly pearl only in the same measure which it has suffered in physical life. The pearl is the outcome of earthly struggles on the part of the soul.

What we have sought to describe as applying to life after death also applies to life before death. The precious pearl, in which a human being can find meaning and value in the soul's evanescent experiences, is accessible to anyone who has learned to get down to basic things, rather than let emotions and impressions swim about on the surface of life. The priceless pearl can be found by the soul's thoroughness, for thoroughness is not possible without grief and suffering.

And again, the parable tells us nothing about unalloyed heavenly bliss. To acquire the field and its treasure means to love earth. To acquire the pearl of great price means to love and to desire pain. What the treasure seeker must sacrifice in order to win the field is the idea of facile heavenly bliss, which comes through turning away from earth. What the merchant must give up is the superficial pleasure of life which ensues with avoidance of suffering.

The third region to be traversed by the soul after death is the region of spirit, where man lays aside even his soul which he has retained after the sinking of physically based memories. And now, whatever the intrinsic worth of that person may be as a spiritual being lies revealed to the eyes of God. The fish net is drawn ashore where stand the angels, ineluctably separating what is good from what is useless. The good is allowed onto the land; whatever fails to pass muster is returned to the sea's uncertain waves. And now those waves burn like the fiery glow of the judgment of the world. The separation of spirits is accomplished in the region of spirits. No further grace is accorded to the human being; he must give account of what he saw of the golden treasure in the field, and of how much he was able to find at the bottom of the sea of the pearl of great price.

The parable of the fish net has relevance into the future, 'So it will be at the completion of the cycle of time.' (Matt.13:49). Nevertheless, everyone at death touches the shore of that world where all that has not yet been purged away is revealed. Once again, what we have here indicated in relation to life after death applies also to life on earth. Those who go prospecting deeply enough will even in life come across the sphere of the world's end, upon the Last Judgment, when every cloak of illusion will have dropped and where the true nature of every human being will stand naked before the eye of God. On the shores of the world of truth stand angels as keepers of the portal, and they thrust back into the sea all who are unworthy of walking on the holy ground. The wrathful fire of judgment is burning now in the bosom of earthly man.

And so, the last three of the seven parables, those directed to the disciples, point the way from the land of physical existence (the field), to the bottom of the sea of souls (the pearl) and thence to the far shore of the region of spirit (the net).

— Learn to stand above circumstance: you will find the treasure.
— Learn to descend into the foundation of life: you will find the
   pearl of great price.
— Learn to know yourself in the presence of the eye of God: you will
   become a fish in the net.

There are those who may be reminded by the style in which we have been sketching these considerations of the old allegorical interpretations. There could however be no deeper chasm than that between our considerations and the allegorical interpretation. The parables do not visualize ideas; nor do they use them as metaphors. These pictures put spiritual truths into words that are the only possible language for spiritual facts.

Let us take note above all that we have tried to emphasize the inward differentiations and their results which are the soul's path; they depict the order of stages along that path by means of the examples we have been discussing.

There is plenty more to say about the thirteenth chapter and about the first four parables. We shall come to them in a later study. Let us for the present turn to the other two series of parables so as to bring out more forcibly a general impression of them and their unique character.

The other parables of Matthew

The second series of parables is not so easily seen at a glance by the reader as those contained in chapter thirteen. Before we can discuss the stages which link up the series of parables, we first have to realize how they belong together. To this end our eyes will have to take in a view wide enough to scan a passage of the gospel ten chapters long, and place it before us as a single whole. Discovery of the seven parables that wind their way through chapters 16 to 26 is only possible if the Bible is no longer looked upon as a book of quotations or an anthology, but as a great, divine tree, an exalted unearthly work of art. There is still many an undiscovered treasure lying hidden in the gospels. Having discovered the series of parables, we shall have received the key to that whole portion which contains them.

The seven parables have a multiple framework. First of all they are embraced by the first and the last of the warnings of suffering:

From then on Jesus Christ began to tell his disciples that he must go to Jerusalem, that much suffering from the elders and high priests and scribes lay before him, that he must be killed and that he would be raised on the third day (Matt.16:21).

And it happened: When Jesus had spoken all these words and had completed his teaching, he said to his disciples, 'You know that it will be Passover festival in two days' time. The Son of Man will be betrayed and crucified.' (Matt.26:1f).

The portion of the gospel that contains the seven parables lies between these two passages. The other two proclamations of suffering are in their turn inserted in between the parables. The first occurs before the first parable:

> Now while they were still living in Galilee, Jesus said to them, 'The Son of Man will be delivered into the hands of men, and they will kill him, and on the third day he will be raised.' (Matt.17:22f).
>
> Jesus prepared to go up to Jerusalem; he took the twelve aside for an intimate conversation and said to them on the way, 'See, we are going up to Jerusalem. The Son of Man will be handed over to the power of the chief priests and scribes; he will be condemned to death and committed into the hands of the foreign peoples to be mocked and scourged and crucified. But on the third day he will be raised.' (Matt.20:17–19).

The second frame placed round the seven parables are words about the return of the Christ:

> The Son of Man will come in the light-revelation of the Father, the Ground of the World, accompanied by the angels who serve him. To each individual human being he will give the destiny which corresponds to his deeds. (Matt.16:27).
>
> When the Son of Man comes, illumined by the light of revelation, surrounded by all angels, then he will ascend the throne of the kingdom of his revelation. He will gather before his countenance all the peoples of the world, and he will cause a division among them, as a shepherd separates the sheep from the goats, the sheep on the right and the goats on the left.' (Matt.25:31–33).
>
> Then the sign of the Son of Man will light up in the spiritual world; in the midst of their cries of woe all the peoples on the earth will behold the Son of Man as he comes in the ether-cloud realm, mightily empowered through the Spirits of Movement, radiantly surrounded by the Spirits of Revelation. (Matt.24:30, between the fifth and sixth parables)
>
> So therefore be prepared, for the Son of Man comes at an unexpected hour (Matt.24:44).

So be alert of soul, since you do not know the day or the
hour (Matt.25:13).

At last, following directly on these utterances, the seventh parable
carries within itself the full theme of the return:

It (the kingdom of heaven) is like a man going on a journey; he
called together his servants and entrusted his property to them
... When a long time had gone by, the master of the servants
returned and settled accounts with them. (Matt.25:14–30).

We are not going to enter upon details either of the proclamations
concerning suffering or of sayings that refer to a return. It will suffice
if we can perceive in a general way the twofold feeling that imbues the
whole of this part of the gospel: the mystery of Golgotha and the coming again of Christ; the first and second revelation of Christ; the imminent appearance of the Christ in the physical; death and resurrection;
the future Christ event in the etheric and his coming on heavenly
clouds.

Between the two great Christ events, humanity will have to pass
along a way fraught with many a trial. That path is to be bestowed on
humans as a respite to enable them to understand and experience the
character of Christ. If humanity fails in regard to what took place on
Golgotha, then that respite will have to mature until Christ's second
coming. That respite ought, however, to be put to good use. There are
seven stages to be climbed if people desire to rise from the physical
plane (scene of the first Christ event) to the plane of etheric existence
(region of Christ's second coming). The seven stages can be recognized
in the seven parables. We are to mature through them as far as experiencing the Christ, as far as experiencing him at his return.

There is a third frame around the seven parables. The frame itself
is made up of two pictures: the shepherd and the lost sheep; and the
shepherd who is also a king, dividing sheep from goats:

What do you think? If a man has a hundred sheep, and one of
them goes astray, will he not leave the ninety-nine in the
mountains and set out to look for the one that is lost? And
when he has found it, yes, I tell you, he will be more delighted
with it than with the ninety-nine that did not stray. So it is not
the will of your Father in the heavens that one of these developing higher beings, however small, should be lost.'
(Matt.18:12–14).

> ... as a shepherd separates the sheep from the goats, the
> sheep on the right and the goats on the left. Then, as king, he
> will say to those standing at his right hand ... what you did for
> the least of my brothers, that you did for me. (Matt.25:32–46).

These two scenes are closely linked by the opening and closing
tableaux that occur at the entrance portal and at the exit of the
temple that leads to the ultimate heights. The connection between the
scenes themselves is perceptible in one instance: it is in the shepherd
who reunites, and in the shepherd who, having become a king, must
from now on discriminate and judge. The picture of the lost sheep
here provides us with a significant key which will prove itself later
on as the key to the whole of this passage of the gospel. In becoming
an ego-being and an individual, a human being separates himself
inwardly from the community to which he belonged before the
awakening of his ego. He becomes lonely. But, should he find his
way back from the wilderness existence of his ego, back to the community, then he would bring with him what he has gained in his solitude and this ego gain, the result of his isolation, would raise him
above all those who still remained in the community because their
ego would still not be awake. The ego person is the lost sheep in contrast to people who have not yet attained to egohood. Those are the
ninety-nine sheep who have not strayed, but have remained with the
flock.

The ego is present within a human being as a frail germ before it
gains in strength and begins to grow. The 'least of these' are people in
whom the ego is still small, inconsiderable and frail. People in whom
the ego is germinating need the love of fellow men. Those who do love
them and help them also love and serve the Christ, because the Christ
can dwell only in man's ego.

Before a human ego has had time to mature it will become clear
whether mounting strength is shaping towards insensibility or
towards the capacity for sacrifice. There are two kinds of ego people.
The shepherd is leader of the flock made up of those who have not yet
attained to the ego. The shepherd who is a king leads the flock composed of ego people. Now there are two kinds of ego people; there are
the hardened, the self-seeking; and there are the unselfish ones, who
go forth in sacrifice and love. These are the true ego people. The
unselfish ones are the true ego people, while those who have become

hardened in their egos only seem to be it. To say 'I' leads to a simulation of the ego; to say 'not I' leads to the true ego.

There are two constellations in the sky that stand above these groups; the constellation of Capricorn, the Goat, expresses the hardening and ossification of selfishness; this is the winter constellation. The constellation of Aries, the Ram, expresses willingness to sacrifice, the power to give; it is the constellation of spring. That is how the two groups of ego people separate into sheep and goats. They are distinguished by the way in which they relate to other egos, to 'the least of them.' The hardened ego person does not cherish, pays no attention to the ego in others and by so doing despises them and fails to recognize the Christ whose desire it is to live in the higher ego of humankind. The true ego person who is capable of love pays attention and cherishes the ego in others, and in so doing serves Christ himself.

The two framing scenes — that of the lost sheep and that of the sheep and the goats — show us that the way from the first Christ event to the second is the way of ego man:

> The great debt and the small debt
> Equal pay for unequal labour
> The two sons in the vineyard
> The Lord's messengers in the vineyard
> The royal wedding
> The ten virgins
> The talents

We immediately become aware of groupings. The second, third and fourth parables take place in a vineyard; the next two deal with a marriage — since it is the bridegroom whom the virgins await. And then a certain similarity exists between the first parable and the seventh — the seventh being a parable of the return.

There are:

> A parable of guilt
> Three vineyard parables
> Two marriage parables
> One parable of the Return (the second parable of guilt).

The history of the ego begins with the fall into sin. Humanity owes its ego to having been released from heaven by cosmic primordial sin. In addressing himself as 'I,' man forgot that everything he was had only been bestowed upon him, nay, that he had actually laid hold of it by force. To be sure, it is part of the cosmic plan for humanity that human beings should be free, that they should become 'like unto gods' and acquire egos. That is why humanity has been discharged from that same original sin through which, in fact, men have attained to possession of the ego. But now man is making demands upon his fellow creatures, referring his entitlement to those demands to his own ability to say 'I.' He demands that right, even though basically he owes his own existence to forgiveness of his great debt. Man's primordial guilt is the ego of man, and yet he sets himself up everywhere as a debt collector in face of his fellow creatures! Here we touch on the cosmically realistic background of the first of the seven parables. A human being in this world can only be a true ego person when he has learned to live in constant awareness of the following situation: 'I am all that I am through the goodness of the divine world, which does not hold the Fall, that tremendous primordial sin, against me. And that is why I have no claims on my fellow creatures, on those who share this earth with me. Rather than press demands, I am going to repay that earliest debt — even though it has been lifted from me — by doing good to my debtors.' Awareness of that primordial debt, of the fall into sin, is the source of goodness. And the true, the exalted ego of man dwells in goodness.

It would not be wrong to describe the first of the seven parables as the 'parable of the fall.'

The question arises in relation to the three vineyard parables: for what spiritual reality is the image of the vineyard an expression and a name? Wine was for men of past ages the ego's elixir. If water was the expression of man's universal, all embracing, as yet pre-ego existence, then wine expresses the ego in the process of learning to find itself within itself. Greece dedicated wine to Dionysus, perceiving in him something of the individuality in man. Man's ego is of Dionysus, who stands for the element to which wine speaks.

Ever since the Fall, earth has been the site for gaining individuality. Earth is the vineyard with all its labour and toil where the wine of ego nature matures. 'Personality is the highest happiness of the children of earth.' The ego personality — this is the aim of earthly life, its reward in the vineyard.

As for the ego, here we have a strange situation. You cannot yourself do much towards achieving an ego; you cannot become a person-

ality through hard work. The very deepest secrets of destiny are concerned in this. No two people are alike in the way they win through to
the ego — and yet everyone is the equal in worth of every other 'I.' The
way towards egohood is what differentiates people. The ego is not a
quantitative but a qualitative dimension. One person must journey far
to reach the dawning of his 'I.' Another receives it as an awakening,
like a flash of lightning. One toils in the vineyard from early morning
to late at night; another begins at noon, and a third may only start an
hour before the close of day; yet the reward in that vineyard is always
the same. The penny which each receives at eventide, no matter
whether he has worked for a long or a short time, is round. This is no
coincidence. We shall see this even more clearly in the five parables of
St Luke. The ring, or circle, is, by its self-enclosing completeness, the
spiritual symbol of the ego or personality. As long as we have not
attained to egohood, our nature is fragmented and splintered. It is the
ego that confers coherence to the disjointed parts. As the marriage ritual has it, in the circle and in the ring let your lives be, so what is separate shall be enclosed to form a whole.

That carries us right into the first of the vineyard parables. Those
who have toiled since morning are resentful because those who started
work in the evening have received the same wage. Up to a point they
betray themselves as traditionalists, and to that extent their egos are
hardened. The ego is indeed the reward for work in the vineyard, but
it is at the same time the most freely given grace of God. We may not
lay claim to the ego; whoever thinks he has a natural right to it is setting out towards an inferior, a false ego. Only those who feel the ego to
be the highest grace, to be guilt forgiven, something of value bestowed
by the Lord of the vineyard — only those are on the way to the true, to
the higher ego, to the Christ. That is why inheritors of the grand tradition can so easily be facing a snare in the struggle towards true freedom and personality, for tradition derives its pretensions from the
ancient past. It is easier for late comers than for heirs of the past: 'Thus
the last will be first, and the first last' (Matt.20:16). The Jews did not
understand the Christ when he turned towards the tax-collectors and
sinners. They believed that they would themselves receive greater
rewards since they had toiled in the vineyard since early morning.

There are more mysteries to the ego besides being qualitative
rather than quantitative in character. It exists within, not on the

outside; it has substance; it is not just a name. Who is the true 'I'? A person who frequently speaks the 'I' or one who says it seldom? Whoever uses 'I' often probably has only an intellectual reflection of the ego. The human ego is, all too often, like the moon, were the moon to reflect sunlight, pretending it was its own. The ego is moonlike, not sunlike. Rather it is an ego consciousness, a feeling of egohood, than a true ego; it is the reflector of an entity, not the entity itself. Someone who is indeed an ego does not speak of it; he may not even be aware of it himself — for the true ego actually reveals itself in its aptitude to forget self. Those who can say, 'So it is not I who live, but Christ lives in me' (Gal.2:20), forget their lowly human 'I' and in so doing gain the exalted divine ego.

> A man had two sons. He went to the first and said, 'Son, go and work in the vineyard today.' He answered, 'Yes, sir.' But he did not go. Then he went to the second and said the same to him. He answered, 'I will not.' Later, however, he regretted his answer and went after all. Which of the two did the will of the father? They said, 'The second.' Jesus said, 'Yes, I say to you, the tax-collectors and the harlots will find access to the kingdom of God more readily than you.' (Matt.21:28–31).

In Greek the answer of the first son is *ego kyrie* ('I, lord.') The words cast light on the whole of the proceedings. The first son is an ego-talker, but not an ego bearer. To talk about the 'I' is no more proof of the presence of a real personality than talk of Christ and Christianity is proof of the actual presence of Christ in a human soul. The better Christians could often be those who do not talk about the Christ, or who even assert that they are not Christians at all.

The third vineyard parable is also the middle one of the series. It is the moving drama of a struggle between the lower and the higher ego. The Lord of the vineyard sends messengers who are to take delivery of fruit from the husbandmen. But the husbandmen have forgotten that they are not masters of the vineyard; they beat up the first servant, kill the next, and stone the third. The same things happen when the Lord sends messengers for the second time. And when he sends his son they actually kill him too. The debased, hardened ego in man kills the true 'I.' The moonlike ego wants to be Lord of life itself.

The sun-ego of true egohood, the ego of Christ, cannot survive in man; it is killed in the region of the skull. That drama is played out in one form or another in every human being. Unwholesome hankering after the ego spells the ego's death. The mystery that took place on Golgotha is the mightiest historical depiction of all this inward drama. It was Jewry, the vehicle of moonlike ego impulses, who nailed Christ onto the cross.

Like the third and the fourth parables, this one is addressed to the Jews. The Christ tells them to their faces what they are spiritually about, and what they are historically on the verge of doing to himself.

The remaining parables, that is, the two wedding stories and the reunion of the return, tell how a human being can grow out beyond himself towards spiritual union, towards the *chymical marriage*, to marriage with the spirit. We have to achieve three things if as egos we desire to grow towards the spirit and be ready for the return of Christ. These things are:

> Purity of the etheric body
>
> Light in our soul nature
>
> The open eye of spirit nature.

The wedding garment is the white garment. Whether a person's etheric garment is white does not depend only on what we usually call moral purity. More especially in our own time, the opaqueness of the garment which we wear, like a more delicate supersensible body, comes from men's dead thinking. Merely intellectual thinking is dark shadow. It does not glow. The white garment is life at its purest and brightest. Anything dead in a person's nature stains that garment. The more exalted ego quality, derived from labouring in the vineyard, first proves itself when deadly human thoughts are transformed into divine thinking. Whoever pushes his way into the bridal chamber with his soul's garment not transformed, having no white bridal robe, must be cast back into the chaos of external life. The white garment is that quality of the sun which a man can have; the higher ego is sunlike. It shines forth from within and blots out all stains with its light. The lower ego is moonlike. The stains on the garment are due to it, for it binds humanity to what is dead.

The oil in the lamps, which does not fail the wise virgins as it does the foolish ones, is the full soul. Love is able to fill the soul. A loveless soul is a hollow, empty soul, a lamp with no oil. Only a well-appointed soul is able to love, a soul acquainted with the art of meditative peace within itself. There can be no power to love unless the soul is collected;

no burning light in the soul devoid of love. The foolish virgins are people who have let themselves be infected by the business of externalized living; they become aware of their own emptiness when it is too late. They would enter into the region of spirit, but they reach a closed door.

If, in this context, we study the parable of the entrusted talents, we find it moving into quite a new light, as did the parables of the buried treasure and the pearl. The parable has all too often been read as if it were the first and not the seventh in the series. If one does accept it as being the first, then its images appear so earthbound that it becomes all too easy to mix some earthly selfishness into religious life. If we take it in its earthly sense, as the foot of the ladder, then the parable speaks up for usury. At all events, the sentiments and atmosphere of usury get mixed up with religious feeling. A kind of 'businessman's Christianity' emerges according to which, in attaining to the kingdom of heaven, not only is a certain turning away from earth praised, but so is resort to questionable methods. This parable is the topmost rung of a seven-rung ladder; it speaks of spiritual gifts (in terms of money) entrusted to people. Even where the cohesion and composition of the seven parables is not known, the proximity of the parable to the stories of the Passion should confer upon it a more exalted level as its sphere of validity. As for usury when applied to the talents — it stands for spiritual schooling, for the awakening and exercising of dormant spiritual organs which have been submerged in human beings. Seen in its own context in the gospels as a whole, this parable is the refutation of countless theological theories which, for example, have been brought forward as arguments against anthroposophy. People say belief is Christian; the visionary seeing discussed by anthroposophy is contrary to Christianity. It is also contrary to Christianity when a person undertakes with religious intent to exercise and train themselves spiritually rather than rely wholly on grace. The spirit of the unsatisfactory servant survives in that objection; he buries the talent entrusted to him and thinks when his Lord returns that he has done well to conserve rather than to multiply.

There are spiritual organs, higher senses asleep in humanity. Luther called faith 'a new sense far above the five senses.' These organs, the eyes of spiritual man, require fortifying, awakening, exercising through inward meditative training. If we leave them as they are, if we dig them still deeper into the ground, the soul gives in when the Lord returns. In order to perceive the returning Christ manifesting in the etheric region, human beings need spiritual organs that are awake. The unsatisfactory servant is to the sphere of spirit exactly what the five foolish virgins are to the soul. Not only does he sleep through and miss the manifestation, but also, instead of lifting himself into spirit, he must be cast back all the deeper into the earthly.

The significance of the key and what it offers through composition will be most clearly seen in this parable. The parable reveals itself as a call to active spiritual training, a call that sounds from the mountain peak of the gospel.

— The parable of guilt (parable of the fall) — the ego aware of its own origin.
— First parable of the vineyard — the qualitative, not quantitative ego.
— Second parable of the vineyard — mere ego consciousness and the true ego consciousness
— Third parable of the vineyard — the lower ego and the higher ego.
— First marriage parable — purity of character (marriage garment)
— Second marriage parable — light in the soul (oil in the lamp)
— Parable of duty (a parable of return) — awakened spiritual organs (increased talents).

Luke's parables

As for the last of the three series of parables, we shall go into even less detailed discussion of them than we did of the two earlier ones. Let us choose one viewpoint of the five parables of St Luke, out of many, and let that view pass before our eyes by way of a brief survey. We are going to look at the last three parables, paying attention to number as it occurs in them. The lost sheep is one of a hundred; the lost coin is one of ten; the lost son is one of two. We notice the numerical circle drawing ever tighter.

One hundred is the number that represents the group soul. Under its sign the many become unity. The Greeks sacrificed hecatombs of animals (one hundred animals) in order by so doing to arouse a more exalted soul element. Individual animals were presumed to be part of the one hundred, but the total of one hundred is equivalent to more than a hundred individuals. The soul of the herd as a whole is added to the many individual animal souls.

The 'hundreds' of ancient armies grew up for the same reason, and a centurion was placed at their head. The one sheep that strayed from the community was the ego-person breaking free from old blood ties.

Ten was indicated by the Pythagoreans as the number of perfection, and was represented by a circle. Ten, however, played a special part in Jewish ritual and passed thence into all kabbalism and medieval esoteric teaching. Contemplation of the *Sophireth* had an outstanding place in the Kabbalah. In Jakob Böhme's writings, for example, the ten, the *denarius*, plays a most important part, splitting up into seven *(septenar)* and into three *(ternar)*. *Denarius* is a Latin word (of Greek origin) for a penny. The penny is round in shape since by its number, the ten, it denotes perfection. The shape of the round coin, of the penny, originated in ritual. An ancient traditional ritual, part of the Christian Last Supper, was to take out one ninth of the consecrated bread, and to dip it in the wine. The host consists of nine parts; the tenth part is the whole host. The host is thus 'the tenth.' Sacrifice of the 'tithe,' which dominated Jewish religious life, passed in sacramental form into Christian ritual. The character of the coin was at first entirely sacramental. It emerged from ritual, from the sacrifice of the tithe, through the use of the round host. The coin host was added to the bread host and quite often replaced it altogether.

So here is the concept that found its way through all ancient ritual imagery: man, on the way to becoming an individual, is himself the host, the 'tithe.' Man was conceived as a nine-membered being, for people thought of all nine hierarchies taking part in man's creation. And ego-man, the whole of him, who is the image and amalgamation of all things individual — he is the tenth member, the tithe, the denarius. The woman has lost the tenth piece of silver, not one of the nine small coins. As she turns out her house she is striving to get back the completeness of her own inward self which egohood confers. The woman finds her own self when she finds the silver coin, the denarius, the sacred ten.

Duality speaks from the parable of the two sons. As a man, the lost son, passes in his destiny through descent to re-ascent, he passes through death: 'For this your brother was dead and is alive; he was lost and is found.' The other son remains on the heights of old heredity. But the ego can only be gained in the profundity of death. The gospel is consistently on the side of the ego.

— The lost sheep (Luke 15:3): Ego man in contrast to the group soul.

— The lost silver piece (Luke 15:8): Ego man as the whole man.

— The lost son (Luke 15:12): Ego man and the man who belongs to ancient tradition.

Duality is paramount in the next two parables — that of the unjust steward and of the rich man and Lazarus — but that duality is withdrawing more and more inward. The utterance, 'No servant can serve two masters ... You cannot serve both God and the powers of all merely earthly existence [Mammon] at the same time' (Luke 16:13), can only be understood when one realizes that Mammon is more than simply the god of money. He is the god of hindrance, of attachment to the old things. He is god of the past: 'No man can serve both future and past.' The steward tears himself free from Mammon in his own way when he turns resolutely to the future. Rather than stay fixed in the past he uses the past as a base for the future, and thereby makes friends with Mammon. This parable is the refutation of all mere traditionalism: you cannot serve at the same time the God who is leading you into the future (Christ) and him who binds you to the past.

We need courage for the future, for the future is poor while the past is rich. We should study the parable of the rich man and of poor Lazarus in such a way as to see duality as having withdrawn completely into man's inward being, making one person of rich Dives and poor Lazarus. (Of course, this is only one aspect of the parable). Dives is the man of soul; spiritual man is Lazarus, the beggar. The rich man represses and stifles the poor one. The poor man lives on crumbs that fall from the rich man's table. After death, the old opulence of soul turns into glowing desire; while spiritual man, however poor, is lifted up into the region of spirit. Dives begs that Lazarus come to him. That soul of his, burning within its own senile heritage, longs for the other's spiritual ego to obtain coolness. Lazarus cannot reach Dives; then at least let him carry the message from the other world to people still alive on earth! This prayer of Dives was heard. St John's Gospel tells us that Lazarus was recalled to life, and he did indeed bring messages from the other world, namely the Gospel of St John, the writer of which Lazarus became.

But people on earth have had Moses and the prophets and the Old

Testament; yet they become no more perceptive. How would they become more perceptive through the message of Lazarus? 'If they do not heed Moses and the prophets, neither will they heed one who rises from the dead' (Luke 16:31). Rightly understood, that parable of Lazarus is a mighty declaration of war on the principles of the Roman Catholic Church. That church is Dives, and desires to maintain each of its members in the condition of the rich man. Lazarus the beggar is truly progressive, the ego-person. He is able to rise again; Dives can only die.

— Fourth parable: The unjust steward: Ego man — a human being of
    the future.

— Fifth Parable: Rich Dives and Lazarus the beggar (Ego man, that
    is, spiritual man contrasted with the soul man).

If we have recognized the truths and the internal ordering of these sequences of parables, then we will have gained much towards our reading of the pictorial language of the parables. They are writings which tell us about the beings and verities of a heaven revealed. Recognition of this has been the aim of the present study.

CHAPTER NINE

The Sermon on the Mount

The Sermon on the Mount as instruction to the disciples

Christ promulgated no ethical or social program in his Sermon on the Mount. Not a lawgiver like Moses, he was a fulfiller. In the circle of his disciples whom he was beginning to train as apostles and priests, he made through his word the strongest and most practical contribution to the solution of ethical and social problems; that is, through the Christian priesthood. The Christian priesthood laid the foundations of a Christian social order.

Quite a new tone is sounded in this connection in the Sermon on the Mount, especially in one commandment. We may perhaps briefly consider that commandment by itself before passing on to the general structure of the Sermon on the Mount as a whole: 'Everything which you want men to be able to do, that you should first do to them yourselves. That is the essential meaning of the Law and the prophets.' (Matt.7:12). If we accept that dictum as being simply a general moral rule, then we are in fact facing something trivial. It has often been seen in that light, but on occasion it has really been adapted as a basic ethical principle, the inspiration of genius. It becomes obvious, however, that this approach does not touch the soul of this commandment because, as an ethical rule, it states nothing peculiarly Christian. Rather, it gives expression to something that was taken for granted as self evident in other religions including pre-Christian ones. Considered as a commandment to apostles and priests, however, those words are a kind of summation of the whole of the sermon.

As leaders, whatever goals towards which you would guide humanity, you must first realize in your own work as priests. Being priests, you must create in the world, through your priestly ministration, a realistic image of the future and of the goals of humanity.

Whatever you would accomplish by way of ethical or social perfection or reforms, demonstrate it by your own priestly conduct. Throw wide the gates that lead from sacrament to life, from the earliest ideal to all the thousands of derivative views of it, from specialized priesthood into the beliefs about the priesthood generally.

How does the priestly instruction continue which the Christ gave to his disciples upon the mountain? Whether one reads the sermon straight through at a sitting in the way that is customary or whether one learns it by heart — there seems to be no prospect of finding any link between the different passages or verses. We can understand how, within the new theology, the notion could have arisen that Matthew the Evangelist is offering in chapters five to seven an assemblage of sayings of the Lord, a collection of precepts which were not delivered by the Christ in that order nor in those combinations but were spoken on the most varied occasions. And yet, if we are to understand the Sermon on the Mount, it is essential to realize that it is an organic whole, a divine work of art, put together in accordance with cosmic laws. Admittedly, that is not possible if we look for a single train of thought through all of it. It does become possible if we peer into the Sermon on the Mount as into a spiritual path that the disciples are to follow, and we ourselves with them.

The Sermon on the Mount begins with the word 'blessed' which rings out nine times in the beatitudes. The picture of the house being built ends it: 'Whoever hears these words and acts accordingly will be like a prudent man who built his house on rock ... But whoever hears these words, and does not act accordingly, will be like a foolish man who built his house on sand ...' (Matt.7:24–27).

That word 'blessed' points to heavenly heights to which human spirituality can be uplifted. The picture of the house built on a rock leads us downward to earthly levels, to which all things must be made to descend if they are to be well grounded in human existence. From blessed heavenly heights, down to rock-bound earthliness — such is the path of the soul to which the Sermon on the Mount points. Jesus brought his disciples together on the mountain's summit at the outset of his own earthly ministry in order to lead them from the heights, so near heaven, down into the depths, into the proximity of people and of the earth. The disciples could become leaders of men only in the depths, upon earth's rockiness. The very beginning of the 'good news' proclaims the ineluctable realism of Christianity, but also its splendid conviction to overcome one's alienation from earth and the world — that is the beginning of every path. Whosoever fails to seek earth first does not deserve to look for heaven.

There is no element of chance about the picture of the house built on a rock. It is a very clear revelation of the character of St Matthew's Gospel. The path of the soul in that gospel is the path of Petrine man — as we have already noted in earlier studies, and as we shall see in more detail later on. Within the meaning of St Matthew's Gospel, Peter is *the* Apostle. 'Peter' means 'rock' (stone). It is the name that the Christ gave Simon when he called him to be his disciple. What did the Christ mean by that name? St Matthew does not record the scene when Christ gave it to him. We find these words only in John: 'Jesus looked at him and said, "You are Simon, the son of Jonah. Your name shall be Cephas (which translated means Peter, the Rock)".' (John 1:42). We could say that the end of the Sermon on the Mount in St Matthew corresponds to the verse in St John where the disciple receives the name of 'the rock.' The Sermon leads the disciples to experiencing the rock-bound base; it calls all of them by the name of Peter, though not in so many words; it places rock beneath their feet.

The Christ's earthly ministry resembles the building of a house or of a temple and, like a wise architect, Christ begins by laying the foundations. Whatever pertains to Peter, whatever is tied up with earth, what, in the disciples' souls, belongs to the solidity of earth, all that is the foundation of the temple of humanity, of the church, which is Christ's building.

The Sermon on the Mount lays the foundation stone of the temple. Had that foundation stone not been laid, then later, by the time the end of Christ's earthly mission was near, these words could not have been spoken: 'You are Peter, the Rock. On this rock I will build my congregation' (Matt.16:18). The foundation stone is laid first, the rock prepared, Simon changed into Peter, and with him the other disciples. That was the first stage in the apostles' education, and the Christ carried it out through the Sermon on the Mount.

A human being becomes Peter, a rock. That is the first step in transforming the disciples into priests, and it is also the first step generally speaking for the successors of the Christ. In our sixth study in discussing the calling of the disciples and the deeds of Christ that followed upon that, we indicated the beginning of the disciples' path in the following scenes: The Christ leads them from the sea to land and, on land, the Christ leads them into the house. The Sermon on the Mount belongs in this context, for he leads from blessedness down to earth, right onto the rock — from heaven to earth.

At this point we can go a little more deeply into what we could only touch upon earlier. In so doing, we cannot, as yet, be led into an understanding of the sermon in detail; nevertheless, we can become familiar with the place that it occupies in the organization, in the composition of the whole gospel.

The Sermon on the Mount and the marriage in Cana

In St John the marriage in Cana, the first of seven miracles, takes up a profound position similar to that of the Sermon on the Mount. The sermon leads from blessedness down to ground level on the rock; in so doing it achieves a transmutation in human souls that can be compared with the transmutation of water to wine. Many an effort has been made to try and understand the miracle of Cana in allegorical terms by saying water is the Jewish religion, wine is Christianity; at Cana, Christ gave us a symbol for the transformation of the water of Judaism into the wine of Christianity.

The law, as delivered for example by Moses, brought ethical ideals close to men from outside; it was a summons to wake up. The law was a revelation of spirit emanating from outside. The law is in itself a revelation. It is of heavenly, not human origin; it belongs to the exalted heavens, not to earth's rocky bed. The stone tablets of Moses were to point the way the law was intended to take. Coming from the heights, it was to be substantiated on earth by human beings obeying it. This is how it was to be written into the rockbound depths of earth. The essential character of the law is, however, of heaven, not of earth. It is not a seed of goodness at rest in earth's womb; it is the moisture of rain streaming down from heaven to waken the seed in the earth. If the era of law is now over, if the seed of man's egohood has become awake in humanity, then moral awareness can no longer draw near from outside; it can thrive only from within outward by natural growth. No longer can rain, the water of heaven, carry the word; it has to be the inmost sap of a creature in the process of growth, the inward wine maturing into blood, the vehicle of the ego, of struggling humanity itself. Water has to be changed to sap, then into wine, then into blood. Law no longer speaks externally from above downward; it pronounces the 'I am' from within outward. Even as Yahweh spoke through the law, so Christ desires to speak in the ego of people: 'You have heard the word that was spoken to mankind in the past: You shall not kill ... But out of my own power I say to you: Even he who allows impulses of anger to burn against his fellow men brings crisis to his destiny.' (Matt.5:21f). That was the law and it is the water; 'I say to you' — here is the ego, the wine. The miracle of Cana finds expression in that utterance of the Sermon on the Mount — the Sermon on the Mount in the form of verbal instruction is identical with the marriage of Cana which was a revelation in the form of a deed. Man's innermost being, acting upon the rockbound foundation of earthly existence, has to take over leadership of earthly things. The Christ gives to men the courage needed for earthly personality.

In transmuting water into wine at the marriage in Cana, the Christ brought about something that, in nature, is brought about by the cosmic interplay of earth and sun. But people of an earlier era entertained no such mechanistic and impersonal concepts as do moderns who rely on the intellect. They saw the divinely rhythmic movement of creative spirits at work, just as they could see angels active in the lives of individuals and archangels in the destiny of peoples. They could perceive external nature dissolving and then reforming, penetrated and governed by beings called Elohim in the Old Testament, and identified in the New Testament as Exousiai. The Exousiai were looked upon as world creators and shapers. The King James' Bible calls them 'powers' (Rom.8:38). Elsewhere in the Bible the Greek term is translated as 'authority.' 'For he taught them as one who had authority, and not as the scribes' (Mark 1:22 RSV). Nowadays that term carries certain legalistic connotations; we should beware of any such implications, keeping in mind the full impact of the word as the name of exalted hierarchical spirits.

The two closing verses of the Sermon on the Mount, and with it the whole of the sermon itself, moves into a new light: 'And it happened: When Jesus had completed his teaching, great excitement arose among the people, for he taught as one in whom the creating powers themselves are at work; not in the usual style of the scribes.' (Matt.7:28f).

This closing scenario is no less significant than the opening one. It introduces a number of profound riddles. The Greek text reads: 'He stood before them as a teacher; he was one who had Exousiai (authority).' A force of nature spoke through him; his speech carried within it the speech of the Elohim, who in the very beginning had created the world by their mighty 'Let there be ...' Utterances in the Sermon on the Mount were imbued with the same powers as was the deed of Cana. The scribes talked about the creation of the world. In the Sermon on the Mount, Christ is himself world creation. The disciples are the building material out of which the Christ was building the temple even while he was speaking, the foundations having been laid. The disciples underwent transformation. The word of Christ moulded them, making building stones of them, foundation stones for the temple of humanity.

This brings us to the words that begin the closing scene: 'When Jesus had completed this teaching, great excitement arose among the people' (Matt.8:28). The passage reads like a crude contradiction of the opening scene where we are told how Jesus, having seen the people, climbed the mountain, called the disciples to him, and taught them there. How could people be amazed at teaching they could not hear and which was directed to a restricted circle of men?

Whenever the gospel speaks in inconsistencies, as it does here, it is invariably revealing to us some weighty secret and it is concerned with unfathomable depths. Those who fail to observe the inconsistencies between the opening scene and the end are too superficial when it comes to profundities. But anyone who really thinks he can establish contradictions in the gospel — such a one is also superficial. The inconsistency is only on the surface. It dissolves at greater depths.

A secret was being played out between Christ and the people. Perhaps we can give a hint of that secret in the form of a picture. A physician finds a seriously ill patient; he examines the patient, peers into his eyes to try to diagnose the roots of the illness. He then says to him, 'Wait here until I come back. I am going away to prepare medicine for you that will heal you.' The patient waits. Meanwhile potent forces are already passing through his system, for he has seen his physician. He has been taking part at a distance with every fibre of his heart in the process employed by the physician in preparing the medicine.

It was like that here. Christ saw the multitude as a straying flock having no shepherd. He ascended the mountain in order to prepare his disciples to become shepherds to that flock. He did this through words that in their effect were like natural forces, like tempests that raged creatively through the soul worlds. They stormed through the souls of the multitudes, inspiring them with powerful emotions. The crowds felt that something momentous was happening to themselves. They could feel the swishing beat of the wings of those who were to become their leaders. The Sermon on the Mount is made known to us through that 'contradiction' as a phenomenon of nature, a soul tempest. It is not words but a deed; it is not doctrine but creation. Its influence extends far beyond those to whom the audible word is directed.

In order to experience in quite elementary fashion the drama that frames the Sermon on the Mount and sets the words of Christ among his miraculous deeds, let us put the opening and the closing verses side by side: 'When he saw the crowd of people, he went up on the mountain. Then he sat down, and his disciples came to him. And he opened his mouth and began to teach them.' 'When Jesus had completed this teaching, great excitement arose among the people, for he taught as one in whom the creating powers themselves are at work; not in the usual style of the scribes.'

Those words give a wonderful picture: crowds in confusion at the foot of the mountain. Up above, at the summit, the solemn scene of Christ seated among his disciples, teaching. The people could not have heard what was said on the mountain even if, now and again, a sound of it had been wafted to their ears upon a breeze. But they could feel, as if they had been able to see it, that scene upon the mountain top: 'Something is going on there that concerns us! The world in which we live is being transformed.' That is how tempestuous excitement passed through the tense souls of the crowds. The Sermon on the Mount influenced them more powerfully because it was not delivered to them directly; its effectiveness would have been less had the people heard it addressed to them. Its influence on them did not lie in audible words; it acted like an event in nature.

The scene that presents itself to us is the metamorphosis of a magnificent scene in the Old Testament: the children of Israel swarming ill-tempered, chaotic and confused, at the foot of Mount Sinai. Upon the summit, Moses is speaking to God in tempest and cloud, in fire and lightning. The people cannot hear the word of Yahweh. They hear only the tumult of thunder and are thereby even more shattered than had they too been able to hear the words that Moses heard. They knew that what was passing between Moses and Yahweh concerned them.

The Sermon on the Mount which Jesus Christ delivered to his disciples up there on the mountain abrogated the law that Yahweh gave to Moses. Terror before the law transfixed the people at the foot of Sinai. Fear of salvation pierced the people at the foot of the mountain where Christ was speaking with his disciples.

The Gospel of St Matthew stresses emphatically, through its inarticulate and yet so insistent language of composition, the way in which the Sermon on the Mount (an event primarily between Jesus and his disciples) reached the souls of the people. Having discussed the first and the last verses which set forth the Sermon on the Mount itself, let us look at the verses which frame the sermon as a whole, that is, chapters five to seven. The last verse of chapter four reads: 'And great crowds followed him from Galilee and the Decapolis, from Jerusalem and Judea and from the land beyond the Jordan.' (Matt.4:25). It is the sight of these crowds who follow him that causes the Christ to ascend the mountain. The opening verse of chapter eight reads: 'As he came down from the mountain, great crowds followed him.' (Matt.8:1). The first of these two verses about the crowds who followed comes almost immediately after the calling of the disciples. The second of them comes after the first major teaching addressed to them. The people felt instinctively that everything that passed between Christ and the disciples was for their sakes. They were led towards him by the very fact that he had gathered the disciples about him in order to make of them leaders and priests of the people. The multitudes followed him because they sensed that in him they would find leadership and leaders.

The beatitudes

Laying the foundation stone is not the real beginning when a house is to be built. Just as conception precedes birth, so descent of the house from the region of ideals, of prototypes, precedes laying its foundations. Building the house starts in exalted spiritual regions with the architect being inseminated in his own spirit with the original concept. It is the same with the Sermon on the Mount which sets forth the process of incarnation of the temple of Christian humanity, right down as far as the laying of the foundations.

The beatitudes and the words that follow on the salt of the earth, on the light of the world, and on the city set on a hill — all of them show us the spiritual prototype of what is to be built; the beatitudes show us the prototype of spiritual man — the words that follow depict the prototype of the spiritual community.

The word 'blessed' has in recent phases of religious development taken a tone that belies all religious vitality. The soul's whole egoism is concentrated in that word, the egoism that has crept into Christian religious feeling. A religious mood, wherein we make achievement of blessedness our highest goal, is foreign to the Christianity of the gospels. It is a mood which was proper to certain earlier religions like some of India's because the time of the ego had not yet dawned, nor had the Christ descended to earth. To seek spirit, human beings had then to turn away from earth towards heaven. Ever since Christ walked this earth, since he was lowered into earth's grave to become Lord of heavenly forces on earth — ever since that time the urge to search for blessedness by turning away from earth has been an aberration of the soul. Christianity that aims only at blessedness is not really Christian.

The Greek word translated in the beatitudes as 'blessed' is *makarios*. It is one of the most splendid and least translatable words in the Greek language. Something of the quietly noble grandeur of the starry skies speaks and exercises power in it. One is tempted to translate it in some such way as this: 'akin to the stars,' 'ennobled by God,' 'imbued with godhead.' But we get no further than groping! No modern language is able to reproduce so elemental yet holy a word as *makarios*. Be that as it may, the ideas and emotions associated with 'blessed' disqualify that word as a translation of *makarios*.

How much misunderstanding has crept in through that word, above all in considering the Sermon on the Mount! We need think only of the first beatitude: 'Blessed are the poor in spirit for theirs is the kingdom of heaven.' Spiritual poverty is widely assumed to be a mental condition resembling that of a child. People imagine that simple, childish innocence will accord with Christ's words and bring them blessedness, bring them closest to the kingdom of heaven.

We could not, however, think like this had we not through our materialistic view of the world lost knowledge of a child's true nature, as well as of that of a childlike adult. A child is not spiritually poor — on the contrary, it is spiritually well endowed. Contrasted with a child, every grown up is spiritually impoverished, the more so if that person is exposed to influences of cultural life that interfere with his normal ingenuousness. Indeed, we could say that those who have perforce passed through an intellectual training, those who are the vehicle of and the leaders in so-called modern spiritual life, are of all people the most impoverished. The first beatitude does not apply to those who are still happy in their simplicity; it does apply to those whom life has made the reverse of unsophisticated, who are not childlike; it means those who feel their own spirituality has reached aridity, that it has stopped short in a dead end. Those are the people whom the first beatitude means. Rudolf Steiner was right when in his lectures on the gospels he stressed that the term 'poor in spirit' is an inappropriate translation of the Greek original, which could read 'beggar for the spirit.' The Greek words actually contain more than a bare indication of poverty. They imply that such people are aware of their impoverishment and are yearning intensely to transcend it.

Many a habit of thought and emotion that has crept into Christian religious life would show up as wrong if we could arrive at a truer understanding of the first beatitude; above all, that selfish striving after 'blessedness' and timid clinging to surviving traces of childish piety. The Sermon on the Mount begins with the word 'blessed,' but it leads straight on away from blessedness, from blessed heights down to the unhallowed depth; it does this by calling blessed those whose souls are unhallowed because of their impoverishment of soul. Herein the Sermon on the Mount strikes out in a direction that leads away from heaven towards earth; it does not turn away from earth and its problems in a search for heavenly blessedness. It keeps right on as far as the laying of the foundation stone in earthly depths and to incarnation in the vale of human life.

Before we attempt any discussion of the nine beatitudes as a whole, let us look more closely at the words that immediately follow them. We shall in that way be able to bring out more clearly what we are aiming at — a general view of the Sermon on the Mount, and recognition of its nature.

Those words about salt, about light and the city set on a hill, are more than pictorial similes. They are exact pictures — letters of a language that is a revelation, the apocalypse of things supersensible.

What is the city on a hill that was hidden, but which is now to be revealed? The Sermon on the Mount stands at the beginning of the New Testament. At its close, John the Seer speaks of the city that is being revealed to him: 'And he led me up in the realm of the spirit to a great and lofty mountain and showed me the holy city Jerusalem descending out of heaven out of the realm of the Godhead.' (Rev.21:10).

The beatitudes showed the disciples the archetype of the new man; the utterances on salt, light and the city showed them the archetype of the new humanity; the new goal of humankind, the heavenly Jerusalem; the disciples were themselves summoned to become fellow builders and foundation stones of this city. We should remember that the spiritual image of the city on a hill would have been very familiar to the disciples from their previous religious life and from the sacred prophetic writings of the Old Testament. Had not great prophets of ancient times, Isaiah, Ezekiel, let that secret sound in the final chords of their prophecies?

They may even have been familiar with the mystical implications of the words concerning the salt of the earth and of the light of the world. Religious tradition and wisdom right up to a few centuries ago knew the secret of salt, even though that knowledge became rarer from early medieval times and was often cultivated only among alchemists and in Rosicrucian circles. We need only take up a little book by the Swabian theologian, Friedrich Christoph Oetinger, which appeared in 1770: 'The secret of salt, noblest of the beneficent deeds of God in the realm of nature.'

Salt was understood to be the divine crystal, the bearer of eternity, implanted into earthly existence. At one time, at the beginning of things, this earth was pure salt, a clear, transparent crystal in the eyes of God. But then, salt came to be entangled in the accursed fall into sin; it became ineffectual, it lost its crystalline sparkle, its power to preserve. Earth became dull and opaque. The time will come however when the divine crystalline power of salt will be implanted anew into a moribund earth. That new process will resume again in earthly substance grown ineffectual and desolate, rendering it translucent again for the indwelling light of God; it will be the mighty cosmic process of transubstantiation. Thereupon earth will again become a holy crystal, spiritually a new earth. The new Jerusalem will grow in it, built of golden crystal: 'The city itself of pure gold which was like a transparent crystal' (Rev.21:18). Earth recovered its salt through the death and resurrection of Christ. The apocalyptic image of the New Jerusalem has in a special sense yet another indication of the uses of salt crystal in the new creation. It says: 'The city lies like a square; its length the same as its width ... Its length and its width and its height are equal' (Rev.21:16).

The city is presented as a huge cube, and salt crystallizes into a cube. So there we have the city before us, a pure crystal of salt. Those words directed to the disciples, 'You are the salt of the earth' are a mighty cosmic commission. They mean: 'Recreate all existence, be architects of the new creation, of the heavenly Jerusalem; let the holy crystallization of God's salt begin in you, where a transubstantiated earth, Christ's earth, can grow.' Basically the words are the mighty commission to priesthood; to bring about the sacrament of change, of transubstantiation.

The utterance concerning the light of the world, the candle that carries light so that it may shine far and wide, would also have been sacred and familiar to the disciples. Was not the seven branched candlestick set up in the Temple in Jerusalem as a reminder of the light of God? His faithful servants were to cause that light to shine far into the world.

Creation was filled in primordial time with the most brilliant cosmic light. The brightness diminished more and more into earthly darkness. It lit up again because of the Christ; those words, well known to the disciples, came true: 'The people who sat in darkness shall see a great light.' The time will come when creation will again be illumined through and through. Revelation says of the city on the hill: 'And the city does not need the sun or the moon to light it. The light of the revelation of God enlightens it, and its light is the Lamb.' (Rev.21:23).

The nine beatitudes and the nine woes

Words that concern the light of the world are once again a cosmic commission to the disciples. Salt is the body, light the soul of the new creation. As priests, the disciples were sacramentally to form the body and by proclaiming it make known the soul of the new creation. They were to become the first fruits, new creatures of Christ's earth.

Together with the beatitudes, this marks the beginning of the apocalyptic exaltation of the Sermon on the Mount. The nine beatitudes, taken together, make up an organism; they resemble nine members of a body, and the body that they form between them is the entity of spiritual man. No matter how intimately the sounds appeal to the heart, that resound even from the very detail of the beatitudes, the task of this study is to achieve a general concept of their structure, and we can be sure that the fullness of the heart's religious echoes will not be the less for that, but richer.

As far as the beatitudes are from the beginning of St Matthew's gospel, that is about how far from the end of it we shall find a certain other gospel passage. It also consists of nine members, and it corresponds exactly to the nine beatitudes: the nine 'woes' (Matt.23:13–36). The Christ addresses the beatitudes to the disciples, bearers and leaders in the world's ascent. The 'woes' are directed to the Pharisees, bearers and leaders of world destruction, of the old, moribund creation. Just as the beatitudes signal the earliest apocalyptic pictorial indications of the heavenly Jerusalem, so the 'woes' pass on to Christ's prophetic lamentation over the destruction of the earthly Jerusalem. Here we meet one of the most shattering of the secrets of gospel composition: 'Jerusalem, Jerusalem, you killed the prophets and stoned the messengers who came to you. How often have I wanted to call your children together as a hen gathers her chicks under her wings. But you did not want to come. See, your house shall stand deserted.' (Matt.23:37f).

The beatitudes and the creation of the heavenly Jerusalem.

The woes and the destruction of earthly Jerusalem.

Let us now take a look by means of a brief sketch at the organization of the nine beatitudes; we are going to compare each beatitude with the corresponding woe.

The first beatitude: 'Blessed are the beggars for spirit, for within themselves they find the realm of the heavens.' (Matt.5:3).

The first woe: 'Woe to you, you scribes and Pharisees, you hypocrites! You shut the kingdom of the heavens against men. You cannot find entrance yourselves, and so you want to bar the entrance to those who can find it.' (Matt.23:13).

By placing these two passages side by side, we can see clearly that our appraisal above of the first beatitude was right. The poor in spirit are those who are impoverished. A spiritually rich life of the soul did exist once. Human beings possessed these riches in the strength of their childlike disposition. Spiritual riches, bestowed on humanity, came to an end with man's childhood. Human beings came up against the hard rock of earthly physicality. They reached for something alive but what they held in their hand was dead. Peoples felt that they were in the dwelling place of earth, frigid, spirit-forsaken. Two possibilities remain: they had either to realize their impoverishment and admit it to themselves, in which case they would yearn for the spirit, would become beggars for spirit. Otherwise, they would turn poverty of spirit into a verity, denying the actuality of spirit, of man's destiny to commune with the spiritual world. People became either beggars for spirit or else Pharisees. Blessedness and woe, both alike apply to those who lack spirituality. Yet those who long for spirit have a promise whereas those who do not yearn for it are under a curse.

Absence of spirituality is in our own day largely a fact of human life. There are however many Pharisees who make an axiom, a truth out of the lack of spirituality, who declare that there is no world of spirit and that human beings cannot attain to perceptive communion with a supersensible world. Even the first beatitude is made use of by the Pharisees. In interpreting spiritual poverty as childishness, they would like to avoid the true meaning of spiritual poverty, turn poverty into a truth, to deny it and cover it up with illusions. In so doing they take away the 'key of realization'; they obstruct the paths that lead through poverty and worldly wisdom towards new treasure, to the simplicity of a higher order.

Rudolf Steiner shows us in his lecture cycle on St Matthew's Gospel how each of the beatitudes is associated with one or another of the physical, soul and spiritual members of a human being. In that way the nine beatitudes taken together describe man as a whole organism, in fact as heavenly man. We shall be observing at every stage how human personality is constituted.

It is because of their spiritual impoverishment that human beings experience their own physical bodies. The experience of matter can become illusory just because we carry matter around with us as those same physical bodies. In such a situation a man could disavow spirit. The experience could reveal to a person his own self; it could enable him to recognize his own spiritual impoverishment; and then he would long for spirituality. The above is the priestly meaning, the 'blessed' archetypes of a physical human body, namely that a person should arouse within himself a longing for the world of spirit, that he should plead for spirit.

> *The second beatitude*: 'Blessed are those who endure earthly suf-
> fering, for within themselves they find the comfort of the
> spirit.' (Matt.5:4).
>> *The second woe*: 'Woe to you, you scribes and Pharisees, you
>> hypocrites! You devour house and home of widows and make
>> out that you have many prayers to attend to. You load griev-
>> ous destiny upon yourselves.' (Matt.23:14).

Man carries in his physical body the weight and the burden of matter. Everything pertaining to soul and spirit is an energizing, creative force, opposed to the force of gravity exerted by what is merely physical; it engenders a buoyancy. Earthly matter has thus become heavier as humanity has grown poorer in spirit. Man possesses yet another sustaining force. By its means he carries the burden and weight of life and destiny, his own and that of others as well. This sustaining power is bound up in us with something that is not so constant as our physical body but nor is it as unstable as the contents of the soul. Whatever is in command between body and soul we can call a person's *character*. The more 'character' a person has the more closely is he interwoven through this hidden buoyancy with the life and fortune of others, the more such a one shares in them. He bears their grief, for he knows what true sympathy is. There are two kinds of sympathy. There is the sympathy that gushes up in the soul but which turns to sentimentality, and there is sympathy anchored in the profound places of life which shares the burden all the time, and which easily turns into melancholia. This last kind of sympathy is characteristic of the priest and is what

the second beatitude means. Priestly man shapes his own temperament through the trials of fate and the experiences of life. Through it,
the priest learns to understand suffering that everywhere threads its
way through life. (In anthroposophy we speak of the *etheric* body as
those same sustaining life forces that pertain to a person's character).

The unjust priest, the Pharisee, does not share in suffering; he
enriches himself at the expense of human grief. The more others need
him, the more he feels his own power. Putting it crudely, 'he is made
happy by every funeral ordered from him.'

> *The third beatitude*: 'Blessed are those who achieve harmony of
> soul [meek], for in their innermost self they will grasp the
> meaning of the earth.' (Matt.5:5).
> *The third woe*: 'Woe to you, you scribes and Pharisees, you
> hypocrites! Restlessly you roam over land and sea to win just
> one follower. And when you have him, you turn him into a
> son of the abyss, twice as bad as yourselves.' (Matt.23:15).

'Meek' is not only a poor translation of the Greek word *praüs*, it is
actually misleading. French has a nearer equivalent in its *brave*. The
Greek *praüs* carries overtones of quiet courage rather than of 'meekness.' It suggests someone who has overcome his own passions and
desires. Those are the only people able to control others; they can lead,
they can 'possess the earth.' Self control amounting to harmony is the
mark of a leader's soul, of the priestly person.

Ambition, and the thirst for power, become involved in every form
of leadership and domination where self control is lacking. This is
especially true in religious life. A state of mind not inwardly under
control, an attitude of soul lacking in harmony, finds outward expression in fanaticism. Proselytizing and the spread of propaganda
through religious activities proceed from ambition and are the antithesis of 'meekness.' Sermonizing with a view to arousing people to
their own sinfulness (that is, making them 'children of hell') is due to
a thirst for disguised power. Those who exhort to remorse are really
out to dominate others. The true priest, drawing upon his own priestly
heart, desires only to heal. (Anthroposophy speaks of an *astral* body as
the seat of soul impulses; it includes soul natures that have been mastered and harmonized, and which we have met as 'meekness').

The fourth beatitude: 'Blessed are those who hunger and thirst for the Good, for their own doing will satisfy their hunger.' (Matt.5:6).

The fourth woe: 'Woe to you! You are blind guides when you say: It is pointless to call upon the power of the Temple; an oath is only of use when it is sworn by the gold of the Temple. How foolish and blind you are! ... And furthermore you say: It is pointless to call upon the power of the altar; an oath is only of use when it is sworn by the gifts on the altar. You blind men!' (Matt.23:16–22).

The first three beatitudes and woes sketch very emphatically the outline of human nature in its sheathlike character, as something that carries inwardness, but is not in itself inward.

In his physical body, priestly man bears earth's spiritual impoverishment.

In his own life forces he bears the sorrows of humanity.

In his soul nature he carries his own self (in human dignity).

The second group of three beatitudes and woes fill in the outline with currents that resemble the circulatory system of blood. This inward part contains an element that thrusts outward; another element that reposes within itself, and one that strives inward. (Anthroposophy speaks of the sentient soul, the intellectual or mind soul, and of the spiritual or consciousness soul).

The element of inwardness that thrusts forth to the outside is akin to the sentient soul; it is related to the stars, it is *makarios* or 'blessed' whenever it expresses itself in longing for the communion that fulfils itself in all living things. It is hunger and thirst for the bread and wine of the divine life hidden in all earthly existence. Whoever goes through life as it were through a temple, and is eager to accept all things earthly as if from an altar, he is the man of true piety. Piety is the air he breathes.

An unjust priesthood provides the contrast to those people. Such priests make a show of mystification derived from parts of the ritual and from life itself. They envisage piety as being embodied in this ritual or that; they issue detailed ordinances; and in so doing they create the basis for pseudo-religious attitudes — hypocrisy and intolerance.

The fifth beatitude: 'Blessed are the merciful, for they, in their turn, will receive mercy.' (Matt.5:7).

The fifth woe: 'Woe to you, you scribes and Pharisees, you hypocrites! You take a tithe of the herbs, of mint, dill and cummin, but that which is weighty in the Law you neglect: Self-knowledge, love and a compassionate heart ... Blind guides you are. You strain off the gnat in your cup, but you swallow the camel.' (Matt.23:23f).

We have now reached the middle of the beatitudes and woes. They address themselves to the central part of human nature, to the centre of gravity that keeps the balance between the outer constitution and the inward self. We can recognize this as being the conformation of the fifth beatitude; it is in the form of a pair of scales, with an equal weight lying in the left hand as in the right hand: mercy. This is where an ego person learns to love as an individual, that is, as an ego person who meets another regardless of emotional or traditional ties. This is the mercy of the Samaritan towards the man who fell among thieves. Only an ego personality rooted in its own inwardness can extend true love from ego to ego. Those who have not yet found themselves are not capable of love. But whoever really finds himself, in so doing also finds the other person.

To become an ego means a definite inward formative process. Anthroposophy calls that form-giving inwardness which shapes the ego, the intellectual soul. The priestly ego figure is a force of mercy. The Pharisaic intellectual soul lingers permanently in mere formalities, in the sophistries of formalism. It makes no allowance for mercy between people, but encourages what might be called 'socially acceptable formal behaviour' which depends on innumerable rules of social interaction. Because people clutch at 'the law' as imposed from outside, they can attain only to a preliminary, shadowy experience of ego in themselves, not as yet to any viability between one ego and another.

Those are the forms that the Christ came not to destroy but to fulfill. Law finds fulfilment when a person sorts his own self out (judgment), when as an ego he is able to love another ego person (mercy), and when he is able to find a new personal relationship to the world of spirit (faith).

The sixth beatitude: 'Blessed are those whose hearts are pure, for within them they shall behold God.' (Matt.5:8).

The sixth woe: 'Woe to you, you scribes and Pharisees, you hypocrites! You cleanse the cup and the plate on the outside, but inside they are full of greed and poison. You blind Pharisee, first cleanse the inside of the cup; only then does it make any sense for it to be clean outside.' (Matt.23:25f).

Inwardness, turned outward aright, is *piety of life;* it is hunger and thirst for the divine that is present in all things.

Inwardness, based aright within itself, is *egohood capable of love:* it is mercy between one ego person and another.

Inwardness, turned inward aright, is *purity of heart* and that is what makes it possible to mirror the divine world in a human being.

Inward purity is a matter of spirit, not of morality. Through purity, the human heart becomes an organ of spiritual vision, an eye with which to see the realms of spirit. Intellectual cognition can be penetrated only by the shadowy world of sensory appearance. It is only when cognition of the heart is married to intellectual cognition, that we become partakers in the treasure of what is worthy of being called spiritual cognition. The realms of spirit are shut against us as long as the heart is impure, or, as the Bible puts it again and again, 'stony.' We ourselves are to blame for our blindness:

> The spirit world is not closed;
> Your own perceptions are shut, your heart is dead.
> Arise, O learner! Be not discouraged!
> And bathe your earthly breast in the rose red dawn.

In those words Goethe summons us to the bathing that cleanses the heart, and which wakens the heart to become an eye. Goethe is often very close in his utterances to the spiritual meaning of the sixth beatitude; more especially so when he says, 'Great thoughts and a clean heart — we should pray to God for them.' Here he opens the way for a truly Christian theory of awareness of the supersensible, of a vision of God. A marriage of head and heart comes about through purity of heart; it brings about the passing of great thoughts through the head; and the human heart vouchsafes a vision of God. Head and heart in a human being are the paten and chalice; inward purity ensures that brain and blood repose in the paten and the chalice like bread and wine; all human cognition is then like the eating and drinking of bread and wine.

The Pharisaic mind puts external ablution in place of inward catharsis; these people wash the outside of the cup and platter rather than cleanse those inward receptacles — the head and heart — in preparation for communion with divine awareness.

> *The seventh beatitude:* 'Blessed are those who bring peace into the world, for they will be called sons of God.' (Matt.5:9).
>
> *The seventh woe:* 'Woe to you, you scribes and Pharisees, you hypocrites! You are like whitewashed tombs. From outside they are beautiful, but inside they are full of dead men's bones and all kinds of uncleanness. You are like that. From outside you appear before men as though devoted to the Good, but inwardly you are full of hypocrisy and discord.' (Matt.23:27f).

This is where the last group of three beatitudes and three woes begins. And now we are drawing near to what is the essential spirituality in man. A human being wins his way through to his own spiritual members; he reaches basic rights of citizenship in spiritual regions when he is penetrated by spirituality, by the transmutation of his earthly nature. Anthroposophy distinguishes three such essential members by means of which a human being grows into the region of spirit, or else reaches up into it. Through the transforming of soul forces he wins his Spirit Self (*manas*). Through the transforming of life forces he gains Life Spirit (*buddhi*) and through the transforming of the physical body he achieves Spirit Man (*atman*). A time will come when abundant light will be shed on the gospels and especially on the epistles of Paul. This will be when people will have realized that in the holy scriptures the same spiritual truths are present behind the same words. Spiritual science describes them in the way we have indicated. Man's soul forces are what the New Testament calls peace, *eiréne*, but permeated and spiritualized by the Christ (Spirit Self, *Manas*); justice, *dikaiosúnes*, man's life spirit forces permeated by the Christ (*Buddhi*); the Christ ego, the *egó eimi*, insofar as a human being can become a partaker, brings about the new, resurrected body (Spirit Man or *Atman*).

That carries us into the region of the three last beatitudes and woes. Anthroposophy explains how in the course of the current aeon, a human being is able to let the Christ penetrate his soul nature, transmuting it to Spirit Self, and thus to achieve 'peace' as an integral part of his make-up. Anthroposophy teaches that the penetration of the human organism by Life Spirit (justice) and by Spirit Man (The Christ ego) will not enter evolution for a long time. Meanwhile, they will be withheld from individual religious experience, nor will they show beneficence to individual destinies. This finds expression in the beatitudes where the seventh beatitude says, 'blessed are the peacemakers,' yet the last two of them are constrained to say: 'Blessed are those who are persecuted because they serve the higher life; the realm of the heavens is within them.' And 'Blessed are you when you are reviled and persecuted, when lying and hate-filled words are hurled at you because my Being lives in you.' (Matt.5:10f). Peace can dwell in people now. As for justice and the Christ ego, these we lack as yet; nevertheless, people can even now suffer for them, be ridiculed and persecuted on their account. That is why the ninth — the last beatitude — is expressly addressed to the disciples: 'Blessed are you.' The most exalted mysteries must continue to slumber; only those favoured ones whom destiny will have placed in close proximity to Christ may partake in a premonition of the very highest things through their own martyrdom.

The Greek word *eiréne*, peace, implies 'those who establish peace,' 'who bring it.' Peace is a very real spiritual treasure, a force. Peace shines out of those who bear it within themselves. Those who have it are no longer children of men; they are children of God. Such people have incorporated into themselves the first higher member, thereby making themselves belong to God's world. A truly peace-creating sun shines from those souls. The Pharisees' piety is not peace of the sun; it is peace of the tomb. A skeleton lurks at the back of it. Death in the inward parts, the soul's death, creates the illusion of peace.

> *The eighth beatitude:* 'Blessed are those who are persecuted because they serve the higher life; the realm of the heavens is within them.' (Matt.5:10).
>
> *The eighth woe:* 'Woe to you, you scribes and Pharisees, you hypocrites! You build monuments to the prophets and adorn the memorials to the men of God and you say: If we had been there in the days of our fathers we would not have taken part in shedding the blood of the prophets. However, you merely prove thereby that you are sons of those who killed the prophets, and so you fill the measure of your fathers.' (Matt.23:29–32).

Justice is the very existence of what is good. We cannot yet have it in the present aeon, but we can accept persecution for it. Insofar as a human being can partake of justice he does actually enter into the sphere of the kingdom of heaven, but that can only be through the Christ. The first beatitude said that such people would reach the kingdom of heaven. The eighth beatitude takes that up again. Begging for the spirit is the beginning of a path which arrives at its goal when it changes to begging for the Christ, to suffering on his behalf, that is, to 'justice.' The Pharisee is the man of self-righteousness. He repels the bearers of a higher life, the prophets and the righteous. Instead of suffering himself, to be persecuted for justice's sake, it is he who persecutes righteousness.

> *The ninth beatitude:* 'Blessed are you when you are reviled and persecuted, when lying and hate-filled words are hurled at you because my Being lives in you. Rejoice and be glad; in the heaven the full compensation of destiny has been prepared for you. Were not the prophets before you reviled and persecuted just as much?' (Matt.5:11f).
>
> *The ninth woe:* 'You serpents and sons of the serpent! How can you avoid the fall into the abyss when the great decision comes? See, I will send prophets and wise and learned men to you. Some of them you will kill and crucify, the others you will scourge in your synagogues and persecute from town to town. But in time revenge must be taken upon you for the shedding of innocent blood on the earth, from the blood of Abel who was devoted to God, to the blood of Zechariah to son of Barachiah, whom you killed between the sanctuary and the altar. Yes, I say to you: Revenge shall be taken upon present-day mankind for all this.' (Matt.23:33–36).

The 'I' means the body of Resurrection, the resurrected Christ. The disciple receives a reflection of it: 'Blessed are you.' Here the disciple finds himself before the very highest of Christ's magic: the change from the corruptible to the incorruptible. That is why the cry of 'woe' has got to strike out at the demonism of the Pharisees' black magic, which confronts the magic of Christ's resurrection. The last of the woes begins differently from those that went before: 'You serpents and sons of the serpent!' The disciple of Christ absorbs into himself the Risen Christ, even when he must suffer death because of that. There is the point at which the Pharisee becomes a black magician. Black magical torture and execution are the nadir of Pharisaic decadence.

Death is the servant of Resurrection (heavenly reward) — that is when the martyr suffers death. Otherwise death is the servant of demonism; in which case it is the murderer and the killer who inflicts death. These are two aspects of the secret of death.

Death suffered leads onto resurrection and to building the heavenly Jerusalem; demonic murder, murder in the Temple, leads to the destruction of Jerusalem, to its submergence. And so the beatitudes flow on into the words about the city on the hill whereas the woes culminate in the lament for a city doomed to destruction.

The nine membered image of priestly man:
1. The physical body carries the spiritual impoverishment of this earth; pleading for spirit will awaken through it.
2. Life forces carry the suffering of the world; consolation is promised them.
3. The soul is the bearer of the ego, as the force through which a person is allowed to become a leader.
4. Inwardness turned outward is life spirit which seeks the divine in all things.
5. Inwardness at rest within itself is the ego personality who is capable of love and enables human beings to become involved in each other.
6. Inwardness turned inward is purity of heart through which a human being can take the divine world into consciousness.
7. Soul forces penetrated by the Christ are the peace that rays forth making its bearer a member of the divine world.
8. Life forces, penetrated by the Christ, are essential justice in which those become partners take upon themselves the destiny of Christ.
9. Physicality penetrated by the Christ is the power of Resurrection which man can win from death through the Christ.

The law and the Sermon on the Mount

The Sermon on the Mount is the very opposite of Mount Sinai, where Moses received the Law. Christ's Sermon on the Mount replaces the Law of Moses. It does not however repeal it. It transforms it, lifts it to a higher level; it fulfils it. Jesus Christ said, 'You must not think that I have come to abolish the Law or the prophets. My task is not to abolish but to fulfil.' (Matt.5:17).

The hand of the cosmic clock has moved on an hour and humanity has evolved. The time of the law of Moses had run out; and that is why, teaching within the circle of his disciples, the Christ gave them what was in fact the law of Moses but metamorphosed.

What distinguished humanity of the law-giving era from the humanity of early Christian times? The answer lies in the way the Christ announced the annulment of law and the beginning of his own fulfilment of it. 'You have heard the word that was spoken to mankind in the past ... But out of my own power I say to you ...' (Matt.5:21f). The 'I' standing up before his people, the Christ ego itself, is the new universal principle. That ego is more than just a unique human personality; it is a cosmic power whose desire it is to come alive in every human being as a majestic inward force. The Christ 'I' is the higher 'I' in every person. The lightning of the higher ego as it enters humankind in the person of the Christ shatters the stone tablets of the law of Moses; yet it does not destroy them: it melts them down in its own divine fire. What becomes of them? Those stone tablets had hitherto appeared before men in order to pass judgment upon them from without; now they have been changed into warmly pulsating human hearts who know freedom within and who offer leadership derived from inward qualities.

The Greek word *nomos*, 'law,' which occurs in the New Testament, is one of the most many-sided of words; it is a mystery word with many a puzzle involved with it. This is most distinctly felt in the letters of St Paul. In chapters 7 and 8 of his Letter to the Romans the meaning of that one word seems to vary from one line to the next. Nor can we get by in the Sermon on the Mount if, in connection with this word, we think only of the Mosaic law. It deserves a brief but far-reaching look at world and historical connotations.

Our thinking at the present time recognizes three forms of law;

first, the law of nature; then the social law (law of society whether it be that of state or church; a law for the dispensation of judgment, a judicial law), and lastly a moral law that speaks to us in our hearts. These three aspects of the law are closely entwined in the universe as a whole. They are like three different revelations of an archetypal law that rests like a basic structure or primal form in all existence. The archetypal law unfolds in the course of the evolution of human consciousness. Its varying forms evolve from that consciousness. There was a time in the beginning when the law of nature unequivocally ordered all life, including that of the human soul and of morality. Human souls and nature's spirituality flowed as one. Sense perception did not present a human being to nature as some detached observer; rather, he was drawn into natural things. A human became whatever he was observing. Not that man actually became aware of those things; it was those things that became aware of themselves upon the stage of the human soul. Human soul nature followed wherever the senses led; when a man beheld a swaying tree top, or clouds moving through the sky, his soul nature rose towards tree top and cloud. It stretched out like an invisible hand for whatever he perceived, much as a child's hand reaches for the sun. Nor did man separate himself from nature as we do now. Whether it was a tree branch swaying in the wind or his hand moved by his own will — both seemed the same, both were distinct from himself, and yet both were members of himself.

Cosmic harmony, as yet totally sheltered within the womb of divine mother nature, streamed from humankind as wisdom and beauty and goodness. Nature's harmonies and laws determined the outer and the inner life of men who were as yet only a limb of the body of nature. There was, apart from the law of nature, no moral law.

At that time of paradisal innocence man had a part in the perfection which still belonged to Mother Nature, who received it as it welled up from the hand of God. Man was perfect, in the same way that his mother was perfect in the universe. That is how Greek mythology presents it, in depicting Demeter (Ceres) as the great mother, as the earliest dispenser of laws, as the very source of law. Schiller has shown us in splendid language Demeter bestowing the law which not only was the beginning of agriculture, but which established civilization and founded orderly living. Demeter (Ceres) speaks:

> The animal in the wilderness loves his freedom; the gods float free through ether; yet Nature's law tames the urgent desires of all their hearts. But man, set in the midst of them all, must stand by fellow men; he is made mighty only by the power of his own moral strength.

While still embraced by and carried around in the arms of the great mother, humankind did in fact possess a soul, but not his own personal spirit, not yet an 'I.' Anthroposophy calls the soul element which humanity had in that early stage of evolution, the sentient soul. Demeter was the sentient soul of humanity. Next came a time when the pain of separation passed through every realm of creation. The lament of Ceres-Demeter was raised for the daughter stolen from her by the powers of the abyss. And man grew ever deeper into intellect, which is bound to the physical brain; so they separated themselves from the very nature that was still embracing them, feeling that they were sufficient unto themselves. A conflict arose between inwardness and the external world, and with it the dualism of nature and morality arose. The ego-bearing intellectual soul awakened in men and brought him the beginnings of a personal life, of an awareness all his own, but at the same time deprived him of the universal morality of the Demeter era.

To replace Demeter's self-directing law, codes were given to humanity through individual initiates and prophet-leaders. Minos on Crete, Solon in Athens, Moses in Israel were legislators inspired by the divine revelation that was still open to them. The era of Demeter had passed into the era of Moses. A rigid, austerely judicial legalism took the place of the harmonies of maternal universality. Men, feeling within themselves the germ of chaos, now clung to the conventions of law and, in so doing, in obeying the law, created the forms of civilization. The world was thrown open to every kind of discord. Now, people had themselves to struggle in order to reach that harmony which earlier the mother had given them. The soul, warring between life and the ideal, in the chasm that yawned between them, was brought up short against the hard tablets of the law; and yet it clung to them.

The formal character of all law-giving was appropriate for the era of the intellectual soul, for the time of the ego's birth. But as the ego waxed stronger, those bonds and restraints were no longer needed. Made strong by those same restraints, the soul shattered the vessel of their formalism in order to awaken to the *consciousness soul*, to awareness of inward law which is the law of freedom. The higher ego is the content not the form of law; it both fills and fulfils it. From then on, the consciousness soul was to pour itself into the intellectual soul.

Not that something merely identical was to be born anew out of inwardness, something that used once to be prescribed externally by the law; but a life totality is to arise from the 'I,' similar to what existed in pre-ego form during the Demeter era. Spiritual man (the 'I') was in Demeter's time still floating high above the earth. Earthly man (body and soul) was kept in communion with heavenly man by the all uniting mother. During the law-giving era each earthly human being lived in isolation. Now, human beings are again to be reunited with heavenly man; not, however, by earthly man withdrawing to the heights of heavenly man in the manner of the sentient soul, but by the incarnation of heavenly man into earthly man in the manner of the consciousness soul.

Perfection, 'human consecration,' stands both at the beginning and at the end. The Greek word *teleios* really means 'having passed through consecration.' The earliest perfection is infantile innocence in the mother's arms. The next perfection is that of the son who, having reached adulthood, takes his place beside his father. 'You are to come close to the holy aims, as your Father in the heavens is the epitome of all holy aims.' (Matt.5:48).

The Son brings to earth perfection, the image of consecration from his Father's realms. He distributes it in the form of a new inward law, the law of freedom among those who are to become leaders of humankind. He enables the disciples to take their first step out of the disintegrating world of formalism and into the dawning world of ego content. He pours wine into the empty vessels of the law.

The structure of the Sermon on the Mount

We have now brought to our consciousness the inmost aims of the Sermon on the Mount, so that we have gone far enough to set about taking a broad overall view of its structure. We can easily distinguish certain divisions.

The nine beatitudes and the utterances on salt, light and the city upon a hill, are followed by a section on law, complete in itself. Of these six passages, five clearly belong together because each begins in the same way: 'You have heard that it was said ... But out of my own power I say to you ...' Furthermore, of these five passages that begin in the same way, the first three belong together since their opening sentence also contains the words 'the word that was spoken to mankind in the past ...' The three groups complete chapter five of St Matthew.

1. The nine beatitudes
2. The words on salt, light, and the city on the hill.
3. The utterances on the renewal of law.

The remaining chapters (6 and 7) are again made up of three groups, each in turn made up of three parts, the parts also being divisible into threes. The first group embraces the passages on *almsgiving*, on *prayer* and *fasting*. The next carries warnings beginning with 'Do not.' The last grouping has three messages about the new life in the spirit: on *prayer* as the way to the region of spirit: the *narrow gate* as the beginning of the region of spirit; and advice on how to distinguish the good from the evil as a weapon in the spiritual region.

SUMMARY

Blessed are the beggars for the spirit (5:3)
Blessed are those who mourn (5:4)
Blessed are those who exercise self control (5:5)
Blessed is the soul's yearning for spirituality (5:6)
Blessed is the love of one ego towards another (5:7)
Blessed is the heart's visionary power (5:8)
Blessed are those who bring peace (5:9)
Blessed are the martyrs on behalf of goodness (5:10)
Blessed are the martyrs of the Christ ego (5:11f)

You are the salt of the earth (5:13)
You are the light of the world (5:14)
The city upon the hill must reveal itself (5:14–16)

I have not come to destroy the law but to fulfil it (5:17–20)

You have heard it said in the past: you shall not kill ... but I say to
you ... (5:21–26)

You have heard it said in the past: you shall not commit adultery ...
but I say to you ... (5:27–32)

You have heard it said in the past: you shall not swear falsely yourself ... but I say to you ... (5:33–37)

You have heard that it has been said, an eye for an eye ... but I say to
you ... (5:38–42)

You have heard that it has been said: you shall love your neighbour
and hate your enemy ... but I say ... (5:43–48)

1 {
1. When you give alms ... (6:1–4)
2. When you pray ... (6:5–15)
3. When you fast ... (6:16–18)
}

2 {
1. Lay not up for yourselves treasure ... (6:19–24)
2. Take no thought ... (6:25–34)
3. Judge not ... (7:1–6)
}

3 {
1. Ask and it shall be given you ... (7:7–12)
2. Enter in at the strait gate ... (7:13f)
3. Beware of false prophets ... (7:15–23)
}

The fivefold renewal of the law

Let us now turn to aspects of the third of the first three groups, namely
to law giving, which we have not yet discussed in detail.

Laws which the Christ expressly confirmed as having been laid
down in the past concern killing, adultery, and swearing. Contained in
those three words we find a clear path from the physical through to
what pertains to the soul, and so to the human spirit.

> Death emanates from the physical
>
> Adultery emanates from the soul
>
> The false oath is a false spiritual attitude.

The next two utterances on law are not expressly defined as having
been said 'in the past': they refer to something that transcends an individual's physical — soul — spiritual life. Those words on vengeance,

'an eye for an eye, a tooth for a tooth,' refer to human destiny and lays it down that the justice of destiny rests on an even balance, on precise retribution.

According to the biblical concept of the universe, destiny is not so much an idea as an entity. An invisible guide of our own, who ordains all things as the 'hand of God,' presides over the destiny of each one of us. That guide is our angel. The next level above mineral, plant, animal and man is that of the angels. Destiny, even balance, retribution, are supreme in the angelic sphere.

The saying on loving one's neighbour and hating one's enemy again carries us up to a higher level of existence. The destiny of a people also governs the destiny of the individual. And this folk destiny is, to biblical thinking, not merely a concept but rather an entity. Just as angels ordain individual destiny, so archangels rule the destiny of nations (for example, the Book of Daniel (12:1) names the archangel Michael the folk-spirit of the people of Israel: 'At that time shall arise Michael, the great prince who has charge of your people.') A 'neighbour' is a member of the same people. In the ancient view of society an 'enemy' is one who belongs to another people. Spiritual life was in ancient times tied to the concept of race: it partook of the archangel. To the Greeks, non-Greeks were 'barbarians.' Intent upon entering forcefully into the ranks of his own folk god (archangel), a man would have drawn a sharp distinction between his neighbour and the 'barbarian,' even when no war raged.

In the last of this group, the Christ confirms the law governing the destiny of individuals and of peoples.

You shall not kill	Body	
You shall not commit adultery	Soul	The individual
You shall not forswear thyself	Spirit	

An eye for an eye, a tooth for a tooth	Individual destiny — Angel
Love of a neighbour, hatred of an enemy	Folk destiny — Archangel

Five trumpet calls announce in powerful terms the dawn of a new cosmic age: 'You have heard that it was said ... But I say to you ...' The ego invades humanity like a shaft of lightning. Christ wields the staff of Moses whose first deed it was to turn water into blood. The inmost laws of human existence were entirely changed by the entry of the ego impulse.

The external forms of society had already been created and they had given humanity some notion of the archetypal, purely spiritual realms that were still soaring above the world of the senses. But now the archetype was to be poured into a form, to become its content. It was to result in a new consciousness. The fact that we now have a new morality is but one aspect of the all-involving transmutation which is taking place in the totality of our way of life.

The old laws on killing, adultery and false swearing had belonged to the conditions of physical behaviour, to external processes in the course of which people could commit sin; killing, adultery, perjury were patterns of external behaviour. But now that a person's archetypal configuration, his own ego, had been poured into his physical and soul sheaths, from that time on the question became what archetypal phenomenon is the basis of killing, of adultery, of the false oath? As inward law took the place of external legality, so intimate, hitherto unconscious inward processes took effect in the sphere of law.

What were the primordial configurations, the archetypal phenomena; what are the deep-seated origins of killing, adultery, of the oath forsworn?

The archetype of killing is the repression by the physical of spirituality. Wherever one person's spirituality is torn down by the superior physical and bodily weight of someone else, there you have the inception of killing. The outward death blow is after all the culmination of physical processes against which the victim's spirit is unable to assert itself. Whatever pushes an ego deeper into the body is already an act of killing.

The Sermon on the Mount points to three kinds of killing: impulses of anger against his fellow men; arrogant disdain against his fellow men; cursing his fellow men out of hate and enmity. Anger lies like an incubus on those against whom it is directed. It kills, even as it presses down, as it forces its way into the other's bodily system. If one person confronts another with disdainful thoughts or words he is pushing that other one deeper into the corporeal.

You have heard the word that was spoken to mankind in the past: You shall not kill. And: Whoever kills brings crisis to his destiny. But out of my own power I say to you: Even he who allows impulses of anger to burn against his fellow men brings crisis to his destiny. And whoever turns against his fellow men with arrogant disdain, sins against the spiritual guidance of his people. And as for him who curses his fellow men out of hate and enmity, he causes his soul to become prey to the cosmic flames. (Matt.5:21f).

We still use the Greek term, *krisis*, for a turning point, especially in disease. The judgment, the crisis, means attainment of a point where direction of movement can still be reversed, where ascent can change to a fall. Especially so in the case of an individual. Anger kills personality. One who kills through anger reaches the *krisis* in his own personality; he is cast forth out of his proper course. Whoever looked on his fellow men with arrogant disdain was killing the human being in a man and in so doing was attacking the nation as a whole, the whole of humankind. That is why the perpetrator would have to undergo within himself a kind of catastrophic falling away from his nation and from humanity in order to compensate for what he has done. Whoever speaks words of hate and enmity is killing the whole earth; he is killing earthly creation present in a man. That is why his soul becomes prey to the flames of hell.

The archetype of adultery is the pollution of spirit by the soul. Every unclean mixing of what pertains to the soul with what is of the spirit, every dragging of the spirit through the mire, is adulterous. For union of what is of the soul with the spiritual is the primal phenomenon of wedlock. In general, prior to the advent of the ego impulse, people were aware of marriage only as something external, and as being still in the area of formal legalism. However, marriage was held to be sacred and divine. At the same time among the Jews, marriages of consanguinity and those born from such marriages definitely expressed a relationship of the person concerned to the spiritual world and of the spiritual world to that person. Any breach of the rules of marriage meant an impure relationship to the spiritual world. A kind of penetration took place — and still takes place to this day in a certain sense — in every marriage. The soul nature of the man is penetrated by that of the woman; the woman's spirit is penetrated by that of the man. That is why the woman takes the man's name. Even if in ancient times women and men were divorced, they still bore within themselves the soul or spiritual elements that had passed from one to the other. A kind of pollution of these elements set in because, unless cultivated, in a sense they rotted — that is, unless the man returned and also received back through the prescribed document of divorce what had flowed from one to the other in marriage.

Once the 'I' had arrived, that interplay between soul and spirit became possible in a single individual. The possibility of adultery can come about inwardly through corrupt sensations of pleasure impinging on spiritual striving; or through disloyalty to spiritual goals already accepted and implanted into the soul. Had those words concerning plucking out the eye and cutting off the hand implied no more than the ascetic ideal of medieval times, that drove people into cloisters, then there would have been no such emphasis on the right eye and the right hand. Failure to notice this point has become one of those traditional superficialities which have made the Sermon on the Mount both trivial and moralistic.

The right half of the human body is the one that takes hold of things earthly; the left half tends rather to draw back towards the soul. The tendency to become too strongly earthbound is due to an Ahrimanic one-sidedness, and it finds expression in the right side of the body; on the left is the tendency to flee from the earthly; this, and fantasy, are a Luciferic one-sidedness. Accordingly, organs on the right side (eye and hand) are the ones that draw the spiritual too far down into the earthly, in perception (by the eye), and in action (by the hand). That is why the right eye is the adulterous one and the right hand the adulterous hand. The right eye, the right hand, forcibly cut off a human being from the spirit even as they drag spirituality forcibly and foully down into the soul. To pluck out the right eye, to cut off the right hand, means to overcome unclean, irreverent emotions in the soul's attitude towards the spiritual worlds; it means sensitivity towards the spirit; not to snatch spirit towards oneself and then to leave it in tatters to rot in the soul; to seek only as much of the spiritual as is bestowed by the spirit itself to any one person, and then only as much as that person is able faithfully to cultivate.

The archetype of swearing an oath is arrogance of spirit in face of the spiritual. 'You shall not swear falsely'; the Greek could be rendered better by 'you shall not over-swear yourself.' Here we have a person's own attitude that matters. To swear is to put a spell on someone or something. In ancient times, when humanity was still in the sentient soul stage, when people were still at one with nature, they were able, by the strength of certain oaths, to identify their own spirituality with that of the cosmos; this was because the human spirit was not yet incorporated in egohood. A man could, as it were, lever himself right up until he was able actually to call upon more exalted cosmic forces as his witnesses; he could himself become one with that spirituality, whether he took an oath or whether he declared his innocence before a judge. An oath was a divine court of justice. If the oath was unclean or perjured, it could even be that people could die of a perjured oath, as many a tradition relates. The true force of oath-taking, of conjuration of the gods, lay in the fact that men were themselves dwellers in heaven, gods as to their own nature.

As the ego entered further into its earthly human dwelling, so the power of conjuration ceased. Nowadays, the deviation lies not in a man overstepping an oath, that is, in calling up as witness a god higher than he should, but in that the man swears an oath at all. We should speak from our own spirit, Yea and Nay are from now on the strongest words of magic. From now on, the deviation of swearing is not only external; it can also be inward. Every kind of arrogance, all spiritual presumption, every extravagant promise, every resolution that is subsequently not carried out — all these are to 'overswear,' a judgment of God which in every case already bears within itself a backlash of retribution.

> To kill: to press down spirit by the physical.
> Adultery: to besmirch spirit through the soul.
> To swear: arrogance of spirit in face of the spiritual.

That ancient utterance of the law, '*An eye for an eye, a tooth for a tooth,*' brings us closer to the secret of individual destiny. As long as humanity was not the bearer of egohood, the law of destiny that demanded even-handed justice for human deeds worked itself out differently from the way in which it works for ego man. Requital invariably took place under angelic governance. This could have been because the angels themselves brought about the process of requital through organic cause and effect, either in that same earthly life, or as resulting destiny at some later time; or even, to put it differently, the angels could find a helper. That helper could be the judge, or else the free human ego itself. In pre-ego times it was normal for leaders of the community, in their capacity as its judicial authority, to impose punishment which embodied a requiting destiny. The further we human beings grow into the era of the ego, the more we choose freely to undertake the role of the angels as well as that of the judge. We become the forgers of our own fortunes, being fully responsible for our own lives. We make amends for the backward step which is the consequence of error; we can make good by even greater devotion to virtue. That is what we do when we 'add the cloak to the coat.'

The fifth utterance on law — 'You shall love your neighbour and hate your enemy' — carries us from individual destiny to the destiny of peoples, from the angel to the archangel. Before individualization everyone served their own folk gods, the archangel of that nation. A person's folk-spirit was also his own ego for as long as he himself lacked one. People were bound by blood love to their 'neighbour,' one who was a relative, and were cut off from all those who were not related by consanguinity. Members of other peoples were barbarians and enemies. In eras before egohood, before individualization, wars were due to conflict between archangels; they were not a matter of human ethics. To the individual, wars were due to some superior fate, as were natural disasters. Barriers of ethnicity began to fall with the advent of egohood. Now, men are not only physically interrelated, through the 'I' we have become related in the spirit with the whole of humanity. It is not just nations that meet each other along national frontiers, but individual human beings. People are acquiring influence over the destiny of the archangels because they are gaining the power to love the stranger and also the enemy. Humanity is beginning to take the place of the archangels. Issues that were previously decided by war are now being decided by the growth among individuals of a frame of mind affecting everyone else, a mood that is struggling towards the light in a fight against personal and national egotism.

We have considered in general terms archetypal phenomena pertaining to law, to which the fivefold metamorphosis refers. We are now going to apply the key we found in earlier studies so as to penetrate further into the detail of the text: namely, we are to think of the Sermon on the Mount as a guide to the priesthood, as pastoral theology. We shall then see that the change from externalized legalism to an inward sense of law was also a change in the priestly function, the change from a judicial and punitive role to one that was more concerned with succouring the soul. The Christian priesthood became the antithesis to pre-Christian priesthood and thus the earliest realization and source of the forward march of the inward law which is the law of freedom.

In pre-ego times the priest was also a judge. He had to inflict punishment on those who came to him for confession or who were convicted of some misdeed; punishment that would bring about the retribution needed for each individual destiny. It was the priest who carried out those words, 'An eye for an eye, a tooth for a tooth.' He lifted their sins from people by punishing them. Nor was it merely right for him to do this, it was his duty as long as there was no ego. After the mystery of Golgotha the same procedure on the part of the priest meant enfeeblement of the human soul. The time had come to implant ego strength and will-power and to cultivate them. Souls were to be united with the Christ ego and filled by it, to enable them to guide their own destinies. They had themselves to bring about whatever was essential to that destiny by virtue of the higher ego, and of the Christ.

That is a secret which Jesus Christ spoke often to the disciples. Instead of inflicting punishment in his capacity of judge, a priest had from then on to learn how to impart strength by merely helping. This is when the pastoral art originated of, as it were, placing into a persons own hands the strength to enable him to undertake the guidance of his own destiny. Every consideration of Christian church history reveals that Petrine Christianity fell back all too soon into pre-Christian times when people were relieved of their sins; their ego was weakened by being punished.

In that way the saying 'Resist not evil' and the words on turning the other cheek, and on the cloak and the coat, became golden rules for the care of souls, and for the part that the priest must play in guiding the destiny of members of his congregation.

Let us once more go through the five utterances on the law and on their transmutation in relation to the priesthood. To the disciples as priests in the making, the words on killing meant: You are no longer to force people back into earthly matter in your role of stern judge. You are to speak no words of banishment. You are not to sermonize at people on the wrath of God! The sacramental act that you are to carry out is by its character bound to egos, of participants who should be united as a community in their spirit. You are therefore not to celebrate at all unless you act in such a way that the nightmare is dispelled which pushes souls down into physical bodies. The last verses of that section contain an especially important direction: 'So, if, as you are making your offering, you become conscious of having done someone an injustice, let your gift lie before the altar, and first go and be reconciled to your fellow man, and then offer your gift.' (Matt.5:23f).

The priest's personal destiny has to be in proper order if it is not to interfere with his sacred task. The priest cannot allow himself to carry about, without resolution, things unresolved in his own destiny. Every such irregularity, even if unknown to the congregation, is none the less sensed by them. The priest 'kills' the truth of the sacrament in the souls of his people.

The words on adultery can be translated for the priest by the following warning: strive towards purity and loyalty in your spiritual endeavour. Live your example of piety to people, a piety independent of the spasmodic and fitful forces in the ebb and flow of emotions. Rather, set the example of piety where soul serves spirit and does not merely seek it in order to keep it for itself. That would indeed be to serve God. Keep in mind that merely emotional Christianity is threatened by an inward adultery. Lead your people into the spirit by your priestly authority by a path where they will be able to unite with the spirit in purity and faith.

Those words on false swearing are for the priest an exhortation towards humility in his awareness. A priest may not set himself up as being nearer to heaven than other people. He must not pretend that he is able through his ritual to command what is of the spirit (that is, by conjuration). He is not to drape himself in a cloak of initiation. The priest should realize and act on his realization that in matters spiritual it is especially true to say that the path to hell is paved with good intentions. Every broken resolution relating to spiritual striving cruelly throws us back in our spiritual path, even though we may not perceive it. The art of a spiritual way of living lies in quiet and patient humility of consciousness. He feels that inward growth is due to divine grace; he allows himself no impatient hankering to 'get moving.' The true priest will set an example of the art of living such as that.

— The first utterance on the renewed law on killing shows the leader the way in which to bring men out of an unfree, authoritarian Christianity.
— The utterance on adultery shows him how to pass beyond egoistic, soulfully emotional Christianity.
— The utterance on false swearing shows how he can pass beyond the hypocritical pretensions of the theurgic Christianity of magic.
— Words on destined restitution transform the functions of a judge to those of a helping priest.
— Words on love for the enemy point out to the priest the path of tolerance.

The last utterance could be put in this way for the priest: Do not take up polemics. Conduct your priestly duties aware that everyone, even 'non-Christians' and opponents, belong to the community that you are to lead. Include all opponents in the community on whose behalf you are to celebrate as priest. Do not set up limitations out of denominational differences in place of old racial demarcations. Think of yourself as priest to the whole of humanity, not of one sect. Be there for all people.

The law, thus internalized, was made a reality for the first time in the priestly ministry. It is the path to the true consecration of man: 'You ... must be perfect as your heavenly Father is perfect' (Matt.5:48 RSV).

— *The nine beatitudes* are an image of Spirit Man in his descent to earth.
— *The words on salt, light and the city:* an image of the new creation.
— *The fivefold fulfilment of the law* points the way to the consecration of man which in turn leads to ultimate attainment of a frame of mind that will embrace the whole of humankind.

The path of consecration

The path of man's consecration continues in chapters 6 and 7. The earlier summary shows three tripartite sections now follow. It is, then, a matter of a threefold evolution, a preparing for the consecrated training of a trinity hidden within men. Let us look first of all at the first two of these sections:

1. Almsgiving — prayer — fasting.
2. To lay up no treasure — to take no thought for the morrow — not to judge.

We find that in each case the human hand, the heart, and the head are, as it were, addressed in turn: will, feeling and thinking. In the first group all these are more concerned with the religious life of day to day living (alms, prayer, fasting); in the next group it is rather a matter of external affairs (amassing treasure, worrying, criticism). The giving of alms is an activity of the hand prompted by the will. Prayer is the religious activity of the heart, borne up by feeling. Fasting, when it used to take place and wherever it is still practised, is the cause of religious awareness. Those who fasted were at pains to enter upon a consciousness undimmed by physicality, and it is in fact possible to bring about by fasting a clairvoyance of a kind that is, however, at the present time, unwholesome and actually harmful. It is the relationship between fasting and the head that motivates these words in the Sermon on the Mount: 'But you, when you practise self-discipline, anoint your head and wash you face' (Matt.6:17).

The danger of avarice threatens the busy hand in the context of daily life (laying up treasure). Enfeeblement and uncertainty threaten the heart ('grey-faced anxiety'). Coldness and lovelessness in one's thinking threaten the head (criticism, judgment).

The *Luciferic temptation* is active in the region to which the Sermon on the Mount would lead us by way of those words on almsgiving, prayer and fasting. These are the powers that would entangle us in a euphoric kind of self-satisfaction and conceit. In the region to which the words on laying up treasure, on being anxious, and on passing judgment would lead us, powers are at work which would bind men in what is too much of this earth, in the bonds of things superficial. They would turn us into ossified creatures with clawlike hands, with hearts devoid of serenity, with calculating prejudiced minds — *Ahrimanic temptation*.

Lucifer lies in wait in the religious sphere, desiring to estrange men from earthly life.

Ahriman lies in wait desiring to entangle men too deeply in the sensual world.

We shall see that this review also sheds light on the meaning and structure of the last and most important trinity of the Sermon on the Mount which brings its teaching to an end.

3. Ask — seek — knock: Enter — beware.

In order to understand aright the transition from the second to the third group of three utterances, we are going to look more closely at the part on judging, that is, at the beginning of chapter seven. 'Do not judge, or the judgment will fall upon yourselves.' (Matt.7:1). In the light of this utterance it is especially necessary — and also especially easy — to trace the transition from the old view to the new. In place of the old, narrowly moralistic concept we shall try to outline a more all-embracing one which will, however, definitely include morality. This kind of outlook I should like to describe as a theory of spiritual perception. The Greek word for 'to judge' is related to *krisis*, and it survives in many a derivative form as in crisis, criticism, critique, criterion and so on. As a matter of fact, that word 'to judge' does not imply anything proceeding from evil intent, from an unethical approach. It implies no arrogance, no loveless criticism, nor pleasure in condemnation; it does indicate a thought form, a manner of shaping ideas which is at a certain stage in human evolution actually the normal one, and proper to all people as they enter upon that stage. The critical mind, the intellect, has to be developed; to acquire and to exercise it is not a moral offence. On the contrary, it is an essential stage of evolution. It is this same critical mind that the New Testament calls 'judgment.' Perhaps we may be allowed to link this up with some observations culled from contemporary life.

In the early days of our Christian Community you could often see opponents at public lectures who wished to inform themselves about the new movement. There were two types — poles apart — easily distinguished and represented by clergy of the two principal denominations, Roman Catholic and Protestant. (It should hardly be necessary to say here that we are passing no generalized verdict; we are describing personal experiences that were typical and characteristic). I have often noticed Catholic priests taking their place in the centre of the hall; surveying everything serenely, they would listen attentively, and would not lose their equanimity when views that diverged from those of Roman Catholicism were presented. On the other hand, one could over and over again observe the following in the case of Protestant ministers. Every unfamiliar view needled them like pin-pricks before they had so much as heard the end of it. Their prejudice constantly urged them to throw themselves into the arena of debate. It happened quite often that their impatience grew to the point where, having ascertained that there was to be no discussion, they would storm out and slam the door behind him.

A third manner of listening seemed to me to be that of Londoners in Hyde Park on a Sunday, when people gather round the speakers' stands to hear all kinds of political and religious opinions. They seemed able to listen to it all, however contrary, with thoughtful detachment. The manner of an Englishman's listening appears akin to that of the Roman Catholic priest. And yet, there is a characteristic gulf between them.

The assurance of the Roman Catholic is that of the sentient soul, which precedes the critical faculty. The irritability of the Protestant is the result of the critical attitude of the intellectual soul. The Englishman's confidence is an example of the behaviour of the consciousness soul — even though it may be something of a caricature. It has advanced beyond criticism. When a typical Roman Catholic hears religious matters being discussed, he is in some way or other detached by the sentient soul. Individual intelligence is silent; only the intelligence of the Church lives, embodied in dogma; it alone is felt to be the mouthpiece for the ordinances of the world of spirit. No matter what a typical Catholic may hear about religion, he will recall what 'the Church' may have to say or teach on that particular topic. It is, however, not emotion but thought that is lifted to supersensible states under the influence of the sentient soul. One is quite satisfied to be moved from one point to the next, keeping in mind to steep oneself in whatever the Church in its superior wisdom teaches. He finds no difficulty in obeying the dictum, 'Judge not.' He does not judge — the Church does! He is excused from critical thinking in the religious field because there exists for him a stratum of tradition and dogma above that of earthly understanding. A sense of security when listening to unfamiliar ideas is his on the strength of the qualities of his own sentient soul which lifts him clear of the region of disputation and argument.

In contrast to him is the person who has lost the capacity of letting himself be carried into an element of the supersensible and religious.

Such a one is wholly of this earth and that is what inevitably his think-ing has to be. Simple folk have to a large extent right up to our own time retained some of the influences of the sentient soul in their reli-gious life. In recent decades Protestant theology, and especially what is known as 'liberalism,' has of necessity led to the weakening of old, pre-critical religious forces. Religious thinking has, through the intel-lectual soul, become totally earthly and ego-influenced. And yet the ego is still too feeble to endure opposite opinions; this results in irri-tability when it comes to discussion. This is where that utterance is ful-filled, 'Judge not that you be not judged.' Eventually, all criticism enfeebles the 'I.' We think we are passing judgment but it is we who are judged. The nervousness of modern living results from intellectu-alism, which reveals itself most glaringly when people think about matters of religion. The condemnation of any weakness, whether the opinion be objectively justified or not, calls forth the same weakness in the soul of the critic. How negative, then, must human thinking be nowadays, and therefore how destructive! 'For with every slighting judgment that you make you actually judge yourselves. With the measure that you use, you too will be measured.' (Matt.7:1f). Had we the choice only between uncritical and critical thinking (Catholicism and Protestantism) we ought still to have the courage to take our stand on the side of critical thinking even if, in so doing, we destroy our-selves.

There is, however, another path out of the intellectual soul besides that of regression into the sentient soul (that is, to 'mere' faith): there is also a way that leads forward into the consciousness soul. The manner in which those English people listen is a one-sided attitude of the con-sciousness soul. Its admirable aspect is that it stems from a certain ego-strength and that it leads onto further strengthening of the 'I.' The art of positive listening is not only a sign of inward strength; it is also the real source of such strength. This is where the words are valid: 'To him who has it, more will be given ... From him who does not have will be taken even that which he has.' (Matt.13:12).

We can recognize in the critical theology and the biblical criticism that arose in the nineteenth century to what unhappy extent those peo-ple were compelled, in the course of developing their own intellectual soul, to overstep the dictum 'Judge not.' The step into the conscious-ness soul is the positive fulfilment of the Christ's command 'Do not judge, or the judgment will fall upon yourselves.' That also means, 'Fulfill rather than destroy.' In the Sermon on the Mount Jesus allows his disciples to peer from the regions of law and of the intellectual soul into the future domain of the consciousness soul. Leaders and priests are no longer to be judges, neither in thought nor in deed: they are to be people who understand and help. They are to be 'those who pity because they know.' They are to be like Parsifal awake, for Parsifal is the true image of man in the consciousness soul. No longer is he to wound himself as well as others; no longer an Amfortas suffering from the wound inflicted upon himself with his own spear.

In the passage on the splinter and the beam in another's eye as well as in our own, which follows the words on judgment, we are again up against one of those traditionally superficial interpretations of the gospel. We have overlooked the circumstance that a splinter and a beam should be present in, of all places, an eye! If we treat that image exactly, then we realize that to have a beam in the eye means to be blind; to have a splinter in the eye is to be partly blind. To have a beam in one's own eye is to realize that one is blind. To see a splinter in someone else's eye is to assume that person to be blind or stupid.

The earthly ego, with its total intellectualism, is the true beam in the eye. It is the cause of blindness when it comes to the world of spirit. Those who have become totally intellectual too easily look down on anyone in whom a residue of the old sentient soul still lingers, perceiving them as naive, retarded, country-bumpkins! In that case, especially if one is a priest or leader, one will turn into a Pharisee. The arrogantly critical intellect despises what is left of the old sentient soul's way of looking at things as stupid, or so much folly. Parsifal's foolishness means nothing to him. Such a leader makes others more blind than ever by what he does himself. The nineteenth century school of critical theology was an essential evolutionary phase even though it regarded the old religious forces, the old strength of faith, as atavism, as splinters in the eye.

If we continue to read the Sermon on the Mount in the usual way, then the seventh chapter, especially, gives the impression of an arbitrary string of disjointed sayings. This is what follows directly on the dicta about judging and the splinter and the beam. 'Do not give what is holy to dogs. And do not throw pearls before swine.' And then, 'Ask, and it will given you.' If we accept it all as intimate initiation teaching we can clearly feel the cohesion in that lucid though seemingly inconsequential sequence.

In cultivating our intellect we create for ourselves a kind of spirituality that we do not desire, that makes of us someone quite different in our feeling and willing. That is why Goethe rejected Kant's philosophy which derives wholly from the intellectual soul, because it enriches our thinking 'but does not make us better people.' On the contrary, if we remain too much 'in the head,' the forces of will and feeling emerge from the unconscious and, enraged at being neglected, they find expression not in human instincts but in bestial ones. The will gets mixed into emotional life in the shape of a ravening dog; feeling is perceived as a rooting pig. The word 'cynicism' is derived from the Greek word for dog, *kyon*. The will, neglected, adds cynicism, the element of the mad dog, to thought. All one-sided intellectualism tends towards mockery, to sarcasm, to cynicism. As for the neglected emotions, they get mixed up with thinking as brutish, as thick-skinned egotism. Should the holiness of heavenly revelation (the good news) or the soul's treasure of true morality (the pearl) sink into the domain of mere intellectualism, then there is no more than a step before the holy thing is torn by dogs and trampled by swine. Only the consciousness that has already passed through the plain of thorns, fraught as it is with temptation, and has reached the heights beyond, only such a one is able to tame and redeem the wild beasts within a human being, the dogs and the swine. Instead of vivifying the divine in us, religious understanding and revelation in intellectual terms serves only to awaken the beast in us.

Christian schooling: ask, seek, knock

How then does the leader among men achieve the redeeming consciousness? How does he attain to thinking about and truly proclaiming the divine thoughts? The Sermon on the Mount goes on to answer those questions. We have reached the transition from the second to the third group of threes.

> 2. — Amassing treasure (the will gone astray)
>   — Anxiety (feeling gone astray)
>   — Judging (thinking gone astray).
> 3. Ask, seek, knock — Enter — Beware.

There, in the very middle, is the narrow gate. We are to strive towards an accurate spiritual understanding of this image. It is clear from the way in which the image of the threshold and the gate to initiation is heralded in what has gone before: 'Knock, and the door will be opened to you.' (Matt.7:7).

What is the narrow gate? It is the same as the eye of the needle in Christ's saying: 'It is easier for a camel to go through the eye of a needle than for a rich man to enter the kingdom of God' (Matt.19:24 RSV). That needle's eye, the narrow gate, is the portal of death, the portal of the 'I.' A doorway looks small at a distance. The nearer we get to it, the wider it seems. Once we are standing right in it, it is as wide as the world itself because it admits us into space; and thereupon we see it no more. The reverse is true of the gate of death. To the physical eye, the starry worlds and the sky are the boundless universe. The world-wide portal of the sense world shrinks to a point at death when we lay aside as a sheath what is of the body. There is nothing we can take with us; we can no longer be 'rich.' We must squeeze through the needle's eye, through the point of our own 'I' nature. Those who are unable to let the earthly drop away are too gross to pass through the needle's eye. On the far side of the needle's eye the human being becomes a sphere that envelopes all earthly existence within itself. Concerning the threshold of the needle's eye, this utterance applies: 'I and my Father are one,' for the Father is the sphere that contains all the heavens. There, the point and the sphere meet as one.

What a human being experiences in death is also experienced by earthly man in the course of real spiritual striving. The 'I' is the 'narrow gate.' The soul has at that stage to become quite poor. The wide portal which leads to destruction is the world of sensory perception. Transitoriness and corruption are masters there. The narrow path is the path of the ego. The wide path, being wide, is no path. To walk along the wide path is not to walk along any path at all. But whoever walks along no path, who saunters through life with no spiritual schooling, loses his way, is lost.

The full and exact truth of those words, 'So it is not I who live, but Christ lives in me' (Gal.2:20), applies to the narrow I-door; here, both death and resurrection take place; sacrifice, and the transmutation of human consciousness. The sentient soul dies; the consciousness or spirit soul, penetrated through and through by the Christ, arises.

Admittedly, only those can respond to the call, 'Enter through the narrow gate,' who have already responded to that other call, 'Ask, and it will be given you. Seek and you will find. Knock, and the door will be opened to you.' Only a life of meditation and striving can lead to that door.

There would be no sense in reopening the trite old problem, often discussed so much in theory — prayer or meditation? Let whatever it may be that the Sermon on the Mount calls upon us to practice, become prayer; it can only mean praying and struggling towards a different kind of consciousness, towards spiritual, holy awareness. Those words 'knock and it shall be opened' testify that those words are meant for the door of the spirit to be opened for revelation. The next words about the narrow way show that it is not a matter of emotional prayer when occasion prompts, but a defined path of regular exercise in prayer.

The person who has something to give, above all a priest, would wish, so far as he is able, that whatever he bestows to be not stones but bread, not serpents but fish. This he cannot do unless he himself follows the way of meditation, himself receiving bread and fish in inward communion. As he meditates, so he gives bread and fish to himself, to his own 'son' who is his ego.

This kind of giving is the same as receiving from God the Father. He who, by meditation, bestows the communion on himself, is able to pass communion on to his congregation. The priest who does not meditate gives stones in place of bread, serpents in place of fish. To have great thoughts and a pure heart and to give of them means to bestow bread and wine, bread and fish. Great thoughts are the holy wafer, the fruit of a brain penetrated by the Christ. A pure heart is the wine. Critical thinking is stony; it lacks the quality of bread. Feeling and willing, not mastered, offer a serpent in place of the chalice (throwing holy things to dogs, the pearl before swine).

The new world order is beginning in the meditative life of the priest. Starting there, it is transplanting itself into all priestly activities, into the social environment of the congregation and of humanity as a whole. The new consciousness, kindled in this world, shines ever more brightly. The taste of communion spreads through the world like leaven.

The last group of threes — ask, seek, knock; enter; beware — builds the trinity of hand, heart, and head, of willing, feeling, thinking. In this context, ask, seek, knock — prayer and meditation — derive from the human will. The inward hand knocks. Then the utterance on the narrow gate is the heart. The true priest will have had to pass through the ego and through death in the strength of his own heart's selflessness. He will strive from the other world, from beyond the needle's eye. If he does, then he will be the bringer of the Tree of Life and of its fruits. Thought is transformed on the far side of the gate into the power of recognizing spirits: 'You can recognize them by their fruits.' Whoever labours from this side of the portal brings only thorns and thistles instead of figs and grapes (bread and wine): 'You can recognize them by their fruits. Can grapes be harvested from a thorn bush, or figs from thistles?' (Matt.7:16). Beyond the I-gate is the sun, and within the sun is the Tree of Life. On this side is darkness. The Lamb is on the far side, the Golden Fleece. On this side is the Wolf of Fenris (darkness). This is the wolf who, in German mythology, devours the sun. The creature who on this side behaves like the lamb is actually none other than the wolf in sheep's clothing.

This is where every priestly activity passes its ordeal by fire. Merely intellectual consciousness, critical thinking, is the Wolf. The new priestly consciousness (or spirit) soul is the shining Lamb of the Sun. But the intellectual soul is able to acquire a pious vocabulary, a pious intonation, a Christian terminology; it can pretend to have passed through the needle's eye. In that case the intellectual soul is the wolf in sheep's clothing. Destruction emanates from such a one in spite of the priestly robes. Talk of the ego does not mean that a person has passed through the needle's eye. Talking about the Christ does not make one a bearer of the Christ nor confer ability to dispense the power of Christ. That is the meaning here: 'Not everyone who says "Lord, Lord" to me will gain entry to the realm of the heavens, but he who acts according to the will of my Father in the heavens' (Matt.7:21). To say 'Lord, Lord' means to talk of the 'I' and of the Christ. The mere words are still thorns and thistles. It is only when talk is no longer of the ego and of the Christ, but when speech emanates from the ego and from the Christ, that the fruit from the Tree of Life ripens, from the good tree which is not to be felled and cast into the fire! And so the Christ addresses the disciples, 'Be on your guard against those who make themselves tools of deceiving spirits.' That means — use the power of your own strengthened thinking to distinguish between the spirits that are within you. Examine yourselves to see whether you are on his side or on the far side of the strait gate, beware of the false prophets within yourselves.

Ask, seek, knock!
This is the call to activity to the will of meditative striving. The spiritual world no longer opens of itself.
Enter!
A call to selflessness, which begins in feeling.
Beware!
A call to strengthen thought to the point where it is able to distinguish and separate spirits.

Let us now set out once more the three groups of threes in chapters six and seven.

1. Almsgiving, praying, fasting   Luciferic temptation
2. Gathering treasure, anxiety, judging   Ahrimanic temptation
3. Ask, Seek, knock, enter, beware   Christian schooling.

If we take the first and the last members of the third group, we could put them thus: Pray and watch! The Christ stands between them as the portal, as the one who said, 'I am the door.' Whoever obeys the first summons (pray) will find the right content, free of Luciferic influence, in almsgiving, praying, fasting. Those who observe the warning: Watch! (Beware of the wolves in sheep's clothing) will find out the true content of what has become Ahrimanic in amassing treasure, in anxiety, in criticism. They will find the true content of religious exercise (prayer) and also of outward living (watching) through Christ, the Door.

1	Willing	Almsgiving	
	Feeling	Praying	Lucifer
	Thinking	Fasting	
2	Willing	Not to gather treasure	
	Feeling	Not to be anxious	Ahriman
	Thinking	Not to judge	
3	Willing	Ask, seek, knock! (Alms, prayer, fasting)	
	Feeling	Enter! Christ is the Door	Christ
	Thinking	Beware, watch! (Treasure, anxiety, judging)	

The beatitudes and the sayings on salt, light and the city give us a picture of Spirit Man descending to earth and of a spiritual earth. Sayings about a renewal of law point the way of earthly man to heaven. The three groups of three sayings each in chapters six and seven show how, despite Lucifer and Ahriman, humanity is able through hand, heart and head to unite with the Christ. That lays the foundation stone of the house being built on rock.

CHAPTER TEN

The Judas Drama

A story has been handed down to us of how, when Leonardo da Vinci was painting his great scene of the Last Supper, he kept interrupting his work because he could not capture what he could see in his heart. The depiction of the head of the Christ and that of Judas caused him more suffering and effort than all the rest. One of the priors of the monastery where the painting was being created became impatient at the slow progress. Leonardo's answer was that he had been unable anywhere to find models for the head of the Christ and for that of Judas; however, now that the prior had visited him he would at least be able to continue painting the Judas.

The figures of the Christ and of Judas stand out in the finished painting through something very strange. The head of Christ is bathed in encircling light; the head of Judas is obscured by a sinister shadow. Neither can be explained by any natural lighting in the group as represented. The visage of Christ shines as if illumined by an inner sun; the head of Judas, as though enveloped by darkness that emanates from within, shrinks away before the figures of Peter and John.

The Christ and Judas; here is one of the deepest riddles of humanity. Why did the Christ accept Judas as one of his disciples, who later betrayed him? And how could one who for some three years had experienced the benison of Christ's immediate presence and leadership, how could such a one turn traitor against the Christ? The first of these problems is solved when we understand the meaning of that number twelve in relation to the disciples. The other will enable us to look deep into the soul and destiny of Judas.

It was no coincidence that the Christ in a unique way bound twelve men into a circle about himself. Of course the number of those who associated with him as disciples or pupils was far greater — the gospels say as much. We can think of the seventy and could imagine a

far larger number. The twelve were a chosen circle; they were a powerful living symbol. Cosmic secrets are revealed by just these twelve
having gathered about the Christ. It is not enough to assume that here
were men who understood the Christ especially well and who were
bound to him in a unique loyalty. A notion such as that is in our time
almost general; it sees the members of the twelve as having been more
or less alike, followers of a great and revered human being. That view
cannot solve the problem of their number, twelve.

Those twelve represented humanity. Each of them was the embodiment of a particular kind of person. Their circle as it were uncovers an
inward twelvefold structure, at the very core of humanity. The circle is
complete; there is no temperament in the whole of humankind that
will not find its ambassador among the twelve apostles who made up
the group of disciples. As the sun has its place in the starry heavens,
passing among them, girdled as they are by the zodiac, so the Christ
takes his place and moves through all humanity, here represented by
the twelve apostles. Behind each of those twelve there stands a human
type who belongs to one or another of the zodiac figures, and each of
them embodies one of the astral possibilities open to man.

The gospel itself in a certain passage gives the star name of one of
the disciples; Thomas is called the 'Twin.' The zodiacal sign of Gemini
is the same in the heavens as the Thomas person is on earth. Were the
gospel to call Judas Iscariot by his star name, then he would be the
Scorpion. Just as there has to be a scorpion among the starry figures,
so there had inevitably to be a Judas among the disciples. To be
amazed that the Christ accepted Judas the traitor as his disciple is like
being amazed that we have the zodiacal sign of Scorpio and the month
of November. What would the year's round be without November's
dread of death? Are those tragic souls who know neither peace nor
light to have no ambassador in the circle around the Christ?

Judas and Oedipus

Early Christianity pointed up the significance of the personality of
Judas by placing him close to one of the tragic archetypal figures of
human destiny: to Oedipus. This is what it tells.

A Jew by the name of Reuben lived with his wife Ciborea in
Jerusalem. Ciborea, being pregnant, dreamed a terrible dream: the

child she was to bear would bring about the greatest evil that could ever come about through a human being. When the child was born, in order to prevent that evil, the parents placed the infant in a little casket, just as Moses' mother had done with her baby boy. They entrusted the casket to the waves of the sea and the sea carried it to the shores of an island called Iscariot. The queen of the island, sad because she was denied offspring, found the infant, gave out that he was her own child, and reared him.

Presently, the queen herself gave birth to a boy on whom she now lavished all her love. The young Judas desired to revenge himself on his foster brother for having deprived him of his mother's love; he quarrelled with him often and, filled with hatred, beat him. At last the queen was provoked into telling Judas that he was a foundling. To avenge himself, Judas killed the king's son and went forth into the world. He reached Jerusalem after many an aimless journey. There he obtained a position as steward in the palace of Pilate. One day, Pilate and Judas were in the palace garden, looking over into that of his neighbour. Pilate wished for some of the apples on his tree. Like the good servant he was, Judas hastened to obtain what his master wanted. He entered the neighbour's garden but a quarrel sprang up between him and the owner, and Judas slew the neighbour, unaware that this was his father, Reuben. To reward his servant's loyalty, Pilate awarded Judas the neighbour's house and the widow for wife. Judas married Ciborea without knowing that she was his mother.

One day Ciborea, seeking relief for her oppressed heart, related how she had exposed her child to the sea; then it was that Judas gazed into the abyss of his own destiny and despaired. Ciborea was a Christian and it was she who brought Judas to Jesus and Jesus Christ accepted him into his circle.

What enables Christian legend in this instance to rise to the heights of myth and to the power of tragedy such as was once alive in Greece? We need not assume that it sets out to recount the story of Judas' youth. The inward destiny unfolds before us in pictures; it is something more than the personal destiny of an individual. What does the myth of the Greek tragedy of Oedipus tell? Oedipus is man at a definite evolutionary crossroads of humanity. Before the oracle concerning him had been fulfilled, namely that he would kill his father and take his mother to wife, Oedipus had solved the riddle of the Sphinx outside the gates of Thebes. (The answer to the riddle was 'Man.') Oedipus is man at that point of evolution when he became 'nothing but human'; whereas he had previously been woven into the universe in childlike godliness with the heavens as his father and the earth as his mother. Now, humankind loosed itself from that all-embracing unity, tore itself out of heaven without knowing what it was about, without even wanting to do it. People became entangled in things earthly. Heaven ceased to be the soul's home. They forgot the 'Father in Heaven.' Heaven came to be populated by dead objects that pursued their courses like so much inanimate clockwork. The Father was killed by the son without the son even wishing to do it. Earth, once holy mother earth, became the scene and the object of lust and instinct, of a craving for power, of egotism; earth became man's whore without man realizing it. True, man has the answer to the riddle of the sphinx, but was not intellect the weapon with which the son, all unknowing, slew the 'Father'? Has not living spirit turned into dead thinking? Do we not with every thought commit murder against the spirit of the Father from whom all of us have sprung? And is it not intellect that at the same time prepares the way for unclean union with earth, with our Mother? Jocasta, the widowed queen of Thebes, gives herself as wife to Oedipus, as a reward for solving the riddle of the Sphinx.

Oedipus became aware of the disastrous fate brought in the wake of patricide and marriage to his mother; he blinded himself. He wandered over the face of the earth as the blind king. Intellect makes people well informed on things earthly but blind to what is heavenly. In the Oedipus destiny, man wakens to blindness; he also wakens to the horrifying loss of the true light of the world.

Judas is Oedipus in a Christian setting. He is therefore a man entering upon the stage of intellectualism. The destiny of Judas and of Oedipus is the destiny of all people. Instead of Oedipus blinding himself, we see Judas' betrayal of Jesus Christ, for the Christ is the Light of the World. In bringing about the death on the cross of Jesus Christ, Judas blinded the eyes of all the world.

The name 'Judas' tells us that the character of Judaism and of the Jewish people found expression in Judas in a special way. The Jewish people were at that time in a peculiar historical situation. The Romans were in the land. Although they were not there as masters, nevertheless they behaved as if they were. It is very important in this context to examine the way in which the Romans had arrived in the country. A century and a half prior to our own era, there was another Judas: Judas Maccabeus.* He too was one of twelve. The five sons of Mattathias the High Priest headed the nation at that time of oppression, together with the seven sons of a widow — although these were leaders in a more spiritual sense. The seven, together with their mother, suffered martyrdom for the sake of their father's faith and for their people. The Jewish people had been waging a desperate struggle for their freedom against the Seleucids, Syrian rulers of the north. The handful of Jews could not assert itself against their crushing superiority despite their bravery. It was then that Judas Maccabeus decided on a step heavy with consequences; he called upon Rome to help. Rome had by then in its pride ascended the throne of world domination. All the world gazed at Rome in admiration. The Jews' call, that of Judas Maccabeus, for an alliance, emanated from that reverential admiration.

The Romans who arrived at the time of Judas Maccabeus were still there at the time of Judas Iscariot. In name they were allies but in fact masters. Judaism had not forgotten its rapport with Rome which dated back to the time of the Maccabees. The Jews faced the Romans with a mixture of admiration and fear. They would have liked to shake off foreign domination but at the same time they were impressed by Rome's greatness and its organization. What they desired for themselves in place of Rome's alien sway was after all a world empire on the Roman model. Judas Iscariot was above all a man midway between Judaism and Rome. It was as though the decisive act of the Maccabees had been repeated within Iscariot. That other Judas invited the Romans into the land. This Judas bore Rome within himself.

Judas Iscariot set his hope on the Christ, his master, that he would some day accomplish the great miracle, overthrow Rome's world dominion and in its place set up on earth a mighty divine kingdom. He pictured that divine kingdom as resembling Rome's world empire.

---

* In his lecture cycle on St Mark's Gospel, Rudolf Steiner represents Judas Iscariot as a reincarnation of Judas Maccabeus.

With extreme impatience he waited for that mighty, magical deed of Christ, for the fall of the Roman Empire, for the setting up of God's realm, the all-embracing *civitas dei* on earth. But the empire of the Romans presented itself no less as the kingdom of a god, for the emperors demanded for themselves the worship due to divinity. Caesar worship made politics into a religious cult throughout the Roman empire. Religions and politics in Rome were on very much the same level. Judas dreamed of another form of divine dominance; here it would not be politics determining religion, but religion determining politics. It would be the grand realization on earth of a divine and mighty social order, a new world where there would be no more poor.

With the utmost impatience Judas awaited the revolution that the Christ would bring about. He could not understand why the Master hesitated so long. There were many things in which he could not understand the Master. Judas was set upon a deed in the social sphere, on reform along lines of a Christian community. Scenes of adoration, like Mary Magdalene's anointing at Bethany, were to him a senseless waste of time and money. 'Why was this oil not sold for three hundred denarii and the proceeds given to the poor?' (John 12:5). As his impatience rose to a climax, Judas felt that he should himself compel the Master to carry out that deed which he was convinced was the earthly goal of Christ. He was sure that he had only to bring the Christ before the Jewish and the Roman courts, and the great miracle would take place forthwith, namely the fall of all earthly powers. The heavenly kingdom would thereupon come into being.

But, when the Christ accepted the death sentence without defending himself, Judas' expectations, and at the same time Judas himself, collapsed. He went away and hanged himself.

The drama was at an end.

The extraordinary orientation of Judas between Judaism and Rome can be a kind of key to the ancient Judas legend. Judea is the seed bed of intellectualism heavy with consequence. It was in Judea that a man killed his father. Only dead thoughts were left over as corpses of the paternal spirit.

In Rome marriage with the mother was supreme. The cult of the emperors was a kind of incest, of prostitution. That cult has been taken into account far too little by theologians as the historical background to events in the life of Christ. From it follows Rome's greed for power, the ravaging of the whole of mother earth for Rome's own ends, for mastery over her. We could put the meaning of the Judas legend in this incisive way: Judas killed his father; that is to say, he was a true Jew. Judas wed his mother; that is to say, in his inmost being he was secretly devoted to the spirit of Rome.

Judas is generally seen as a traitor, the faithless one, the evil man. He was no more that than was Oedipus, the blind king. Judas' destiny is the tragedy of all humanity. We begin to understand the fate of Judas as we peer into the most shattering tragedy of human nature.

The political situation of Jerusalem at the time of Christ was more than coincidence. The interplay between Judea and Rome resembles a concerted step forward of the two powers who act as tempters for evolving ego-men. Ahriman was at work in Judaism, killing spirit to the point of ossification in the letter of the law — that is, corruption of thought, patricide. Lucifer was busy in Romanism, in corruption of the will; marriage with the mother. That is one reason why the Christ had to become man precisely among the Jews and at the same time under Roman domination. He had to be born between Lucifer and Ahriman if he was to win the fight, this dual victory of redemption. As for Judas Iscariot, the historical and political situation of Jerusalem was his soul's fate. Through their destiny, the Jewish people were at that time at the centre of humankind, and Judas was at the very midpoint of the people's soul. He was ego-man in his dual tragedy. Judas fulfilled the Oedipus myth — he was the true Oedipus. Just as Christ could become man only among the Jewish people if he was indeed to enter into the centre of defiled humanity, so it was inevitable that Judas should enter the circle of Christ's disciples. It was there that humanity came to Christ. These words were spoken to the Christ before the palace of Pilate, 'Behold, that is the man.' *Ecce homo*. Judas was that man, meaning he was the lower ego, filled by Lucifer and Ahriman. Christ is *the* Man, meaning the higher ego, who victoriously overcomes Lucifer and Ahriman.

The tension between Christ and Judas, which acted itself out with such ineluctable drama, is a tension that exists in everyone. It is the tension between the higher and the lower ego. As a person becomes an ego-being, so that person becomes a Judas, entering upon the path of the Oedipus — Judas destiny. That destiny begins with being turned out of the paternal home. But were that person to remain caught up in the lower ego, then he would become a traitor to his own genuinely higher existence; and so, a traitor to the Christ. It is only when we realize that our lower ego can and must become the receptacle and vessel for our own higher ego, that the Judas in us can become the Christ.

The Old Testament prophecy of Judas

The mystery drama that was acted out on destiny's stage in Jerusalem is, down to the last detail, a disclosure of inmost secrets, of their historicity in the human soul. It records all this as historical fact. Through the profoundly based continuity between the Old Testament and the New, between prophecy and its fulfilment, the Bible lets us see how in that mystery drama the character of Judas was being led in a peculiar way, symbolically but also humanly, through its various destinies.

From that shattering moment, pregnant with evil, when Judas left the holy company of the Last Supper and went out into the night, his fate unfolds in the manner of a stupendous drama: Judas in the Temple accepting the thirty pieces of silver; the Judas kiss in the Garden of Gethsemane; Judas breathless and tense, following the court proceedings before Pilate's palace; the collapse of his illusion; Judas in the Temple hurling back the thirty pieces of silver; the grim end of Judas.

There are many scenes that lead from the Old Testament straight on to the image of the thirty pieces of silver. There is in the Old Testament a dark Judas who sells another one, a bright one, for pieces of silver, and that also happens among a group of twelve. It happens when, of the twelve sons of Jacob, Judah is the one who, for twenty pieces of silver, sells Joseph to Ishmaelite merchants to be carried into Egypt (Gen.37:26–28). Can the harmony between events in the Old Testament and those of the New be a coincidence? Or is it simply a case of comparable legends? No, the story of the people of Israel, like the life of Jesus, is the realization, the divine dramatization of inward truths. Wherever similar inward secrets become historical events, there those external events take on similar forms. There is many a closely related sequence of events passing along a silent yet strong bridge from the Old Testament to the New.

More than any other, a certain prophetic passage in the Old Testament leads into the final stages of the Judas drama; its climax is in chapter eleven of the Book of Zechariah. Let us look at the verses that follow:

> Then I said to them, 'If it seems right to you, give me my wages; but if not, keep them.' And they weighed out as my wages thirty shekels of silver. Then the LORD said to me, 'Cast it into the treasury [*or* to the potter]' — the lordly price at which I was paid off by them. So I took the thirty shekels of silver and cast them into the treasury in the house of the LORD.' (Zech.11:12f).

The thirty pieces of silver that Judas hurled back into the Temple, were they not given to the potter in payment for his potter's field, which was then used for a cemetery?

We would be underestimating the Bible were we to see the link between prophetic utterance in the Old Testament and details of the Judas story in the New as merely the first passage foretelling the second. The Bible sets out to do more other than dishing up minor miracles. We have first to understand the prophetic utterances entirely for their own sakes.

This part of the Book of Zechariah is concerned with the crisis in the function of the shepherds among humanity: 'Woe to my worthless shepherd, who deserts the flock!' (Zech.11:17). At the beginning of Jewish history stand the great personalities, the patriarchs, Abraham, Isaac and Jacob. At the beginning of the Old Testament, when history was just emerging out of myth, to be a shepherd was not the same thing as minding animals. Myth is history too, but we must be able to decipher the pictographic writing in which mythology expresses history. The 'shepherd' was the personification of the man about whom a community gathered, who was leader of that community, who was not only the bearer of a personal soul, but also of the spirit which informed his people. Not for nothing has the word current in ancient languages for 'shepherd' come to designate a 'priest,' like the Latin *pastor*. Even if the patriarchs were 'shepherds' in the accepted sense of the word, they were shepherds first and foremost in its deeper meaning. Abraham was the shepherd of all peoples and also their father; Jacob was the first to bear the national name of 'Israel'; he was the shepherd of his own people and the bearer of the national spirit of a society that was to come.

The scope of the pastoral calling kept contracting from Abraham to Jacob, and then ever more so from the time of Jacob. Abraham was pastor to all humanity. Jacob was the shepherd of his own people. At last the community building power of the shepherds shrank right down to the individual. The ego nature of the individual detached itself more and more from the racial and social element. It became in a sense the special task of the Jewish race to lead humankind into the egotism of 'individualization.' The great flocks under the earliest of the outstanding shepherds became the 'lost sheep of Israel.' The more isolated ego-man became, the more his own community's power became irrelevant for him; he himself, the Israelite, was the 'lost sheep.' When, at the destruction of Jerusalem, its people were scattered to the four winds of heaven, that was only the external fulfilment of what had already taken place as inward fact. Judas it was in whom the separation of the ego was complete. From Abraham to Jacob, and right down to Judas, here is the story of the submergence of the shepherds; first came the great shepherd fathers. The story ends with a flock having no shepherd or with only a pseudo-shepherd, a hireling (John 10:1–5).

The Greek word for 'to destroy' is *skorpiyei*; it is the word from which 'scorpion' is derived. The scorpion's sting is involved wherever a community is disintegrating, where nothing remains but the isolation of the 'I.' The constellation of Scorpio hung over Judas. He was the man of destruction. Abraham had the biggest flocks. Judas was all alone.

Man, as he passes on his inward way, has to tread humanity's roads from Abraham to Judas. The part in the Book of Zechariah which is relevant here describes this. Step by step it goes into man's gradual impoverishment and abandonment. That inspiration which streams down from above is beginning to give out. Decadent atavism is taking the place of priestly revelation. 'For the teraphim utter nonsense, and the diviners see lies; the dreamers tell false dreams, and give empty consolation. Therefore the people wander like sheep; they are afflicted for want of a shepherd.' (Zech.10:2). As the old spiritual priesthood disappears, so the community disintegrates. The 'I' is born in travail. A destroying tempest of wrath passes through the world, felling trees and forests (11:1f). 'Hark, the wail of the shepherds.' (11:3). Man undergoing the trial of isolation is set the task of himself becoming the shepherd of the sheep condemned to slaughter. 'Thus said the LORD my God: "Become shepherd of the flock doomed to slaughter. Those who buy them slay them and go unpunished; and those who sell them say, "Blessed be the LORD, I have become rich." And their own shepherds have no pity on them.' (11:4f). Of necessity the man becomes a shepherd himself; two staves are given him: they are 'Grace' and 'Union.' Grace is the touch of spirit from above; Union is the unanimity of spirit below. 'And I took two staffs; one I named Grace, the other I named Union. And I tended the sheep.' (11:7).

The result is that now, more than ever, he feels the doom and ruin of instituting the shepherd's office. In a single month, in a single passage through the lunar cycle, he witnesses the triple death of shepherd man. The ego, arrested by forces of the moon, is the cause of their ruin. 'In one month I destroyed three shepherds. But I became impatient with them, and they also detested me.' (11:8). The moon ego becomes the murderer of the shepherds. All the ego can do is abandon to ruin whatever is there to be ruined; all it can do is relinquish to death what is already at death's door. The moon ego can do no more than leave those who have separated themselves to tear one another to pieces. In so doing, the first shepherd's staff is broken, Grace. The connection with the spirit world is thereby broken. As well as losing the community, the ego loses heaven but finds a dim perception of its own self: as murderer and at the same time as murder victim.

During that stage of inward evolution, man reaches a point when he is tempted to deceive himself into disbelieving the fact of ego death. The mirror-like experience of the earthly ego desires to cover up the death of the true ego, of the shepherd ego, of the heavenly ego. The moon-wolf is out to devour the sun, having scattered the flock. The man thinks that he is of some importance, and asks what he is worth — he is weighed on the universe's scales, and gets the answer, 'thirty shekels of silver.' What does that mean? Thirty is the moon number, the number of days it takes to pass through a lunar cycle. Silver is the lunar metal. Thirty pieces of silver are the night's coins that become visible in the skies through a month. So here is the meaning of the answer the man gets to his question, 'Your ego is only moon, and not sun — it is only the illusion of light, but it is no more than borrowed, reflected light. You do indeed say 'I,' but you are lying as you say it.

You have received everything in the same way as the moon receives all its light from the sun.'

This is where man is confronted by a decision. Will he think the thirty pieces of silver a 'goodly' sum after all? Will he think himself a sun, whereas he is only a moon? Will he be caught in the madness of reflected light, in the moon-cold silver of earthly consciousness? Or will he see through his own ego and learn to tell himself in true self-revelation, 'I am no I.' The constellation of Scorpio is preceded in the heavens by that of Libra. On Libra, man is weighed. If he fails the test of the thirty pieces of silver, then he is stung later by the scorpion; he is threatened by the destiny of Judas.

At this crucial moment a helping voice becomes audible: 'Then the LORD said to me, "Cast it into the treasury [*or* to the potter]" — the lordly price at which I was paid off by them' (Zech.11:13). The man who passes the test is he who throws away the thirty pieces of silver and is able to say, 'So I took the thirty shekels of silver and cast them into the treasury in the house of the LORD.' (11:13).

Ordinary self awareness exists in man's intellectual thoughts. These are associated with physical decay. That is because the forces of intellectual awareness are transmuted forms of what normally would be pulsing through the human body as living, formative forces, shaping and fashioning the body like the potter who shapes and moulds it. Living matter dies whenever formative forces turn into intellectual awareness (the thirty pieces of silver).

He who is not trapped in moon consciousness, and who can see through the illusion of his intellectual thinking, has the chance of reviving what is dead. That is the art of forgetting, which has something in common with eating. Thoughts that are the content of lunar consciousness have got to be 'eaten up' — they have to pass over into 'flesh and blood.' Essentially, by not repeating the 'I,' as well as by forgetting, man restores to the formative forces (the potter who fashions the body) those powers which have been withdrawn from them; he sends them back into the body where they become once again formative forces. He casts the thirty pieces of silver back into the temple of the body where they are given to the potter. The content of the intellectual consciousness which one forgets turns back to formative forces. All content idly retained withdraws formative forces. It is necessary to say 'I' but doing so only leads to the lower ego, an illusory ego, the

Judas ego. Inward progress towards a non-ego clears the way towards the higher ego, 'So it is not I who live, but Christ lives in me.' (Gal.2:20).

What the prophetic book describes imaginatively as the path of the 'shepherd' becomes history in the destiny of Judas. When Judas received the thirty pieces of silver he held more in his hand than a mere sum of money, his reward. Significantly, legend tells us a good deal about those thirty pieces of silver. The coins are said to have been temple treasure, some valuables of Alexander the Great to have reached Jerusalem. The treasures that Judas held in his hand are an image of his own nature. What took place there sprang from roots more profound than all too human motives, like greed and treachery. We shall have to come back to this again later. Human destiny is symbolized here; a mystery play about human destiny takes shape upon the stage, scenes that reveal secrets of the soul. It is too late by the time Judas throws back the thirty pieces of silver in the temple. The lower ego, that of the thirty pieces of silver, had already left the higher ego, that of the golden sun, to die. In turning traitor and murderer of the higher ego, the lower ego at the same time destroys itself. Murder and suicide walk hand in hand. The creature found to be too light-weight on the scales perishes from the scorpion's sting.

It is true that the thirty pieces of silver are given to the potter, not however for him to shape and mould into vessels, but rather to stop him from fashioning them. The potter has hitherto made his vessels from the clay in his field. But then that field became a burial ground where the bodies of human beings decay. The thirty pieces of silver set up a putrescent fermentation in place of a formative impulse. The world is turned by Judas into a grave. Christ, who conquered the grave, bestows on those with a higher ego a new communal force. He restores the care of the shepherd: 'I am the good Shepherd.' In him, whatever was lost along the way from Abraham to Judas returns on a more exalted level.

Judas and Christ: hireling and good shepherd. The shepherd keeps his own flock; the wolf and the scorpion scatter that of the hireling.

The anointing in Bethany

Of the gospels, the first and the last, Matthew's and John's, strike quite a special note whenever the character of Judas appears on the scene of the holy story. It is St Matthew who tells the tragedy of the thirty pieces of silver. The other gospels do not mention it. Matthew tells this story rather than any other because in it Judas passes through the tragedy of Jewry, the tragedy of ego awareness. In two different scenes, John depicts Judas in unique colours.

We have here the two final sacramental scenes, that of the anointing in Bethany, and that of the Last Supper in Jerusalem. John especially stresses Judas because it is here that Judas lives through the tragedy of all humanity, of devotion in general.

Matthew and Mark also describe the anointing in Bethany, but John is the only one to name the disciple who raised objections to Mary's action. By setting this solemn scene of the last anointing so close to the raising of Lazarus, John gives it a magnificent backdrop and a sense of drama. There at the table sat Lazarus, so recently risen from the grave, together with the Christ, his awakener, the twelve disciples and Lazarus' two sisters. It was a festive meal, imbued through and through with the secret of death and resurrection, a fact recently fulfilled at the graveside in the sight of everyone. A profoundly human understanding comes to us of what was happening in the soul of the sister of Lazarus if we think about the circumstances at that time. The very deepest feeling of holiness that was hers, this Mary could express in no other way than through that sacramental act of hers, an act of sacrifice and worship. This sister's deed was like a response from the heart of Lazarus. Lazarus and Mary were like one single soul. They belonged closely together. The gospel describes how, when the ointment was poured over the feet of Christ, the house was filled with the odour of sacrifice; was not that the great thanksgiving for the deed of conquest over death that Jesus Christ had just fulfilled at the tomb of Lazarus? It was more: Mary Magdalene's great confession was a confession of faith in the deepest Christian mysteries. It was not a confession in words, but with heart and hands, with the whole of her humanity. Near Caesarea Philippi Peter had said, 'You are the Christ, the son of the living God.' But his confession and recognition applied only to the living Christ. When, immediately after the confession, Jesus

Christ began to reveal his imminent death and resurrection, Peter spoke thus: '... do not allow this to happen to you.' (Matt.16:22). Peter confesses the Christ but not Christ's death and resurrection. But Mary's act of anointing also says, 'Thou art the Christ' — for 'Christ' means 'the anointed one.' She said even more. As the echo of Lazarus' death and resurrection, she sensed in advance the death and resurrection of the Christ, and her sensitive heart accepted it, and confessed it. For her deed towards the Christ was a sacrament of death, an extreme unction. The Christ accepted Mary Magdalene's act as an avowal of his death.

If we have vividly thought of what preceded the anointing, Judas' protest seems to us to betray a lack of understanding: 'Why was this oil not sold for three hundred denarii and the proceeds given to the poor?' (John 12:5). A wide chasm yawns between Mary Magdalene and Judas. Two attitudes of heart, totally different, are here revealed. We could think of the scene given in St Luke, when Christ was at the house of those two sisters, Mary Magdalene and Martha, in Bethany. The anointing that Mary carried out on the Christ, stooping over his feet, pouring oil over them, bathing them with her devoted tears, drying them with her hair — is a sublimation of her sitting quietly at the Master's feet, listening to his words. And is not the frame of mind evinced by Judas' words the culmination of Martha's restless diligence in external service, of Martha to whom the Christ said that Mary had chosen the better path?

Those at table in Bethany fall into two groups. The two sisters of Lazarus, Mary and Martha, are like soul-doubles of two characters who are at the same time infinite extensions of themselves. On the one hand, by their very nature, Mary Magdalene and Lazarus belong together; as do Martha and Judas on the other. With that, the true polarity becomes clear in the difference between all those assembled about the Christ. In Lazarus and Judas we shall have to consider more of this duality, especially when in later studies we shall be speaking in greater depth of the awakening of Lazarus. We shall then see that Lazarus is the evangelist, St John himself. So we have here before us that tremendous polarity, Lazarus and Judas. We can begin to understand why, in the Gospel of St John, in this scene Judas is mentioned by name. Judas is the antithesis of Lazarus-John, of him who rose from the tomb. Judas cannot understand Mary Magdalene's behaviour, nor can he understand Lazarus-John on his re-awakening by the Christ.

The contradiction between John and Judas stays silently in the background of the scene. The difference between Mary Magdalene and Judas finds expression in the foreground. The sister stands in for her brother. Confronting one another are the woman bowed reverently over the Christ's feet, and the exasperated protester, springing angrily to his feet.

The gospel does not preach morality in abstract terms. As the mouthpiece of holy scripture, it sets before us profound object lessons; moral wisdom take fire there. In the scene of the anointing in Bethany it has a message for our own time on the social problem.

It has been said often enough that the social problem is a religious one. It is not a community question in the sense that is most often meant. It has been frequently stated that humanity has got to improve before we can approach any amelioration in social conditions. But that is no more than a phrase. Why would anyone really prefer being made better, even someone depraved? Such a one is not shown ways to improve, is not offered the strength nor the assistance he needs. Thrown back on his own resources, nobody could bring about in himself the transformation that would be able to carry in its train a transformation in social conditions.

A person can be very willing to help in the community; activated by that good will, the more he does, the more complex the social environment becomes. Do we nowadays do too little, socially speaking? Yes, indeed. We may fall short in many ways. But overall too much is done. That is a strange assertion. But let us ask where in the human heart does the root of communal need lie? What is the reason for the decline in community building tendencies and forces? Lovelessness is not a matter of morality to be cured by 'preaching love.' It is a quality of civilization. We lose the art of loving because of the kind of civilization into which we have evolved. Loving kindness is an art. Maybe the most exalted of all the arts. There was a time when people were artists in loving kindness. Now that art has to be learnt all over again from the ground up. We need a religious life which instead of preaching love could create a school of loving kindness where the exalted art of charity could be regained, step by step. That would be the contribution of religious living to the solution in the social problem.

The first condition to fulfill where love is to exist would be that human hearts should harbour at least a minimal tranquillity. In modern parlance that is to say, 'the art of having time to spare.' There is nowadays an epidemic, rampant but not recognized, in our cultural life: it is the sickness and the illusion of not having time. A nervousness, a restlessness, has been dripped like poison into human hearts. It causes people to rush past each other, to bore one another, to fob each other off with some conventional form of speech in situations where the chord of serene heart-to-heart contact could and should sound. People drive each other apart with their haste; the impulse toward community evaporates. For it is not true that people have no time. With a few exceptions the cause of restlessness does not lie externally in having too much to do but in a lack of spiritual communication. In business, hustle and bustle are the mask intended to disguise a weakness.

In our time the community and the religious life of society alike are in the grip of the same hustle, an illusory 'busy-ness' that has the effect of splintering the personality. Is it not symptomatic that in some social welfare organizations workers are the last of all to attain to self-realization? There is the feeling that somehow, and in spite of every effort, one is not getting to the roots of what is needed. To that extent we could say that too much rather than too little is being done. There is so little love because there is so much to do. We could say, communal need is today so great because Ahasuerus, the Wandering Jew, keeps passing through our ranks. Ahasuerus is not some loveless creature opposed to community beneficence; in fact, he is ruining the strength of society by his over activity. The scene of the last anointing at Bethany draws a contrast in Judas and Mary Magdalene between sacramental man and a socially conscious man. The character of Judas shows up the roots of the community's need. Mary Magdalene reveals the springs of its healing. Ahasuerus, the Wandering Jew, is present in Judas. He is possessed by that unhealthy restlessness which imagines that it must at all times be up and doing. But that is simply the self indulgence of an isolated ego soul. Ahasuerus cannot find repose in the present moment. He has to think ahead, to plan, to make decisions, to resolve on things and more besides. He confronts Mary Magdalene's deed without understanding it. In that way he misjudges the one thing that could heal him. He is caught up in the illusion which is nowadays a common habit of thought; that we can be 'doing some-thing' all the time, and need take no heed of the sources from which new strength could be drawn.

Judas is the man with no understanding for worship. Worship, sacrament, is the source of communal renewal. Mary Magdalene exemplified it by living it. The sacrament is the school of love. The first thing people learn in that school is to have time, to pause within the moment for inward quietude. The next lesson to be learnt is to draw strength from the divine source for serene loving kindness, but also for action. Modern civilization is Judas. It has lost the habit of worship in developing abstract thought in matters religious, having become entangled in the fallacy of 'busy-ness.' We can read from the Bethany scene what is needed to cure Judas and also Ahasuerus, who keeps passing through our ranks; we must establish seed beds of sacramen-tal Christianity as the source of group community building forces, as schools of inmost peace and love. Sacramental human beings, the Mary Magdalene people, will be not less but more influential than the social activists, the Judas people. For theirs are creative deeds. The activities of Judas people are deceptive, and bring about chaos. That is the meaning in St John's Gospel when it goes on from Judas' protest against the anointing, 'But he did not say this because he was con-cerned about the poor, but because he laid claim to what did not belong to him. He kept the accounts and had charge of the donations.' (John 12:6).

That is not meant as a clumsy piece of moral disparagement. Two chapters earlier the gospel speaks of the good shepherd and the hireling; of Christ and Judas. Christ says of himself, 'I am the door to the sheep' (John 10:7) The higher ego is the door, that which binds people together. Of the hirelings he says they are thieves and murderers. All those who came before him (that is, those who place themselves ahead of the higher ego, the bearers of the lower ego, the Judas ego) are thieves and murderers. They are thieves because they pretend to be something that they are not. Their inmost life is without control. Outwardly they seem active, busied with many things. What fruit can their activity bring? Martha and Judas on the one hand: Martha serving at table, Judas talking of serving the poor; Mary Magdalene and Lazarus on the other hand. Lazarus sits at table with the Christ at the Last Supper. Mary Magdalene bestows on the Christ the sacrament of death. And the word of Christ goes like this; 'Mary and Lazarus — they have chosen the better path.'

Judas at the Last Supper

The second sacramental scene where St John's Gospel sets the personality of Judas clearly into the foreground, is the Last Supper itself. The Christ had foretold that a certain one would betray him. Peter and John seek to find out who it could be. 'And Jesus answered, "It is he to whom I shall give the morsel when I have dipped it." And he dipped the morsel and gave it to Judas, the son of Simon Iscariot. And after he had taken the morsel, the power of Satan entered into him. And Jesus said to him, "What you are about to do, do it soon!" ... So, after receiving the morsel, he immediately went out. And it was night.' (John 13:26–30).

We are given a devastating key to the last act of the Judas drama. It is not Judas himself who carries out the betrayal and accepts the thirty pieces of silver; Satan has already entered into him; Judas is no more than a tool. Judas' actions take on a symbolic character which make them the fulfilment of Old Testament prophecies; this is because the actions are no longer human but demonic.

What the gospel calls Satan entering into Judas, we in our day would describe as the onset of psychosis. Judas' illusionary expectations were strained too far; neurosis advanced into psychic illness. As Satan entered into Judas, so Judas' 'I' passed out of him. This lack of inward control led to the loss of ego. The death of Judas did not occur when he committed suicide, when he hanged himself. His 'I' had left him at the supper table. Only the sheaths were left to bring about their own end by suicide. What they had hitherto contained had already vanished into that world to which souls go after death. Judas' betrayal and suicide had taken place earlier, during the night that engulfed him.

There is something utterly shattering in seeing Satan enter into Judas, as he accepted the morsel from the hands of Jesus Christ and carried it to his mouth. Acceptance of the sacrament, of communion, broke the link between Judas' 'I' and his physical-spiritual nature. The catastrophe of Judas actually ignited from the sacrament. We have before us the tragic fulfilment of St Paul's words on the improper receiving of the communion: 'Whoever eats and drinks without considering the exalted mystery of this body, causes grievous destiny to fall upon himself by so eating and drinking' (1Cor.11:29). This implies no moral condemnation. It means that a minimum of inward peace and sacramental reverence are necessary. To him that has shall be given, from him that has not, even what he has shall be taken away. Because of his inmost agitation Judas had no appreciation of the sacrament at Bethany; how then could he have been equipped for the sacrament of the Last Supper? People are inevitably either healed or shattered by the sacrament. Judas was broken by the only thing that could have healed him.

Just as Judas and Mary Magdalene are contrasted at Bethany, so are Judas and the Christ at the table of the Last Supper. This is intimately depicted by Leonardo da Vinci. For the Christ, the path led from the Last Supper through the night of Good Friday to the morning of Resurrection. For Judas it led from the same Last Supper, out into the night of suicide. Suicide and resurrection — the greatest opposites in human destiny. In our present day civilization, marked as it is by the sign of Judas, there is a good deal of suicide and not much of resurrection. On the scales, the dish that carries resurrection is given weight against that of suicide by the cultivation of sacramental Christianity. Judas was dead already on Easter morning. Mary Magdalene stood at the tomb, the first witness of the resurrection. Here we see the manner in which the paths of those capable of worship diverge from the path of those incapable of it.

Judas' betrayal and death

Lastly, here is a brief indication intended to lead into the next gospel study. The fate of Judas cast its shadow over the whole circle of the twelve. Its doom struck down not Judas alone, but it hit him hardest; he was stung by the scorpion. By that scorpion's sting Judas was bereft of his human 'I' and of its consciousness; he was cast forth into the night of insensibility.

As Jesus was passing from the supper table to the Mount of Olives with his disciples, he said to them, 'In this night you will lose your faith in me and lose your inner certainty. For the scripture says: I will strike the shepherd, and the sheep of the flock will be scattered.' (Matt.26:31).

The original text also uses a word in which 'scorpion' is embedded. The sheep are to be scattered by the sting of Scorpio. That would be a verbatim translation. The utterance refers to the twelve, and it is in fact fulfilled among them. It does not mean a scattering in the external sense. It implies something that happened to their perceptions. The scattering of the twelve disciples began when Satan entered into Judas. It was completed when, after the kiss of Judas, the guards laid hands on the Christ (Matt.26:50). If we imagine the disciples' flight as having been external and spatial, then the deepest problem of the Passion story will remain unsolved.

The disciples' flight is like the scattering of the sheep, and it took place within their consciousness. That the disciples went to sleep in Gethsemane is part of the same thing; so is much else besides. It was not the consciousness of Judas that dissipated at the death of Christ. The consciousness of each and every one of the disciples was led into the most extreme temptation. The consciousness of one only stood firm; that was John. He was the only one of the twelve to stand at the foot of the cross. Judas and John are the extremes; Judas' consciousness broke down into possession, into psychic illness. John was lifted to apocalyptic vision. The remaining ten were ranged between Judas and John. The mystery of Golgotha brings out into the light of day the degrees of human awareness. Whoever comes in contact with the mystery swings between madness and initiation.

The disciples' 'flight' demonstrates the feebleness of the human soul. It came to light when the grandest mystery in earthly evolution was fulfilled.

Gazing down on the Temple from the Mount of Olives with his disciples, Christ spoke of the ruin of the old creation, and he gave an early prediction of flight: 'Then those who are in Judea should flee to the mountains ... If then someone says to you, "See, here is the Christ," ... do not listen ...' (Matt.24:16f). 'Then, when you see the aberration of the human self set up, a hideous form, where it should not be (let the reader penetrate what he reads with his thinking) let all those who are in Judea seek refuge in the mountain heights' (Mark 13:14).

Every merely superficial view of Christ's apocalyptic utterances spoken on the Mount of Olives comes to grief. The Christ was saying that a time of decision would come when for those who have entered upon the region of the 'I' (Judea) there would be nothing left to do but to transmute their own consciousness. Such people will have to raise themselves out of the depths to the heights of spiritual perception (flight to the mountains) if they would avoid being swept into universal ruin. Human beings will then be utterly unable to continue in the old consciousness. They will have no choice between 'staying' and 'fleeing.' Flight will be a fact. May the transmutation of consciousness not cast down people into the night and into the void into which Judas staggered when his consciousness was changed by his acceptance of the morsel. Human awareness has entered into the region of spirit. And now it must become apparent whether it is a time of harvest there, and whether humanity will be able to gather ripe fruit; or whether it is winter; whether flight be in summer or in winter. Judas' flight took place in winter under the constellation of Scorpio. It will also need to be made clear whether the spiritual region upon which humanity will be entering is to be bright or dark, sunlit or partaking of the nature of Saturn. Judas entered upon the world of spirit on a Sabbath (in the meaning of Matt.24:20), that is on a day of Saturn, the day of the dark grave. Flight for him was a sabbath flight, not a Sunday's flight.

The time has come when humanity really has no choice left between summer and winter transmutation, between sunlit perception or that of Saturn. And that choice lies between John and Judas: a choice between awakening of the spirit on the one hand and psychic illness on the other.

CHAPTER ELEVEN

The Apostle Peter

From the beginning Simon Peter occupied a special place among the twelve disciples. He is always referred to as the first. St Matthew's Gospel actually stresses that he was 'first' when the twelve were sent forth (10:2). He was the one to receive the apostolic commission from the Christ (Matt.16; John 21). He was 'first' among the apostles, the apostles' leader. And yet this position of pre-eminence cannot mean that Peter was spiritually the most mature of the twelve, or that he was closest to the Christ. He was not 'the disciple whom Jesus loved'; he it was who three times disowned him.

The internal structure of the disciples' group sets profound problems. Errors on the part of historical denominational Christianity are tied up with a superficial, undifferentiated view of the individual apostles, of their tasks and destinies. There are two questions through which we gain panoramic views into the immeasurable vistas of Christianity. The first of these questions was basic to the last chapter. The second is to be the subject of our present one.

How is it that Judas belonged to the twelve when it was he who betrayed Christ?

How is it that Simon Peter was first among the twelve although he was the one to deny him?

Franz Werfel, in his fascinating trilogy, *Der Spiegelmensch,* touches on the human riddle contained in the second of these questions. Thamal, a seeker of the way, asks to be admitted to the brotherhood of a Tibetan monastery. Many things, however, are strange to him. He has to understand at the outset that the man who welcomes him in his capacity of abbot and master of the monastery is not one of the most exalted of initiates. One of the monks explains to Thamal that the one who has been most recently admitted to the brotherhood has to undertake the office of abbot.

MONK: He stands on a lower step. Only those are suited to command who are themselves half servants.

THAMAL: This inferior one is he who wears the girdle?

MONK: Because he is the youngest in the order of incarnation. His soul is as yet moist from the probation. It has no rank in the higher austerity. Corruption is still pulsing through it. A multiplicity of interests calls shrilly in him. That is why he is chosen to rule and give orders. The anxieties of power are suitable only for those of low estate. He who still dreams and cries out by night, he it is who must wear the girdle of gold.

[*Eventually, Thamal is admitted to the brotherhood and is invested with the abbot's girdle.*]

THE ABBOT (*approaching him*): You are the youngest in order of incarnation. Take then the golden girdle of office. A dark vapour of preoccupation with human time rises from your head. You are thus still bound to Maya. You have first of all to direct your soul towards selfless goals, in sorrow, in the performance of duties. Only then can you attempt to climb the rocky steps of that Love that has summoned you hither. Thus you may in the end find final perfection in sweet extinction and in a fading out from your own self.

Notwithstanding the orientalism which we may discern in these words, they do disclose a universal law that is embodied in the character and destiny of Peter: it strikes us like pictorial drama. Peter gives off a 'dark vapour of preoccupation with human time.' There is no one among the twelve disciples whose soul we see so tossed about by storms as that of Peter. Peter is pre-eminently a man whose personality actually demands psychological study.

Jesus Christ himself gives the first and most significant interpretation of the character of Simon in calling him Peter 'the Rock.' 'You are Simon, the son of Jonah. Your name shall be Cephas (which translated means Peter, the Rock).' (John 1:42). If we remain within the image carried by that name, we cannot but remark on the contradiction between the nature of Peter and the name bestowed on him by the Christ. A rock is hard, firm, immovable. Is not the heart of Peter more like a stormy wave? 'And if I had to die with you, never would I deny you!' (Matt.26:35); but then later he collapses, 'I do not know the man.' Where is that rock-like firmness in the heart of Peter?

St Mark's Gospel links the naming of Simon by Christ with that of the brothers James and John: 'There were twelve whom he chose to be always with him. They were to be sent out to proclaim and to be given the creative power to drive out demons. Thus he founded the circle of the twelve and gave Simon the second name Peter. The others were James the son of Zebedee and John the brother of James. He gave them the name Boanerges, that means the sons of the thunder.' (Mark 3:14–17).

The Bible itself points to the internal ordering of the disciples' group which is also that of the order of their calling and of their being sent. It gives the names of those disciples who were later to form the closest and most intimate circle about him. The names then refer to individual personalities and their tasks. They reveal that in gathering them about the Christ, there was a cosmic ordering. Within ancient sensibilities towards the universe it went without saying that those names, Cephas and Boanerges, referred to the elements: Peter to the earth element, the Boanerges to the water and air elements. Christ summoned to his side representatives of the life elements in the person of these three disciples Simon, James and John. Peter represented the firm mineral earth element; James represented the fluid, etheric water element; John represented the ensouled air element. The fourth spirit-bearing element, that of fire, was alive in Christ himself. 'Boanerges' is usually translated 'sons of thunder' in the belief that its meaning is the choleric temperament of those two which became evident, for example, when James and John wanted to call down fire from heaven on the Samaritans. The exact meaning however is 'sons of the weather', 'sons of the storm,' and weather dwells in the clouds where water and air elements are united. Early Christian legends confirm this; they depict James as the apostle of the sea, patron saint of seafarers, in which capacity he played an important part right through the Middle Ages. And how closely St John was bound up with the essence of the soul-bearing air element, the element covered in Greek by the word *pneuma*, emerges from every line of St John's Gospel and from Revelation.

The human element to be carried by each of the three disciples makes itself known in the cosmic meaning of the names bestowed on them in their capacity as disciples. Peter 'the Rock' received his nature from the profundities of earth, which hold mastery with vulcan-like force, like deep-seated unconscious and primitive instincts. James bore the cosmic spaces in his personality, like dreaming sea-currents; and John spread a spiritual mantle from the waking heights of existence about all creatures, just as air envelops the earth. Earth is Peter, the Rock. The Christ, engaged in building a heavenly temple, begins, like a wise architect, not with the roof but with the foundations. He lays the foundation stone, setting Peter, the rock-man, into the foundation of earthly Christianity. If Christianity was to be firmly established within humanity, like a temple resting on firm rock, then it had to be sunk first of all into the depths of the human will, even though these depths are in the main unconscious and instinctive like a volcanic stream. Peter is the man of will. That is why he received the name of Peter and was appointed the first leader at the time of the establishment of Christianity. He was first among the apostles and became the earliest leader in Christendom at the time when the mineral, Petrine epoch began, when Christianity had yet to live within the sleeping depths of the human will.

The sign of Jonah

'Peter' was not the only name the Christ bestowed on Simon. There are some very telling moments when Jesus Christ calls him 'Simon, son of Jonah.' The translation is misleading since it creates the trivial notion that Simon's father was Jonah. We are going to consider more closely an example which will at the same time lead us towards one of the most important scenes in the gospel concerned with Peter.

In chapter 16 of St Matthew's Gospel, the elemental flash of light flamed forth from Peter's soul: 'You are the Christ, the Son of the Living God.' And Jesus Christ said to him: 'Blessed are you, Simon, son of Jonah.' This chapter, more than any other, shows clearly to anyone with a sense for the composition of the gospel that the name of Jonah added to that of Peter is intended to stress something more than family descent. For that name Jonah occurs earlier in chapter sixteen. Christ answers the Pharisees and Sadducees when they demand a sign, 'Only a humanity which has become degenerate and unfaithful to the holy order and harmony of life demands a wonder. But no other sign will be granted it except the sign of the prophet Jonah.' (Matt.16:4). It is out of harmony with the spirit of the gospel to see coincidence in this repetition of the name Jonah in this passage and to say that the Old Testament prophet who had the adventure with the whale and Simon's father happened to have the same name.

The name, Jonah, conceals an important secret. The Hebrew word means 'the dove.' The names Jonah and John are closely related. That relationship stands pictorially before us at the Baptism of Jesus when the dove appeared. The Jonah secret contained in the name John is also what links the two Johns — the Baptist and St John, the disciple. In order to understand the appellation of Peter we will have to let Peter himself retreat into the background for a while.

Where does the word of the Christ come true to the effect that the sign of the prophet Jonah is to be fulfilled? The answer is to be found if we can understand the true meaning of the Jonah story. The Book of Jonah describes an initiation in imaginative, pictorial language. Jonah is one who passes through death and resurrection. For three days he reposes in the womb of earth before waking to a new life. Earth is the great fish that swallowed him as he was swimming in the etheric sea. The dove rises from the fish at the moment when Jonah is awakened from his temple sleep. Herein lies the meaning of the name Jonah. Man belongs by nature either to what is earthly, the great fish when death is strong in him, or else he belongs to what is exalted or heavenly — to the dove. He has struggled through death to life.

If we accept this interpretation of the Jonah miracle, then we can recognize that fulfilment of the word of the Christ is twice illustrated by the sign of Jonah the prophet, firstly in the death and awakening of Lazarus, and secondly in the death and resurrection of Christ himself.

Here we have the dual New Testament 'sign' of Jonah. The first three gospels only tell us of the second of these, the greatest of the New Testament Jonah miracles. The fourth gospel also describes the first of them. The re-awakening of Lazarus is the middle point of that gospel. But to understand this Jonah miracle as told by St John is to hold one of the most significant keys to the gospels in general, and at the same time a key to the destiny of Peter.

The awakening of Lazarus should not be regarded as an isolated, self-contained miracle. It is the highest and the last step along an exalted path, the seventh of the mighty deeds to be found in St John, deeds that within the first half of the gospel determine the inmost path. The reawakening of Lazarus would have been impossible without the preceding six deeds, each a step along that way. The first six deeds were not carried out on Lazarus. The first of them took place at Cana on the water in the pitchers; the second on the centurion's son; the third on the sick man at the pool; the fourth on the five thousand; the fifth on the disciples in the boat at night; the sixth was the healing of the man born blind. These are stages along the way along which Lazarus advanced until, at the seventh and last stage, he himself became the external object of the deed of Christ. This happened when he was called from the tomb, from the whale's body, to become Jonah-John.

An early Christian legend helps us to see the connection between the first six miracles and the seventh, in fact to gain more understanding of the awakening of Lazarus. According to this legend, Lazarus was a wealthy young man, a member of a royal house. He owned a large part of Judea, including the area of Jerusalem. The young prince had been amongst the disciples following the Christ and had witnessed his deeds. He was there outside the city of Nain where the Christ raised the only son of the widow. This deed of Christ made so mighty an impression on the young man that he went away and sold all his possessions, distributing them among the poor. This was in order to belong, from then on, wholly to the Christ.

A legend such as this one becomes transparent if we refrain from reading it as being concerned with physical facts, rather then with the inward processes of the soul; yet they are set forth in scenes of external life. The wealth and possessions of the young prince are inward — they pertain to the soul. In saying that the prince sacrificed these goods under the influence of the deeds of Christ, the story tells us that he sacrificed himself, his own soul with all its riches. There we are face to face with the death of Lazarus; anyone who can understand that secret will also be able to understand the awakening of Lazarus.

We can hardly imagine nowadays that anyone could die of emotion enkindled by some powerful impression on the heart. Perhaps events may serve to enlighten us, such as those handed down to us from the fourteenth century. Johannes Tauler, the renowned Strasbourg preacher, recognized through the influence of the great but anonymous 'Friend of God,' who visited him from the mountain regions, that his preaching was of no avail until, through meditation, he had brought about decisive changes in his own spirit. He withdrew for two years from his preaching and sought the peace and tranquillity of meditation. When he reappeared before the public, his preaching brought about such emotional storms that forty people fell dead to the ground.

The present era places the life of the body and physical health above everything else. It will thus be inclined towards seeing happenings like those in Tauler's life as an outrageous gamble with human life which should be forbidden. Earlier periods felt differently. They felt greatness in a death brought about by self sacrificing emotion called forth by the spirit. Be that as it may, in our time, because human beings are so firmly embedded in the physical, they have lost the power of receiving spiritual impressions so strongly as to die for them.

The death of Lazarus was a consequence of the deeds of Christ. We could also say it was the fruit of the six preceding stages of experience. That legend regards the awakening of the young lad at Nain as a summation of the deeds of Christ. The greatness of Christ had so overwhelmed Lazarus that, having witnessed those deeds, he was transformed by them stage by stage. At last, after he had watched Christ Jesus heal the man born blind, the scales fell from his own eyes — the restoration of sight had become a deed accomplished within himself. The Christ being stood before his now open eyes as the Light of the World, far outshining Jesus of Nazareth. His soul was filled with desire to give himself utterly to Christ, so as to lose himself in him. Accordingly, he offered up all that he had. He let himself, his whole life, flow into that of Christ. We can imagine how, as he fell sick in Bethany ('The House of Poverty' or 'The House of Sickness') gradually wasting away, this illness was nothing but the soul's impoverishment, proceeding from the limitless desire for self sacrifice.

In his book *Christianity as Mystical Fact*, Rudolf Steiner described the re-awakening of Lazarus as an initiation. Lazarus' sojourn in the tomb he represents as the three and a half days of sleep which the neophytes of old had to undergo in the temple. One difference however is remarkable between the ancient temple initiations and the initiation bestowed upon Lazarus by Christ. The temple neophytes were plunged into deathlike slumber through the priests' magical rituals. Christ as hierophant brought it about while performing his life-bringing deeds. He did not exert his influence on Lazarus from close quarters. Lazarus had observed him perform the miracles and thereby passed through his own soul's destinies. In general terms that is the

way in which Christ influences human souls. How deeply the influence of Christ will penetrate into our own souls will depend on our
receptivity as witnesses of the deeds of Christ. The gospel shows us
the Christ when he receives the news of Lazarus' sickness and death.
Despite deepest agitation of soul, the confident assurance of the hierophant is nevertheless his. When he had heard that Lazarus was sick, he
stayed where he was for two days. Then he said to his disciples, 'Let
us go to Judea again' (John 11:7). The Christ suffers destiny to fulfil
itself and does not intervene. He waits until the temple sleep of the disciple whom he loves has run its full course. Then he approached the
tomb. Since Lazarus died because of the Christ, Lazarus could also be
recalled by Christ into his earthly sheaths even though those sheaths
were already falling into decay. To give himself wholly to the Christ
was the desire of Lazarus, a desire that governed him entirely and
which tore his soul from his body. Lazarus' soul was all in all with
Christ. That is why the Christ was able to guide it back into the body,
even into a body swathed head to foot in grave clothes. The Christ fulfils in Lazarus the sign of Jonah.

Primitive Christian art in the catacombs reveals that in the early
days of Christianity an awareness of these mysteries was still alive. We
find the image of Jonah and the fish beside the scene of the resurrection of Lazarus in many a sarcophagus and on many a mural. Through
his re-awakening, Lazarus became Jonah-John. He received the name
of Jonah-John in its fullest sense. We have several times mentioned in
the course of these studies that Lazarus is identical with the St John
whom the gospel refers to as 'the disciple whom Jesus loved,' namely,
the evangelist, John. We see on the paintings and reliefs in the catacombs, the Christ standing before the tomb of Lazarus, the priestly
staff held aloft. The sign of Jonah is the continuation of the temple
mysteries dominant in pre-Christian humanity; it was this that survived into early Christian consciousness.

Peter and the seven stages of John's Gospel

The earliest strong realization of the word of Christ concerning the
renewal of the sign of Jonah is to be found in the sevenfold path of
John right up to the resurrection of Lazarus. The sign of Jonah was no
isolated miracle. Rather it was a way consisting of seven stages.

Having grasped that, we can turn back to the personality of Peter, because the Christ bestowed on Peter the name of Jonah; a breath of the air of the sevenfold path of John must also have been poured on Peter. The way of Peter had to come in contact with the sevenfold way of John. Peter had to stride along the sevenfold way of the sign of Jonah. What point had he reached along that path when the Christ addressed him saying, 'Blessed are you, Simon son of Jonah'?

When, in the first of these studies, we made some attempt to sketch the structure of St Matthew's Gospel in relation to that of John, we discovered the scene of Peter's confession, and we pointed out that the scene of Peter's confession near Caesarea Philippi corresponded to the sixth miracle of St John, that is, the healing of the man born blind. Petrine man had attained to the sixth stage of the sign of Jonah.

The first stage (changing water into wine, the Sermon on the Mount) brought him the step from 'sea to land' away from pre-ego existence in heaven into the ego-centred life on earth; away from externalized law to the freedom of inward decision making.

The second stage (the nobleman's son, the centurion in Capernaum) brought about the 'step into the house'. This healed the rift between soul and body.

The third stage (the man at the pool of Bethesda, the man sick of palsy). These took place wholly 'within the house'; it enabled Peter personally to experience the healing by Christ of 'sin engendered sickness.' Forgiveness of sin became the strengthening of his true self, a strength which penetrated his very body.

The fourth stage (the feeding the five thousand). Having passed through the stages of personal evolution, Petrine man was lifted into the super-personal element of community, into the element of intercommunion. Once again 'he went forth from the house to the sea.' He learnt how to live by the power of the spirit.

The fifth stage (walking on the waters). This led him right out upon the waters and straight into the realm of spirit. Here Petrine man had to learn for himself the true character of the Christ, which revealed him to be Lord of the region of the spirit. Peter must stand upright in the spirit. For the first time the soul of Peter revealed itself here in strength, as in weakness. The vision of Christ walking upon the waters struck like lightning into the most profound regions of Peter's will. Those profundities of will reacted immediately without first calling up

awareness, just as if lightning had enkindled the glowing lava of a volcano. Peter desired also to walk upon the water, to stand upright in
spirit, but his soul as yet lacked the strength for what the soaring will
wanted to do. Peter sank into the waves. The Christ had to take him by
the hand, to say to him: 'How weak is your heart! Why did you
become unsure?' (Matt.14:31). The will stormed forward to be succeeded by the soul's ebb tide.

The two last stages of the sign of Jonah still lay ahead of Peter. At
the sixth stage he was to learn how to become awake in the spirit (the
healing of the man born blind). The seventh stage should have brought
him to a new birth in the spirit (The resurrection of Lazarus).

When the Christ directed his question to the disciples, 'Who do men
say that the Son of Man is?' it struck Peter like the sudden rending of
a curtain that had been hiding a light. The same kind of thing happened to Peter in his conscious relationship to Christ. It often happens to people in some unimportant situation that they are asked a
question to which they do not, at that moment, know the answer. Yet,
at that very moment they do know it. The question enkindled the
answer in Peter. The holy name of Christ rose for the first time from
a human mouth. It was as if for the first time the memory was awakened in Peter of his encounter with Christ walking on the water. That
memory rose out of the womb of night into broad daylight. That is
when it was brought home to the disciples that their Master was
more than a human being, more than Jesus. Jesus was earthly man,
one who walked upon the earth. What Peter had received into the
subconscious depths of will, now rose illuminated by the question
posed to him by the Christ; it arose into regions that were fully
awake. From existence in the spirit, Peter attained to awakening
within the spirit.

The following simple synoptic observation enables us to pass to the
scene in St Matthew of Peter's declaration at Caesarea Philippi which
does in fact correspond to the account in St John of the healing of the
man born blind. Let us compare the gospels of Matthew, Mark and
John by looking at the confession of Peter. We shall find the scene
given very vividly and in detail by Matthew (16). Mark presents it very
briefly (8:27–29). In John, coming as it does in chapter six between the
healing of the man born blind and the walking on the waters, it sounds

like a far distant echo. The reverse is true of the healing of the man born blind. It occupies a prominent place in John. Mark tells it briefly just before Peter's confession (8:22–26). It is missing altogether from Matthew. Mark shows the interdependence of the two stories by ranging them one after the other.

Peter had been granted a sudden vision of the true being of the Christ, the Light of the World, thereby breaking out of the congenital blindness of his own soul; in drawing near the point at which the sign of Jonah fulfils itself in death and resurrection he had climbed to the sixth stage in the way of Jonah — these were the reasons why the Christ addressed him thus: 'Blessed are you, Simon, son of Jonah.'

Peter was given a share in the essence of Jonah; he became one of the sons of Jonah: 'You have not received this revelation from the world of the senses but from the world of my Father in the heavens.' In recognizing and looking upon the very being of Christ, Peter had broken through the stratum of sense perception — he had penetrated all the way to the realm of 'the Father in the heavens.'

Here is one of the great mysteries of the personality of Peter, his closeness to John. But just as Peter's impulsive excursion onto the waves was followed by his sinking into them, so the summit of Peter's closeness to John was succeeded by the profound and dark abyss of the proximity of Judas: 'Leave me, power of Satan.' Only once more do the gospels confront us with so sheer a plunge as that one — it is the change of mood on the part of the Jerusalem crowd from 'Hosanna' to 'crucify him.'

Here is the other aspect of the mystery of Peter, namely Peter's closeness to Judas. The Gospel of John says of Judas, 'Satan entered into him.' The Christ had to drive Satan out of Peter because the threat of the destiny of Judas loomed over him. St John's Gospel clearly points to the mystery of Peter and Judas where there is an echo after the feeding and the walk upon the waters: 'Then Jesus said to the twelve, "Will you also leave me?" And Simon Peter answered him, "Lord, to whom could we go? You have words full of unending life. We have perceived with our hearts and recognized with our thinking that you are the Holy One of God." And Jesus said to them, "Did I not choose you, as the twelve? And yet one among you is an adversary".' (John 6:67–70). Here the Christ replied to Peter's confession by pointing to Judas. In this way the gospel itself warns us to think of the nearness of Judas to Peter: 'Leave me, power of Satan.'

Peter stands between John and Judas. Actually the affinity of Peter's nature to that of John lay hidden until Easter and Pentecost when it began to unfold. His proximity to Judas makes ever stronger demands and at last turned him not into a traitor, but into one who denied the Christ. The reversal, the shift in the drama of Peter, the plunge from the exaltation of John to the abyss of Judas took place at Caesarea Philippi. What is the reason for the plunge?

Peter was drawn into his experience of the sixth stage, the healing of the man born blind, as if by a storm of revelation. Would he have the strength to gain his footing for this experience? Would he ever be able to advance towards a true achievement of the sign of Jonah? Christ put the strength of Peter's soul to the test. Nevertheless he had hardly uttered his answer to Peter's confession than he began to direct the disciples' thoughts to the mystery of Lazarus which was to be fulfilled by the disciples and by himself. Having reached the sixth stage, Peter had to listen to the content of the seventh stage as being a foretelling of the Christ's suffering, death and resurrection. From that time forth Jesus began to show his disciples how he must go into Jerusalem and suffer many things from the elders and chief priests and scribes and be killed and be raised again the third day (Matt.16:21).

Just as on an earlier occasion Peter's will-nature had burst out like a volcano, bearing him to the very highest revelation 'You are the Christ, the Son of the Living God.', so now his will surfaced again, this time as a fighter against death, 'Do not allow this to happen to you.' But the death which Peter attacked here was a holy death; Peter thought he was fighting against a hostile will; instead, he was opposing the will of Christ himself. He was not yet mature enough for the secret of the death of Lazarus and that of Christ. He had struggled through to stage six; he was shattered at the seventh stage.

We are here confronted by a psychological phenomenon which life repeats in a thousand basic variations. Those who make themselves out to be strong are often not the most steadfast souls. An intense or impulsive upsurge of the will is usually the result of an inward susceptibility, a frailty; it is no more than a safeguard from being overcome by some impression. People who are less self-aware have within them a stronger individuality than do others who are constantly stressing or parading their own personality, their self sufficiency. How often does the arrogant trumpeting of one's own opinion only prove that person to have suffered a blow from something new, from something that could force him towards a change, a change which his soul can not accept. Much opposition to anthroposophy derives from the fact that many people, deep down in the subconscious, have already been convinced of the authenticity of anthroposophy; and yet because they are afraid lest that impression become too compelling, they fight back with a counterblast of non-acceptance, or with hatred. Vehemence directed outward is often a cover-up for inward weakness; the reticent open mind of many a quiet person reveals true strength of soul.

Lazarus and Peter stand side by side. Lazarus does not outwardly step forward. He lets the being of Christ strongly influence his own soul. So great is his inmost strength that it does indeed let in these impressions. His death through those impressions was not due to softness or weakness but to the greatness and maturity of Lazarus' renunciation of self. He exposed himself to the fire of spirit until it had utterly burnt him up. That is why he was able to rise from his own ashes — an eagle-phoenix.

Peter was also an observer of the deeds of Christ, but Peter's inmost being was, like an open wound, reacting whenever it was touched. He was fortunate when that same reaction enkindled his will, called forth the touch of spirit which led on to impulsive recognition of the Christ, to confessing him. Woe to him when it led to a warding off, to active opposition. The fact that Peter cried out, 'Do not allow this to happen to you,' did not come from any lack of perceptiveness; it was due to the fact that he was only too susceptible to the spiritual reality of 'die and live anew,' when the Christ began to speak of it. The exposed nerve was touched. This is where Peter was weak. Death to him, in any situation, was the enemy. He wanted to preserve his own life and that of his Master as well.

And it was then that Christ spoke the solemn words through which humanity was to learn to grow in inward strength in relation to death, 'Whoever would follow me must practice denial of self and bear his cross. Only so can he follow me' (Matt.16:24). The destiny of Lazarus-John stood in the illumination of the saying: 'Whoever is concerned about saving his soul will lose it, but whoever loses his soul for my sake will truly find it.' The fate of John-Lazarus stands in the light of that 'will find it.' Peter wanted to keep his life. Would he, on that account, lose it, as Lazarus was to find his again, not outwardly but inwardly? And that took place in Gethsemane and in the courtyard of the denial.

Peter, the first Christian priest

Peter's relationship to Lazarus-John is like that of stage six to seven in the sign of Jonah. Lazarus-John had passed through this consecration to perfection before the death and resurrection of Christ. Peter could not do this. So the Christ must die and rise again for his sake. We can consider the relationship of stage six to stage seven from yet another side. The organic build up of the seven miracles in St John is the same as that of the seven sacraments. The seven miracles are in fact like basic phenomena, like pictorial imaginations of the seven sacraments.

Marriage in Cana (Sermon on the Mount)	Evolution of personality	Baptism
Centurion's son	Harmonizing personality	Confirmation
Bethesda (Man sick of palsy)	Healing of personal sin	Sacramental Consultation
Feeding the 5000	Living out of the Spirit	Eucharist
Walking on the water	Standing upright in the Spirit	Marriage
Man born blind (Peter's confession)	Waking in the Spirit	Ordination
Awakening of Lazarus	Rebirth in the Spirit	Anointing

Having attained the seventh stage, Lazarus became the bearer of Christian initiation. Peter, who belongs to stage six, became the first bearer of the Christian priestly commission. Christ committed Christian priesthood to Peter in the words: 'You are Peter, the Rock. On this rock I will build my congregation and the gates of the abyss shall not swallow it up. To you I will give the keys to the kingdom of the heavens. What you bind on the earth shall also be considered bound in the heavens, and what you loose on earth shall also be considered loosed in the heavens.' (Matt.16:18f). We have for the most part applied these words concerning the power of the keys to the sacrament of confession and absolution of personal sin. This is because Christianity has in fact only unfolded its truths within the first sacramental stages, stages in personal Christianity. In fact there were, beside the three existing sacraments, four other mysteries which transcended the merely personal — the Eucharist, Marriage, Ordination of priests and Last Anointing; but these can all be experienced at the same time with concepts and emotions only appropriate to the first three. The Christian sacramental system was in this way held back at stage three.

The Eucharist was looked upon not as an event to change the cosmos, but one to create a community experience. Luther found that the principal abuse of the Mass lay in the fact that it was treated as a 'sacrifice,' as something one offered in the form of pious works of some sort and by means of which one strove to make atonement for one's sins. The sacrament at the altar had been debased from stage to stage. It was not long before within Protestantism too, the Eucharist suffered a similar fate. The atmosphere of fear of personal sin was carried into the Eucharist instead of allowing the communion to bear the participants aloft, above the personal into the cosmic. Those who could find a relationship to the cosmic aspect of the Eucharist felt that nature (bread and wine) was separated from spirit by a deep abyss.

The same inclination comes naturally to Christianity even to this day, namely for the mystery of the fifth stage to fall back to stage three.

We need only look at the Catholic Church's patronizing of marriage, but also at the lowly status taken by women in religious affairs and leadership. More particularly, it is all that prudery towards matters of sex which belongs here and which historical Christianity has exemplified. Everything to do with sex was branded sinful, subject for confession. In that way the church also became answerable for the corruption that prevails nowadays in that field. Perceptiveness of the eternal feminine came to be shackled, and yet only perceptiveness of this kind could ward off the danger inherent in stage five. Having slandered nature, we deprived ourselves of the cosmic Christ feeding humanity. By slandering sex, we have deprived ourselves of Christ walking on the waters, and stilling the storms; of Christ who would have restored the eternal feminine to humanity.

A true perception of the consecration of priests as the mystery of stage six has remained repressed because absolute power of the keys was assumed to be restricted to personal absolution. A large part of humanity refuses all priests because all they can see in them is so many father confessors. However, many people in our time quite rightly wish to be their own father confessor. To be a priest is not only to be a father confessor. Confession in the Christianity of our day and age has taken a quite special character because it is a wholly optional matter. The image of the key presupposes the image of a gateway. By accepting the keys of heaven, Peter became the bearer of an all-embracing commission for sacramental priesthood.

The closed gates outside which humanity has been living are now to be opened to man. All spiritual grace and power of blessing are now to be poured out on us. The Christ was able to give the keys to Peter, for Peter had just won the Christ for himself. Those words, 'You are the Christ, the Son of the Living God,' were uttered not before the closed door of heaven, but before an open one. To Peter, to struggle and to recoil were one and the same thing. They will be the same for all who pass through to priestly activity in the light of the sixth stage of St John. The priest has no advantage over any other man. He can be both vessel and tool for the Christ, who only bestows what we are able to achieve by virtue of our own maturity.

To try to dispute from the New Testament that the Christian priesthood was conferred on Peter would be a piece of prejudiced stupidity. Similarly, it is nothing but denominational prejudice when Protestant historians question Peter's residence in Rome (Tradition tells us that Peter was for twenty-five years bishop of the community in Rome). Undoubtedly, the Papacy's claims are mistaken when the Church of Rome bases these claims on chapter 16 of St Matthew. Peter became the bearer of the commission to the priesthood but he did not carry it as an absolute and infallible precedent to be passed down to those who were to follow him. In quoting from chapter 16, the Church of Rome wisely stopped short after the words that deal with the rock and the keys. The simplest way of refuting the Roman theory is to read on in the gospel where, 'Blessed are you, Simon, the son of Jonah,' is followed by, 'Leave me, power of Satan.' The gospel defends itself against misuse. It took two millennia before papal infallibility was made dogma. It is refuted by the fallibility of Peter into which he plunged as soon as he had climbed to the summit of revelation.

At Caesarea Philippi the greatness of Peter and his invitation are revealed at one and the same time. We see its relevance, and with it the relevance of the whole of historical Petrine Christianity. We are confronted by the question: why was not John rather than Peter called to be the first of the apostles and bearer of the Christian commission? Why had the Christian initiate and Christian priest to be two different people?

One answer especially meaningful for our time can be deduced from the words 'the gates of the abyss shall not swallow it up.' The gates of hell stand opposite the gates of heaven which the golden key fits. It is a law of the spirit that the doors above never open without the doors down below also opening, as if in a mirror reflection.

St John stands beyond the gates — the portals have stood open to him ever since the grave had to unbar its doors before him. Were he to be the leader of Christianity, then humanity would already need to possess sufficient strength to encounter the most virulent onslaught by the devils; otherwise the church would be overwhelmed.

Peter had the key but he was not the man to open the portals of heaven. He is the earthly rock. Near Caesarea Philippi he was favoured, just like children may be on Christmas Eve, by being vouchsafed a peep through a chink in the door — a glimpse from the dark cell of earth into the gleaming light of the spirit world. What he then saw of the Christ he carried around in his heart from that time on and with it that Petrine part of humanity which belongs to it. Vision lived on as faith. Since the gates of heaven do not stay open, the portals of the abyss also remain closed, nor can they subjugate the throng of Peter's people.

As long as Peter remains humanity's leader, Christianity has been given a breathing space in which to gather strength for the satanic war which is to break out when the era of Peter has run its course.

The common view of the reign of a thousand years of chapter 20 of the Book of Revelation is that the pinnacle of perfection will have been reached. There is a good deal of nonsense being bandied about concerning the imminent dawn of a golden age and of the millennium. But the motif of the thousand year era is in reality not leading to a

Utopia, but to the gates of the underworld being opened to destruction. All this, however, is the shadow of a new dawning light, for at the same time the portals of the heavens are opening. Only humanity, having lost its spiritual perception, does not notice this.

The time is now approaching when the exalted spiritual portals are opening and John takes over from Peter as the leader of humanity.

The Petrine era is identical with the millennium. Peter had to carry Christianity through the dark ages; this darkness was intended to provide humanity and Christianity with a protective breathing space of a thousand years. Now is the time when the millennium of Peter is to be replaced by the era of John. And it makes no sense to enter upon the future with illusions. The greatness of our future is that humankind must face mighty satanic struggles before the open gates of heaven. St John emerges; stage six yields the leadership to stage seven. Christian priesthood and Christian initiation are to become one under the Christianity of John. It will have to prove itself as one.

For as long as stage six held the leadership under Peter in the way we have discussed, a natural inclination persisted for all Christian mysteries (Eucharist — Marriage — Ordination of Priests) — to slip back a stage, to the stage of the personal soul life, back to confession and the forgiveness of sins. Petrine Christianity is of the soul. What pertains to John has to be of the spirit. It casts its anchor upwards inside the threshold into stage seven. There, sustained from above, each sacrament and mystery will be able to evolve its own spiritual character. Impoverishment of the soul through indifference to religious life will come to an end and give way to the riches dispensed by manifold mysteries of the spirit. The mystery of personal redemption is joined by the mystery of metamorphosis, of the eternal feminine, and of the spirituality of priesthood. The newly won kingdom of mysteries is to be the arsenal in the struggle against the devils at large roaming the earth.

Peter between Judas and John

The Gospel of St John shows us Peter at the very pinnacle of events, midway between Judas and John, at the Last Supper. Christ speaks, 'Yes, I tell you, one of you will betray me.' Peter was one of those at whose heart the question, 'Lord, who is it?' knocked most stormily.

Did he feel his own closeness to Judas? Peter did not himself address his question to the Christ. 'Now one of the disciples was at the table, lying close to the breast of Jesus, the disciple whom Jesus loved; so Simon Peter beckoned to him and said, "Ask who it is of whom he speaks".' (John 13:23f). Peter addressed his question concerning Judas, through John. And through John came the image of Judas, as in a warning mirror, of the danger that lurked within himself. Judas came to feel the decisive crisis in the truth of the Last Supper, of the communion. 'And after he had taken the morsel, the power of Satan entered into him.' What happened to the soul of Peter under the effect of the same truth? Was the nearness of John, or the nearness of Judas (Satan having entered him), to be victorious?

Three times a powerful experience of the Christ was to become the testing ground of Peter. First of all he apprehended an image of the spiritual nature of the Christ; that happened at the time of the walk upon the waters. Next he heard the Word that awakened him to recognition of Christ; that was in the question at Caesarea Philippi. Lastly, he apprehended the self immolating being of Christ as he strode into the mystery of death; that was at the Last Supper. Each time the soul of Peter responded with an impulsive upsurge of will. Because the will had risen from depths of the unconscious, that upsurge could not hold its ground and it fell back again.

It was experience of the Christ that brought about such an upsurge of will and also, on that account, its collapse. The Gospel of St Matthew tells us: 'They went out to the Mount of Olives. And Jesus said to them, "In this night you will all lose your faith in me and your inner certainty. For the scripture says: I will strike the shepherd, and the sheep of the flock will be scattered".' (Matt.26:30f). Peter said to him, 'Even if all lose their faith in you, yet I will never lose my faith.' Jesus replied, 'Yes, I say to you: In this night, before the cock-crow you will deny me three times.' Peter said, "And if I had to die with you, never would I deny you!' And all the disciples said the same. (Matt.26:34f). St John's version is: 'Peter said, "Lord, why cannot I follow you now? I will lay down my life for you." Jesus answered, "You will give your life for me? Yes, I tell you: Even before the cock crows you will deny me three times".' (John 13:37f).

A powerful desire for self sacrifice was kindled in Peter by the self sacrifice of the Christ who in the Eucharist had joined his soul to the bread and wine and to the souls of his followers. Peter was in earnest: 'I will lay down my life.' The Lazarus-John intention awakened in him. Would he be able to do what he wanted to do?

Gethsemane followed. The gospel tells us that Peter, one of the three disciples, was sunk into a strangely deep sleep. 'And he comes to the disciples and finds them sleeping and he says to Peter, "Could you not keep awake with me one hour?"' (Matt.26:40). The sleep of Peter at Gethsemane was no ordinary sleep. His consciousness had succumbed under the overwhelming force of impressions made by the Christ. The saying of Christ was fulfilled, first of all on the one who had recently so forcibly contradicted it, 'You will lose your faith in me and lose your inner certainty' (that is, you will lose consciousness). Lazarus-John experienced in himself the overwhelming power of the deeds of Christ. He sank into the temple sleep of death that led on to resurrection. Judas felt the overwhelming power of Christ upon himself; he was lost in the night of possession that led to a horrible end. Peter was half way between these two; he was sunk into the sleep of unawareness.

Peter, asleep in Gethsemane, is one of the deepest world symbols — the slumbering rock. The sleep nature of Peter's character which made him akin to the rock of earthly existence is here evident: The sun nature of Christ brings the birth of Peter's character into the light of day. There lay Peter like the lava of some volcano that had cooled into rock.

From that time Peter moved about like a quenched fire. He was like a somnambulist, incapable of rousing himself to awareness of what was taking place. The company of the high priests' servants arrived, led by Judas. It was they who were to prepare the death of Christ. Despite his protestations that he would lay down his life, Peter's real character rebelled against death, 'Simon Peter had a sword. He drew it and attacked the High Priest's servant and cut off his right ear. The servant's name was Malchus.' (John 18:10).

That blow with the sword is none other than Peter's 'this shall not happen to you' translated into action. The sword thrust was the final twitching of the Luciferic storm-tossed consciousness.

We shall have to pause a moment at that thrust from Peter's sword. The sword with which Peter lunged at the priest's servant may really have been there — we can let that stand. Be that as it may, something else comes to light in Peter's sword thrust.

The mighty hierarchical cultures of the distant past, in Egypt and in Babylon, were governed entirely by means of the magic word of the priests. It was always represented by a sword issuing from the mouth of him who was wielding it. The magic word had the power to kill and to bring to life. When the sun passed across the skies from the constellation of Taurus, the Bull, (which formed the human larynx as the organ of the word) into the constellation of Aries, the Ram, (which formed the forehead), the era of the magic priestly work expired and then dawned the era of ideas derived from the forehead. Peter, unable to rouse himself to thought consciousness, had fallen back into a night of numbness. At the time of the arrest in Gethsemane, he went through a kind of lapse from the human condition. It was then that the ancient, magical, priestly word, which killed through curses and brought back to life through blessings, shuddered once more to life out of his soul. That is what lay hidden behind the image of Peter's sword thrust. That is why he cut off Malchus' ear. The will of Peter desired to ward off death by means of ancient powers common to all humankind. He was calling upon the past to fight the present.

Such an interpretation of the episode of the sword is important for two reasons. In the first place it gives us ground on which to build our understanding of Peter's part at Pentecost. At the feast of Pentecost when Peter awoke from the torpor of Gethsemane, the ancient power of the priestly word was transformed into speaking with tongues and put into the service of Christ. At the same time, the sword episode, properly understood, offers a significant key to certain tendencies within Christianity under Peter. For the personality of Peter is in all its features a pictorial prophecy of Petrine Christianity. The sword of Peter still survives in the magical mantric manifestation of the ritual word within the Church of Rome. This is indeed the most profound reason for holding on to the Latin language. The wording of the Mass is not intended to strike the consciousness of the people; just as Peter's sword was aimed at the ear of Malchus, so it is aimed at every individual, maintaining him in a condition of unawareness comparable with that of Peter. Egypt survives in the Roman Mass. Egypt still clings on to humanity by means of it.

Following the impulsive swing of the sword, Peter's nature sank right back into the nothingness of the night of unawareness. When, in the courtyard of the high priest's palace, Peter answered questioners with, 'I do not know the man,' he was not telling a lie through cowardice. He was uttering the tragic truth; he had been deserted by his own consciousness. The text of St John's Gospel sends a shaft of light deep into the riddle of Peter's soul. His reply is consistently 'I am not.' That is the truth. In denying Christ, Peter was speaking the truth about himself. His 'I am not' is the truest contrast to the 'I am' uttered by the Christ. A chasm yawns between Jesus and Peter. Not only was the prediction concerning Peter fulfilled here, but also Christ's words 'Whoever is concerned about saving his soul will lose it.' Peter had fallen from nearness to John to nearness to Judas. He had lost his ego. Only the grace of the Christ's gaze still resting upon him prevented some demon from taking possession of the vessel deserted by the 'I' of Peter.

Peter had slept through all the nightly events that followed. He did not see Christ crucified. He was absent from all that took place. The Risen Christ shed no light, in the form of a dreamlike vision, into his sleep until after the morning of Easter. Future interpreters of the gospel, regarding the treachery of Judas and the denial of Peter, will need to move from a narrowly moralistic appraisal to a spiritual exegesis. For here is not merely paltry human wickedness, but a mystery of the soul on a grand scale making itself evident. We recognize ourselves in those shattering scenes of the tragedy of human nature. Not that spirituality is lacking in the world: 'the spirit is willing.' On the contrary spirituality is present, too much of it and too strong. The human vessel cannot contain it; it cracks — 'the flesh is weak.'

The charge, 'Watch and pray,' sets out to make Peter into John; to break the walls of the era of Peter and to lead humanity into the radiant fields of life in the spirit.

Petrine Christianity

Lastly we shall take a look at a scene which stands there in the gospel like a hieroglyph: in answer to the Roman's question, Peter can only say, yes indeed the Christ pays tribute to Caesar; nevertheless Peter has to admit that for his own part he can neither understand nor approve. For is not Caesar in Rome the devil, the wild beast? The Christ bids Peter go to the lake-side and tells him that he will find a coin in the mouth of a fish that he will catch. With that coin he will be able to discharge the tax not only for him, but also for his own self.

We should no more look for this fish in the physical world than we would look there for the whale in the Jonah story. Simon Peter, having received the name of Jonah, was to find help in the spiritual picture of the fish. He was to find strength in the 'sign of the fish.'

There was a time when Christ had directed him away from the external occupation of fishing to the spiritual calling as fisherman: 'From now on you will be a fisher of living men' (Luke 5:10). Now he is pointing Peter away from the external meaning of the fish to its spiritual meaning. The symbol of the fish was very much alive in early Christianity. Numerous representations of fish in the catacombs in Rome, where Peter later worked, testify to this. Early Christians perceived many a secret embodied in the fish symbols. They saw in the sign of the fish, just as in the Jonah event, a hint of the mystery 'die and become.' They could feel within it a secret of the future: 'die to find a new life.' For just as the sun had passed from the constellation of Taurus into that of Aries, the Ram (the Lamb), so in the future it would pass from the constellation of Aries into that of Pisces, the Fishes. (That took place in the fifteenth century).

Lastly people saw in the fish a symbol for the Christ himself who, through death and resurrection, leads on into the future. In the Greek word for 'fish' they saw the initials as spelling out 'Jesus Christ, Son of God, Saviour.'

Peter could not accept the destiny that had put Caesar on the throne in Rome. He saw in the Emperor a satanic power whom he fought, as he fought death and the devil. Christ was attacking neither death nor the devil. He imparted strength to what was good to the end that evil might be broken. He overcame the contrary powers by allowing himself to be crucified by them. The sacrificial wish, the wish of Lazarus-John, infinitely magnified, was alive in Christ. The Christ paid the tax to Caesar, not because he acknowledged Caesar as master, but because he wished in majestic freedom to make his own word come true, 'I say to you: Do not resist evil.' (Matt.5:39).

A glimpse into a future age will explain the significance of something that appears to be without meaning. To contemplate the Resurrection gives meaning to the death that precedes it. We could also say, if we look ahead to the dawn of the era of John (which is the time of the fishes), then we will see the era of Peter justified and strengthened so as to pay its own tribute money.

Christ endorsed a Petrine Christianity which through the pact between the successors of Peter and the successors of the Caesars became the Roman Church. He endorsed it even though he knew that thereby he would experience his second crucifixion. He endorsed it as being the necessary path to the Christianity of John. He desired it as he had desired death before the Resurrection. His acceptance of the Roman Christianity of Peter is the stage setting on a world scale of the Jonah sign for Christianity. For the sign of Jonah manifests itself in three grand crescendos: following Lazarus and the Christ, all Christians themselves will have to pass through death and resurrection. Christianity must die then rise again, at least by contemplation of the image. Peter had to win through to the courage of Jonah in order to move along the inescapable path that would take him to Rome. From the sign of the fish he was to learn by what means he was to pay his own tribute to the opposing forces, instead of blindly attacking them. What Christ had achieved in Peter's soul through the fish with the coin in its mouth, he achieved again before the gates of Rome. In the apocryphal Acts of Peter, Peter had fled from prison in Rome; suddenly along the Via Appia the Risen Christ met him. Surprised, Peter asked *'Domine, quo vadis?'* (Master, where are you going?). And Christ replied, 'I go to Rome to let myself be crucified a second time.' This time Peter did not say, 'Lord, this shall not be.' This time he realized how far he was from the Christ's willingness to die. And he returned to Rome, to that hell from which he had sought to escape.

Peter's Roman Christianity was the second crucifixion of Christ. Peter was not there at the time of the first crucifixion. He gained courage to be present the second time, to introduce it by his own martyrdom on the cross. He derived that courage from the glory of John that brooded above him and found expression in the name of Jonah; from the image of the fish that the Christ had given him; and he derived it from that part of his personality that was close to John.

CHAPTER TWELVE

Simon of Cyrene and Joseph of Arimathea

It is a feature of true drama that significant answers and solutions are often given to questions not in words but by dramatic means, as by the appearance on stage of a new character at the most climactic moment. Rudolf Steiner offered a classic interpretation for an important passage in Goethe's *Faust* by drawing attention to this principle. Faust has summoned the Earth Spirit who describes himself thus: 'I surge up and down the flood of life, in the storm of deeds.'

Faust is elated and desires to experience the sensation of his own relationship to this mighty spirit: 'I feel how close I am to you, most vibrant spirit who ranges the length and breadth of Earth.' But the earth spirit repels him forcefully: 'You resemble the spirit whom you can understand, not me.' Faust is humbled; he poses this question after the Earth Spirit recedes, 'Not you? Who then?'

There is a knock at the door and Faust's servant and familiar Wagner, clad in dressing gown and night-cap, a lamp in his hand, enters. Wagner's entrance is no merely inopportune intrusion on Faust in his heart' desolation and struggle in face of the Earth Spirit; it is an answer, in dramatic form, to the question, 'Who then?' Wagner, a second-rate repeater of other men's sayings — this is the spirit whom great Faust resembles because he understands him. Wagner is the mirror in which Faust, the genius, is to see himself.

Recognition of this basic phenomenon in drama opens for us many profound things in the gospels, since the mystery of Golgotha is the greatest drama of all; Earth is its stage and God its master.

This dramatic nature appears most strongly in the gospel accounts of the Passion. The sequence of acts and the advancement of the dramatic theme are given there in seven gradations of initiation, beginning with the washing of feet and continuing right up to the Ascension. Earlier Christians meditated on these in their hearts; this was when people still knew something of the spiritual secret of the 'stations' of suffering. In our own time, in places of pilgrimage, all that remains of the spiritual stations are crude remnants, and those 'Ways of the Cross' with their chapels for prayer.

The following are the seven gradations:

1. Washing of the feet
2. Scourging
3. Crowning with thorns
4. Crucifixion
5. Deposition
6. Resurrection
7. Ascension

Before examining more closely the dramatic development of this succession of deeds, we should look at the organization of the seven gradations so as to recognize the plan which they enclose. Matthew's Gospel lucidly describes the middle five of the seven stages. The first and the last, the washing of feet and the Ascension, seem to have been poured out into events rather than to have been presented in their own pictorial stature. The atmosphere of the washing of feet is infused into everything that enfolds the Last Supper. The resonance of the Ascension is to be inferred in the command to baptize that Christ entrusted to the disciples on the mountain in Galilee. Although the beginning and the end seem to be as it were hidden in the clouds, St Matthew's Gospel nevertheless manifests very clearly a splendid symmetry, a harmony of the seven-act drama with cosmic law. Similarly St John's Gospel presents the first six gradations most vividly, but it merges the last one with the Resurrection stories.

If, without going into the content of individual grades, we simply follow the sequence of scenes, then we will see the first three and the last three as being two equal symmetrical curves. In both we can see a powerful urge from below upward. The first time the scenes climb in accord with the human body, from the feet (washing of feet) to the chest (the scourging) and to the head (crowning with thorns). The second time it rises along a similar path, but now by way of the body as a whole, the body which we can call the macrocosmic body of man; this accords with the wise saying to the effect that man is a small cosmos while the universe is man on the grand scale. The sepulchre, the world's feet, is the deposition. The etheric ambience, as the place of Resurrection, the circle of earthly air, that is the world's breathing chest (Resurrection); the heights of heavenly spheres, created in the likeness of man's head — these are earth's head (Ascension).

Both microcosmic man and macrocosmic man, as they move from below upward, are built up in their threefold nature, from the feet to the head, from the profundities of earth to the heavenly heights. Between these, that is, between the two triads, stands the cross at Golgotha.

What is the cross? Following completion of the first triad — that is, of the washing of the feet, the scourging and the crowning with thorns — the mystic words are uttered before the palace of Pilate: *Ecce Homo*, 'Behold there is the Man!' And indeed, a vision of the Man rises pictorially before us from the first three stages. But the saying, 'Behold there is the Man,' belongs to the vision of Christ crucified in another sense.

The secret of the human form is revealed upon the cross. The cross is the actual secret of the human body. Not for nothing is the spine in German called *das Kreuz*, the cross. The physical body is in truth the cross from which man's destiny arises. The body is the cross that humanity must learn to take up.

But when, our arms spread wide, we unfold what is hidden of the cross within our earthly existence, whether it be in blessing or in death — that is when the cross becomes a doorway leading from the microcosm into the macrocosm, out of ourselves into all humanity and the universe. The cross becomes the threshold to two worlds. One of those worlds is small and constricted, we are alone there; that is our personal existence, and it is tied to our physical body. The other world is great and wide; there we are in a common bond with all things created; we are lifted beyond our own selves.

The Egyptian represented the key secret of the cross through the sacred Tao sign, which is none other than the runic sign for the human figure. The Tao is the key that unlocks the gate leading from earthly life to that of the spirit.

Matthew's Gospel sets the cross at the midpoint between the three microcosmic and the three macrocosmic degrees, framing them between two dramatic personages.

The path of the cross-bearer leads from the first three degrees on towards the cross. Now the first of these two persons appears: 'And they ... led him away to be crucified. On the way they came upon a man from Cyrene, by name Simon. Him they forced to carry his cross.' (Matt.27:31f). Simon of Cyrene, the cross bearer, leads from the three degrees of the microcosm towards the cross. And, after the culmination of the drama is over and the Christ has died upon the cross, that is when the second personage appears: 'When it was evening there came a rich man from Arimathea, named Joseph, who also was a disciple of Jesus. He went to Pilate and asked him for the body of Jesus. And Pilate ordered it to be given to him. And Joseph took the body, wrapped it in pure linen and laid it in his new tomb which he had had hewn in the rock. And he rolled a great stone before the entrance to the tomb and went away.' (Matt.27:57–60). Joseph of Arimathea, having freed the body from the cross, leads on to the three degrees of the macrocosm. They begin with the deposition in the sepulchre.

1. Washing of feet	the feet	
2. Scourging	the chest	the microcosm (man)
3. Crowning with thorns	the head	

Simon of Cyrene, who bears the cross

4. Death on the cross	transition from microcosm to macrocosm

Joseph of Arimathea, who took down the body of Christ from the cross

5. The deposition	the feet	
6. Resurrection	the chest	the macrocosm (the universe)
7. Ascension	the head	

We could easily say Simon and Joseph are quite unknown and unimportant. The gospels have not so far mentioned them at all. Why were they introduced at this most holy moment of the drama? Is it not distracting to do so?

We are confronted here by an enigma similar to that of the appearance of Wagner, the familiar, in Goethe's *Faust*. In our first example, during Faust's struggle with the earth spirit, in walks Wagner! Now at that most awesome moment of cosmic withdrawal — the Christ and the cross — two strange *dramatis personae* become involved. In accordance with the laws of the cosmic dramatist, two people are led by the destinies of life to reveal the way the knot is drawn tight. Preceding Golgotha and subsequently, there are secrets that may not remain as mere thoughts and emotions; they must become a part of every human being. Simon of Cyrene and Joseph of Arimathea demonstrate how two deeply serious states of the soul do turn human. This growth into humanity will have to advance, will have to grip all humankind. Whenever any one of us lives through the gospel's Golgotha, and thereby becomes a Simon of Cyrene, a Joseph of Arimathea, then the soul's mystery of these two men is realized and incarnated in us.

That is how the gospel should be read and lived through. It should not be used as a compendium of historical information, nor as an anthology of wise sayings for us to ponder, but as a holy choir of fellow human beings; we should transform ourselves into a likeness of them. The gospel should not be a mirror wherein we are able to see ourselves as we are; it should be a mirror where, at every stage of our development and experience, we should behold a vision of what we are to be. The mysteries we are to bring to human life in contemplating Simon of Cyrene and Joseph of Arimathea are the mysteries of bearing the cross and the deposition from the cross.

We have attempted here to give a schematic sketch of the seven degrees of suffering and of the group of people gathered about the heart of them. All we can hope to do is to cast a light from one side or another; we seek to make possible recognition of the golden figure hidden within the gospel, and the divine ordering and law that are supreme there. Naturally, the same could be done from many aspects instead of from a purely compositional viewpoint that rests on the two groups of three degrees. The cross stands between them, as the median. It is a basic requirement for our own times that we should have a general survey. This is essential not only for Bible reading but also for meditation. Any series of biblical scenes, such as that of the seven degrees of the Passion, is there to be meditated upon. It is advisable to point to what is simply pictorial, to what seems to be externalized, what is there seemingly only to be looked at — this is good

advice. Gospel scenes are so pure, so potent, that they imprint themselves in our hearts, cleansing and transforming one's character,
changing us into the personalities present in whatever scene is before
our hearts. We are to become Simon of Cyrene, and Joseph of Arimathea too. What does that mean? Here we turn wholly to the pictorial
element, to what one can look at.

It is man himself who has to tread the path of the degree of the
cross and to pass through it. Man himself becomes the cross-bearer,
even before he has gone half his journey, before he and the cross
become one. In the meantime, while bearing his load, he must gradually unite himself with it before, at the midnight hour of his own
life, he passes through the portal of the cross, to become wholly
identified with the cross of all the world. Again, it is man himself,
striding along the narrow path, who is able, at the descent from the
cross, to free himself from the cross, becoming the liberator from the
cross. That is when, borne up by angels, he learns to float above the
cross.

At the stage of Simon of Cyrene, as at that of Joseph of Arimathea,
we are but loosely bound to the cross. The loosening, however, takes
place in opposite directions in the two instances. The cross itself stands
in the middle, having carried the body nailed to it. Both before and following this midpoint, a man is the bearer; Simon carried the cross
while Joseph bore the body of the Christ. Here is the religious meaning that painters and sculptors have presented over and over again in
these two scenes. We are peering right into two of the most significant
basic phenomena of religious striving.

If the cross is the innermost secret of man's earthly body and
thereby of the destiny conditioned by the body, then 'to bear the
cross' means to accept unreservedly our human incarnation; it means
willingly to bear our destiny on earth. Simon of Cyrene was carrying
not his own cross but the cross of Christ. The thought of sharing the
suffering of Christ, a thought that sounds through all the letters of
Paul, helps us to find ourselves, to accept our destiny. If that is so, the
'descent from the cross' is what releases humanity from its fetters.
From confinement in our own body, we are lifted up above what is
merely personal to oneself; we are liberated from the body. Joseph of
Arimathea took down the body of Christ from the cross. Once again
it is Paul's thinking about entombment with the Christ, and rising

again with the Christ, that shows us the way from an awareness tied down to the body, to a way beyond oneself, a way to find universality.

Between those two paths lies the 'I' in its sacrificial death, the light of the sun being darkened. Upon the cross that Simon has carried, hangs the body of Christ which Joseph has yet to bear. To think of suffering crucifixion with the Christ, of dying with Christ, helps people to endure the midnight hour of attainment to the absolute 'I.'

Bearing the cross comprises the three first of the seven degrees of suffering, namely the microcosmic degree of personal testing and purification. We could designate Simon of Cyrene, bearer of the cross, as the patron saint and archetype of 'personal piety,' which is on its way to the 'I' (that is, the death upon the cross).

The three last degrees, the macrocosmic degrees of earth and heaven, are contained in seed form within the descent from the cross. We could call Joseph of Arimathea the patron saint of macrocosmic Christianity; itself free of the body, it transcends the personal, and ripens beyond the death of its 'I' towards love that will release the world.

The descent from the cross contains within itself the fundamental mystery of the sacramental life. Joseph of Arimathea's reception of the body took place at the uniquely historical hour of Christ. The tomb was Joseph of Arimathea's; when the body he had been given was laid in the tomb, he took it fully into his own existence. Acceptance of the body of Christ lives on in the mystery of holy communion. We ourselves may become Joseph of Arimathea if, in the form of bread, we receive the body of Christ into ourselves in the right way.

Simon of Cyrene bearing the cross is a picture which reveals for me what I have to cope with in my own religious life. Joseph of Arimathea and the deposition of the body of the Christ reveal to me the secret of the communion by receiving the body of Christ. I am to be guided by it, freed of the body, to awareness of the cosmos, and thereby to find priestly tasks to serve the cosmos. The significance of the deposition from the cross and of Joseph of Arimathea himself to the Last Supper is very great. There is an addition to the gospel scene from early Christian tradition: Joseph of Arimathea standing at the foot of the cross, in his hand the holy chalice from which the Christ bestowed the Last Supper upon his disciples. The soldier is piercing the side of the crucified one with his spear; Joseph of Arimathea is catching the blood and water that spurts from the wound. This is the beginning of the story of the Holy Grail. The lance and the chalice, symbols of the Grail, are together. There stands Joseph of Arimathea before the altar of all the world, the first king of the Grail, holding high in sacrificial gesture the chalice, as the priest lifts up the chalice in a re-enactment in the sacred ritual of the Act of Consecration of Man.

If we can describe the deposition in these words: 'Humanity receives the body of Christ' — then we could express the Grail scene beneath the cross thus: 'Man receives the blood of Christ.' In both cases Joseph of Arimathea is destined to take part in the Eucharist as the prototype of all men throughout the passage of sacred history.

Joseph of Arimathea stands for humankind receiving the body and the blood of Christ. Through the gift of the Last Supper we penetrate into the realms beyond death, into the realms of the three macrocosmic gradations: Burial, Resurrection, Ascension. But those are realms of life and of consciousness freed from the body, where man is master over his own physicality, where he is no longer the servant, but is, together with the Christ, Lord of destiny and of heredity.

Christ's body is taken from the cross. As our bodies receive something of the quintessential body of Christ, so we too are taken from the cross. If Joseph of Arimathea awakens within us, and with him the secret of the Grail, then he lifts us also from the cross. We learn to walk, freed from the body, in the land of spirit.

Deposition from the cross has the deeper meaning of the Eucharist and of sacramental religious life; carrying the cross has the deeper meaning of personal religious life.

The weakness of the disciples

Why were there not two members of the group of disciples in the place of Simon of Cyrene and Joseph of Arimathea? The mystery of Golgotha is surrounded by a circle of the unknown who, by belonging to the mysteries, may have been more advanced than the disciples themselves in the experience of spiritual matters. A company of the great unnamed may have sent two of their own number to take the forefront of the stage for such a fateful moment. Initiates of every age were witnesses of the drama on Golgotha. Destiny prepared them to step in where the disciples had failed.

The disciples fell asleep in Gethsemane. Their consciousness had been stung by the scorpion. They fled. John was the only one of the twelve who did not sleep through Golgotha; he stood at the foot of the cross. The others were not present at the *Ecce Homo* before the palace of Pilate; nor did they share the bearing of the cross or the crucifixion. Admittedly, Peter did say 'Even if I should die with you ...' Yet he was not even there when he could and should have carried the cross. Peter, who was fated later to suffer crucifixion in Rome, ought to have trodden the way from Jerusalem to Golgotha as cross-bearer. He was the one who should have laid the personal and human experience of the first three gradations on the altar: unconsciously, he hung back in the region of what is only individual. Simon of Cyrene stepped in for Simon Peter. The similarity of the names may not be coincidental and irrelevant here, where the world's dramatist has ordained all things with infinite wisdom.

Every weakness is uncovered at this time, when the deep solemnity of world decisions is speaking. The deepest hidden weakness of Peter's nature is revealed in the carrying of the cross, and with it that of the whole of Petrine Christianity; it was not Simon Peter who carried the cross for Christ. Of the seven gradations of the way of John, Peter seems to have struggled through the first three which are concerned with the development of the personality. He passed not only the mystery of community (feeding the five thousand) which abides in the fourth gradation, but went as far as the sixth (healing the man born blind / confession near Caesarea-Philippi) when he received the commission to the priesthood. Was Petrine man's involvement in the feeding of the five thousand, in the walking on the waters, in the acceptance of the priestly mission, really genuine, or was it not? Peter's personality was quite steady in the first three grades, in what is individual. Anything beyond that is in constant danger of falling back. We can understand something of the tendency present in all Petrine historical Christianity to lapse back into the atmosphere of the third gradation, into the atmosphere of personal redemption and the forgiveness of sin. Petrine Christianity, having failed to bear the cross, only seems to have discovered the mystery of the Last Supper. Nor did it even really discover the cross; still less could it find the world of the macrocosm where, together with Resurrection and Ascension, abides the Grail secret of body and blood.

Joseph of Arimathea took the place of the third of the Gethsemane disciples, of James. James could well have had the task of fulfilling the Grail. He should have caught the blood in the holy chalice and taken down the body from the cross. This we only need to mention here. Fate enabled James to make up for the task he had left undone. He was the first of the apostles to die a martyr's death, after he had carried the 'good news' to the West, to Spain, to the land of the Castle of the Grail. In due course his grave in Santiago di Compostella became for centuries the sacred goal of pilgrims travelling by land and sea.

Unlike Simon of Cyrene, Joseph of Arimathea did not have the same name as the one whose place he took. He bears the same name as that Joseph who, in the Old Testament, gave to his eleven brothers in Egypt corn and a goblet.

Simon, Joseph and Nicodemus

Each of the gospels, including that of St John, mentions Joseph of Arimathea by name. Only the first three mention Simon of Cyrene. St Mark identifies him more closely by referring to him as the father of Alexander and Rufus. It is not easy to see why this closer identification should have been given, since we know nothing of the two sons. There is a hint, in that a Rufus is mentioned in the last chapter of the Epistle to the Romans (16:13). We may infer that Rome was the home of Simon and of his sons. That is what theological tradition has accepted, and it is supported by the assumption that the Gospel of St Mark was written in Rome.

Another significant aspect of the cross bearing scene may light up if we associate Simon of Cyrene with Rome. Rome stands at the centre of Petrine Christianity. The other Simon, Simon Peter, incorporated his Roman destiny into the history of Christianity. One feature of the bearing of the cross does stand out: Simon of Cyrene did not willingly carry the cross. When the Christ collapsed beneath it, it was a Roman soldier who grabbed Simon and compelled him to carry the cross; perhaps Simon was known to them from Rome? If we paint in some more detail, we could perhaps assume that the soldiers, knowing Simon as a leader of some special mystery sect, mockingly invited him to give support to a fellow prophet.

It seems as if the spirit of Petrine Christianity was already fore-shadowed in that episode. The admixture of the spirit of Rome to Christianity brought it about that people were actually compelled to carry the cross under the church's tutelage. Personal life in its struggle with destiny was subordinated to the compulsion of Roman law. Confession, made compulsory, became a means of dominance over souls.

On the other hand, the gospels tell of how Joseph of Arimathea had the courage to go to Pilate, the Roman, and to ask him for the body of Christ (Mark 15:43). True eucharistic man stands up free before Rome, whatever face Rome chooses to put on. The freedom of the cross is freedom from every kind of bondage. And the sacrament is the garden where grows the freedom of the man of Christ.

St John's Gospel does not mention Simon of Cyrene. It names Nicodemus in place of Simon of Cyrene. It was he who helped Joseph of Arimathea with the descent from the cross, with embalming the body and the deposition in the grave. The first mention of Nicodemus in the Gospel of St John is in the scene by night, after the marriage in Cana. Nicodemus there spoke with Christ of reincarnation. Then, following Christ's death on the cross, there came the greatest reincarnation of all. Microcosmic man was dead, macrocosmic man was about to rise again. Like Joseph of Arimathea, Nicodemus stood at the threshold of the experience of cosmic worship. He shared in the reception of the body of Christ. He too was a man of the Eucharist. Significantly, tradition tells that Christ celebrated the Last Supper with his disciples in the house of Nicodemus.

Just as John places Nicodemus beside Joseph of Arimathea, so St Luke's Gospel ranges a group of weeping women with Simon of Cyrene. Along the way of the cross, Christ turned to the women and spoke to them: 'Daughters of Jerusalem, do not weep for me; but rather weep for yourselves and your children! For see, there will come times when mankind will say: Blessed are the barren, blessed the bodies that have not given birth and the breasts that have never nursed. And they will say to the mountains: Fall on us! And to the hills: Bury us! For if such things are possible while the tree is yet green, what may not happen when it is dry?' (Luke 23:28–31).

Christ was pointing in powerful apocalyptic terms, away from his own bearing of the cross to the vast bearing of the cross by the whole of humanity, which lies in the future. A Christianity of soul alone is like the women lamenting before the unique historical event, the carrying of the cross and the crucifixion on Golgotha. By and large, in the manner in which Christianity has so far regarded the Christ, in pain, suffering and dying, it has behaved like the women who wept along the way. A Christianity which can grow into cosmic and spiritual spheres, and yet not lose its own personal character, can see scenes prophetic for humanity right down to every detail. One of these days a huge bearing of the cross and a crucifixion will befall the whole of humanity. Men will die the great death of humanity. Those who are born will be born unto death on the grand scale. They will have to decide how much strength of soul humankind possesses; whoever does not outgrow his own self, whoever is caught up in what is personal, will then perish. Those, however, who by the contemplation of the Christ, will have acquired the cosmic power of love that transcends the personal — those will all pass from human death to human resurrection.

It is possible to lose touch with the advance of universal mysticism through a false religiosity. Whatever is concerned only with one's own person too easily turns into a sentimental phrase. The women's lamentation is an image of a religious quality that lacks a future. Sympathy with this one or that one — even with the Christ — does not carry us forward. Only sympathy with man, with all humanity, does that; only suffering with the Christ.

The wood of the Tree of Life was green when the Christ was nailed to the cross. Its inheritance of life forces was far from being extinguished. Christ has said that humanity will be nailed to the cross when the time comes of the dead wood.

In our own day anyone who is honestly sensitive to the times can see with his own eyes that the time of green wood is running out and that the dead wood is staring us in the face from every quarter.

The hour of humanity's Golgotha is upon us. Bearing the cross has to be a matter of will. Each must carry not only his own cross, but also the cross of all humanity. Each one will have the courage to enter with

Christ into the darkest hour of universal history, where humanity is hanging on the cross and when the sun is darkened of its own accord. If, at that time, the spark of the nature of Joseph of Arimathea, the spark of that sacramental life, be enkindled, then that spark will carry us through to the new dawn of humanity.

Bibliography

Bock, Emil, *The Apocalypse of Saint John*, Floris, Edinburgh 2005.

—, *Caesars and Apostles*, Floris, Edinburgh 1998.

—, *The Childhood of Jesus*, Floris, Edinburgh 1997.

—, *Genesis*, Floris, Edinburgh 1983.

—, *Kings and Prophets*, Floris, Edinburgh 2006.

—, *Moses*, Floris, Edinburgh 1986.

—, *Saint Paul*, Floris, Edinburgh 2005.

—, *The Three Years*, Floris, Edinburgh 2005.

Madsen, Jon, *The New Testament*, Floris, Edinburgh 1994.

Steiner, Rudolf, *According to Luke*, Steinerbooks, Great Barrington 2001.

—, *According to Matthew*, Steinerbooks, Great Barrington 2003.

—, *The Apocalypse of St John*, Anthroposophic Press, Great Barrington 1993.

—, *Approaching the Mystery of Golgotha*, Steinerbooks, Great Barrington 2006.

—, *The Background to the Gospel of St Mark*, Rudolf Steiner Press, Forest Row 1985.

—, *The Book of Revelation*, Rudolf Steiner Press, Forest Row 2008.

—, *Christianity as Mystical Fact*, Steinerbooks, Great Barrington 2006.

—, *The Fifth Gospel*, Rudolf Steiner Press, Forest Row 2007.

—, *From Jesus to Christ*, Rudolf Steiner Press, Forest Row 2005.

—, *The Gospel of St John*, Anthroposophic Press, New York 1962.

—, *The Gospel of St John and its Relation to the Other Gospels*, Anthroposophic Press, new York 1982.

—, *The Gospel of St Mark*, Steinerbooks, Great Barrington 1986.

—, *The Reappearance of Christ in the Etheric*, Steinerbooks, Great Barrington 2003.

—, *The Sun Mystery and the Mystery of Death and Resurrection*, Steinerbooks, Great Barrington 2006.

—, *Turning Points in Spiritual History*, Steinerbooks, Great Barrington 2007.

Index

Biblical Index

Floris
Books

For news on all our **latest books,**
and to receive **exclusive discounts,**
join our mailing list at:

florisbooks.co.uk

Plus subscribers get a FREE book
with every online order!

We will never pass your details to anyone else.

Lightning Source UK Ltd.
Milton Keynes UK
UKHW050755290422
402152UK00011B/432